A Journey

25 Years of the Green Party in Irish Politics

Green Party council meeting in 1989. From left: Margie Bach (Joint Co-ordinator), Tom Simpson (Energy Spokesperson), Mary Bowers (candidate for Dublin South Central), Alison Larkin (candidate for Dublin North West), Colm Ó'Caomhánaigh (Foreign Affairs Spokesperson), Roger Garland TD, Gerry Boland (Urban Conservation Spokesperson), John Gormley (Election Campaign Director) and Stephen Rawson (Press Officer). **Courtesy *The Irish Times.***

AUTHOR

Dan Boyle TD for Cork South Central was the first Green Party candidate to have been elected to Cork City Council in 1991. He is Party Whip and spokesperson on Finance, Social & Family Affairs and Community & Rural Affairs.

EDITORIAL TEAM

Sean O' Flynn has been a member of Comhaontas Glas (Cork South Central) since the foundation of the party in 1981.

Laura Wipfler is a graduate in European Integration Studies and French from University College Cork. She has been Parliamentary Assistant to Dan Boyle since 2005.

A Journey to Change

25 Years of the Green Party in Irish Politics

By Dan Boyle

NONSUCH

Nonsuch Publishing
73 Lower Leeson Street
Dublin 2
Ireland
www.nonsuchireland.com

British Library Cataloguing in Publication Data.
A catalogue record for this book is available from the British Library.

ISBN 1 84588 559 7
ISBN-13 (from January 2007) 978 184588 559 5

Typesetting and origination by Tempus Publishing Limited
Printed in Great Britain

Contents

Each chapter is written by Dan Boyle and followed by a contribution from various party members.

Introduction

This project is not a conventional publication. It is a compendium, as well as an attempt to record a piece of political history in Ireland. The book seeks to convey the collective sense of how a group of like-minded people, sharing common goals, sought to bring about a more just society, and a better environment in Ireland. I hope that it can serve as a resource that records what the Green Party/Comhaontas Glas is; how it came about; and where it might go in the years to come.

I am grateful to all those members and staff of the Green Party who, in one way or another, have been involved in this publication. In particular I would like to thank my editorial team of Sean O'Flynn and Laura Wipfler. I am grateful to Sean for sharing his ideas on the structure of the work and for proofreading the book. Laura has my gratitude for her research and her collation of the numerous source documents and materials. I would not have been able to undertake this project without the transcription and drafting skills of my constituency secretary, Edel Boyce, who constantly encouraged me despite this imposition on her workload.

A special acknowledgement to my nearest and dearest for their tolerance and patience as I struggled to bring this book into being. My old self will return soon!

I would like to thank Nonsuch Publishing for having faith in this project from the beginning.

Finally I would like to acknowledge our collective debt to Christopher Fettes and Máire Mullarney for daring to think differently, and then for having the courage to act on those thoughts. Without your actions the Green Party might never have been formed.

The book includes two special contributions from Harry McGee, Political Editor of the *Irish Examiner* newspaper, and Trevor Sargent TD, the leader of the Green Party. Harry's piece is that of an outsider looking objectively at the party. Trevor's piece is unashamedly partisan and seeks to outline a vision of the contribution the Green Party can make to Irish life in the future.

Dan Boyle TD,
Dáil Éireann, October 2006.

Please note that the generic term, the 'greens' (with lower case), is used throughout this book to denote the 'green movement' except when referring specifically to the Green Party or the Green Alliance.

Preface

The pains of gestation. The evolution of the Green Party into a fully corporeal political entity in Ireland has taken almost all of its twenty-five years of existence. In that time, there have been peaks. But there have also been troughs, with all the political misery and soul-searching that go along with them.

Each encouraging milestone has, more often than not, been followed by a discouraging falter. Reading through Dan Boyle's personalised history of the party, the phrase that constantly recurs is: 'We learned a valuable political lesson'. That's a euphemism for 'false dawn'. Or if you want to be unkind about it: 'That was one spectacular bellyflop'.

Slowly, slowly, the greens have gradually emerged from their first meeting at the Central Hotel in the depths of winter in 1981. Yes, the party can argue – with a great deal of authority – the continuity of the the grand ideals that compelled that small group of eighty people to form a movement back then. But it could be equally argued that the party of 2006 has changed beyond all recognition from the 1981 template. It has learned the painful lesson that it too had to change, that it needed to attune its message to the ears of a wider electorate and not just the already converted.

The metamorphosis has involved two name changes; fundamental organisational changes; changes in its decision-making process; a conscious effort to escape its 'middle-class-Dublin-o-centric-letters-page-of-*The-Irish-Times*' image; embracing 'personality' politics (i.e. electing a leader); and the tactical and pragmatic approach of the 'realos' (realists) prevailing over the 'fundis' (fundamentalists) who wanted no deviation from core principles. If you want to put it in lay terms, the Green Party realised it needed to get real.

The journey has been a slow one, sometimes tortuously so. It is over twenty years since the first electoral breakthrough – the highly unusual and unexpected success of Marcus Counihan in Killarney in 1985. Those that followed are more familiar to those with an interest in Irish politics: Roger Garland's remarkable breakthrough in 1989; the party's splendid performance in the 1991 local elections; the even more remarkable victories of Patricia McKenna and Nuala Ahern in the 1994 European Parliament Elections (a trick they repeated in 1999); and, of course, the quantum leap of 2002, when the Green Party tripled its Dáil representation from two to six, and announced its arrival as a real force in Irish politics.

But there have also been a series of disappointments. There was the mediocrity of the 1992 and 1997 General Election campaigns, where the party failed to galvanise its support base and failed to live up to its own expectations. There was the abject reversal of the 1999 local elections. Even when you thought that it had gained a kind of critical mass after the 2002 breakthrough, there were further disappointments. Both European seats were lost in 2004 and the local election performance, while an improvement, was still nothing to write home about. Each was explicable (for example, Nuala Ahern's decision to step down as an MEP instantly made the retention of the east seat a huge – and in hindsight, impossible – task). Having said that, for a party at this stage of its development, more might have been expected.

There is a theory that the Green Party's journey to where it is now has taken too long: in other words, that the party has underachieved or has failed to build on its electoral successes or is just now belatedly turning its attention to the considerations of governing, rather than eternally opposing. But that theory needs to be put into context. To that end, there's no harm in giving an axiomatic and self-evident cliché another outing – politics is a cyclical business. You only have to glance at recent Irish electoral history to realise that. Look at the Spring Tide that delivered thirty-three seats for the Labour Party and created an expectation that the '90s might be socialist after all. And then look at the tide in 1997 that carried the party all the way out to its lowest ebb point, punishing it for linking up with Fianna Fáil and for its failure to live up to the new vision of Ireland that emerged from the Robinson presidential campaign.

Or look at the Progressive Democrats. During its two decades the party has more than once stared near obliteration in the face only to bounce back.

Or look at Fine Gael, which is now primed to rebound strongly from the nadir of the 2002 elections, when its future survival was also questioned.

Notwithstanding similar vagaries and reverses, the Green Party has survived and established itself as a party for the long-haul, at all three levels of political representation (unlike in Britain, where the greens have signally failed to replicate in Westminster their successes in European elections).

And at this moment in time, the Green Party stands at its strongest, every position going into an election. It now has six TDs (all of whom punch above their weight in terms of profile, integrity, and ability). There is a feeling abroad among those of us who write about politics, that Trevor Sargent has grown in authority as Green Party leader over the past eighteen months. If you wanted to pinpoint his tipping point, to use Malcolm Gladwell's fashionable phrase, it would be his more robust contributions to leaders' questions in the Dáil, plus his impressively crafted and well-delivered speeches at the last two Green Party national conventions. The party's organisation and presentation is more professional, its potential TDs are all well embedded in their constituencies, its policy papers nowadays seem to be far more focused, realistic, realisable, and *ergo* less prone to the abstract and the ideal.

Underlying this is an acceptance of three basic political realities. Change, even radical change, happens by degrees and by increments. To effect real change in society, you need to be in a position to influence, and that means you need to be in government. To be in government, you need to be prepared to make difficult compromises (and the ultimate example of that is the concession the German Greens made in relation to nuclear power).

Strategically, the party has become clever at positioning itself, focusing its message, without betraying its convictions. 'It won't frighten the horses,' said one candidate in 2002, as he explained one of its more elector-friendly policies.

One of its TDs, as 'realo' as you will find, told me that he has never used, and will never use, the word 'sustainability' in his suburban constituency because it is has little purchase with people who live there.

Perhaps the most pellucid example of this is the shift in the tax policies of the greens since the turn of the millennium. In four years the party has leap-frogged from a position where it was calling for corporation tax to be pegged at 17.5 per cent, to an interim period where it settled for 15 per cent, to the current policy where it will leave corporation taxes unchanged at 12.5 per cent.

There are two separate forces at play here. There is the 'mainstreaming', as evidenced above. And there are increasing numbers of citizens coming around to identify with the party's core policies, such as the need to address dwindling fossil fuel supplies as continuing environmental profligacy creates greater urgency.

Translated into the geometry of electoral possibilities, the Green Party's stock has risen sharply in recent opinion polls. In the summer of this year, it reached a support level of 7 per cent for the first time, a figure that had been maintained over two tracking polls at the time of writing. And so, once again the Green Party seems to be on the cusp of something new. When you look back at the pre-election press-cuttings going back to 1992, there were brave promises of significant 'breakthroughs'. Sometimes those expectations were realised. But invariably, they were not maintained afterwards. The General

Election of 2002 did not constitute such a breakthrough by any measure. Pundits' predictions are as fallible as anyone else's, but on the basis of all the indicators, the 2007 General Election will allow the Green Party – perhaps for the first time in its existence – to consolidate. That means holding most or all of its six seats. That means making gains elsewhere (and I sense that here the party will spring one or two surprises of the Sadhbh O'Neill variety). And that also means – most critically of all – the real possibility of the greens going into government for the first time.

The entity that emerged from the winter of 1981 was to become the first wholly original political party to emerge since the foundation of the State. Most other parties were the result of splits or splinters from the civil war parties, from the wider republican movement, or from the main socialist party. Some were eventually subsumed into larger parties (like the Worker's Party and its offshoot, Democratic Left); others eventually withered on the vine (like Clann na Poblachta and a host of tiny left-wing parties). Of all those, only one other party, other than the greens, can claim to have survived over the long term: the PDs, which itself emerged from a split within Fianna Fáil.

The survival of the party through the lean years of the 1980s is a tribute to the perseverance of those who drove it in its earliest incarnation. The political climate at that time was hardly conducive to a new party with such a radical message and such an unusual approach. The political system was in turmoil. The country was experiencing economic stagnation and hopelessness of Albanian proportions, with the younger generation ('our greatest national asset' as the hackneyed political phrase put it) the country's largest export.

To be sure, though, there were straws in the wind that suggested that an ecological and environmental party might gain electoral purchase, if only at the fringes of political life. The campaigning groups, Greenpeace and Friends of the Earth, had raised awareness of important environmental and conservation issues, as had the early successes of nascent green parties elsewhere in Europe. Domestically, the one event that could be pinpointed as bringing an influence to bear was the (successful) campaign in the late 1970s against Des O'Malley's plans to site a nuclear facility at Carnsore Point in County Wexford. Reading about it now, there seemed to be an element of a peasants' revolt to that particular campaign (none of the established parties had developed anything like a considered policy on nuclear power). That campaign captured the public imagination to such an extent that there would never again be popular support for nuclear power in this country.

During the course of an interview with Trevor Sargent in the autumn of 2003, I put it to him that the Green Party had travelled some distance over the previous decade, mollifying some of its more hard-core messages as it moved from marginal to mainstream. He disagreed vehemently, pointing out that most of the movement was in the other direction, with the established parties gradually accepting and absorbing the major underlying principles of the greens. In the same breath, he mocked the 'We are all green now' claims made by bigger parties here and in Britain, saying that not only had they barely scratched the surface when it came to adopting an environmental and ecological outlook, but their pronouncements instantly betrayed their lack of appreciation or understanding of what the green movement was about.

Sargent was making a vital point. The Green Party has developed and evolved over twenty-five years. But in all that time, it has remained remarkably consistent in its message. The arguments made by two of its two founding spirits, Christopher Fettes and Máire Mullarney, in the early '80s are – extraordinarily - the selfsame ones used by its political leadership today, give or take a variation or two.

In particular, a phrase used by Fettes at the very first gathering continues to resonate powerfully today. 'I believe,' he said, 'that the basic political philosophy of all these people can be summed up in the saying: "We do not inherit the earth from our parents, we borrow it from our children".'

That still gets to the heart of what the greens are about, perhaps in tandem with its other clever slogan that can be read on more than one level: 'Green politics is clean politics'.

In terms of hitting the nail on the head, the seven-point manifesto agreed in early 1982 is a model of concision, stated in simple, easily understandable, terms.

- The impact of society on the environment should not be ecologically disruptive.
- Conservation of resources is vital to a sustainable society.
- All political, social and economic decisions should be taken at the lowest effective level.
- Society should be guided by self-reliance and co-operation at all levels.
- As caretakers of the Earth we have the responsibility to pass it on in a fit and healthy state.
- The need for world peace overrides national and commercial interests.
- The poverty of the two thirds of the world's family demands a redistribution of the world's resources.

From our perspective here and now, it is hard to imagine anybody even beginning to quibble with any of those seven aspirations. But placed in the context of the time, many of those issues were not even on the political radar.

The first challenge facing that small group of concerned people was to convince and educate people that these fears were real, were imminent, and were not abstract (i.e. so far off in the distant future as to be negligible). But beyond that there was a larger challenge – the need to find solutions that were grounded in some kind of reality and did not leave the party open to be besmirched as off-the-wall, apocalyptic, or as out-and-out Luddites.

Unlike other Irish political parties, the outlook of the greens was, by definition, international and global, rather than local. And while other parties invariably promised a better future through the miracle of continuous economic growth, more investment in industry and services, more development and 'progress' (that great catch-all word) the Green Party's message ran counter to all this. The intellectual difficulties that arose were formidable. When it came to localised and practical solutions, the party was way ahead of the posse in its calls for more recycling, substantial investment in public transport, bans on smoky coal and on unleaded fuel, cycle paths, a strong environmental agency, and strict planning control to prevent rampant and moronic development.

But in a wider context, its calls for greater collective responsibility sometimes came across as Cassandra-like, with what seemed like over-shrill warnings about an approaching Armageddon. The harsh and unfortunate reality, of course, is that this analysis is neither alarmist nor over-dramatic. The NGO Christian Aid recently estimated that 184 million people could die in Africa alone because of water and food shortages caused by climate change. Global warming, the rise in carbon gas levels and the quick-thrust acceleration in the depletion of the world's natural resources are huge issues that are beginning to touch on this generation. But politically, there is also the countervailing reality that you just can't frighten the horses too much.

The Green Party, in staking out its philosophical territory, has always boasted that it is a party of neither the right nor the left, nor of the centre. But if it isn't any of these, what is it exactly? The need to come up with sustainable solutions may have moved beyond debate or argument. But floating the message of sustainability is a tricky proposition indeed.

The political quandary stemmed partly from very divergent views within the party on some issues, which often led to fudge, masquerading as consensus. But even when there was accord, the solutions were too often vulnerable to attack for having slightly Quixotic characteristics. It seems to me that the party persisted for too long with some core policies that were admirable, highly idealistic, etc. but neither practical nor achievable.

One such solution was floated by Fettes at the very first meeting in 1981 and continued to be party policy into the 1990s – in fact it provided part of the basis of Trevor Sargent's maiden speech to the Dáil in 1992. This was the concept of basic unearned income, a salary that was payable to all irrespective of work or social status.

In his Dáil speech, Sargent argued that a radical change in work practices was needed for a post-industrialist society.

'A shorter working week as well as work-sharing, workers' cooperatives, early retirement options and an unconditional guaranteed basic income for everyone paid by the State, need to take their place to ensure that dignity is restored to all and that the mountain of work which needs to be done, such as food growing, house building, tree planting, road sweeping and child rearing can be done by people who are willing to work.

A guaranteed basic income would end the concept of unemployment, it would end the effective prohibition on work for those who are in receipt of benefits and, above all, it would give citizens real choices so that they can work or not work, study, rear their children, do voluntary work, without the farce of pretending that they are looking for formally paid work.'

This is more than a radical change. This would involve a fundamental re-ordering of society. It might just work in the smallest community but such a system implemented across a complex, urbanised society of four or five million people seemed unimaginable. How would society pay for the basic income? How would people be encouraged to do the jobs that nobody wanted to do? Wasn't there a basic inequity in giving a reward to people for doing nothing, while not commensurately rewarding those who put their hearts and soul into the 'mountains of work' that needed to be done?

As early as 1981, the idea of basic unearned income was drawing the wrath of some who were highly supportive of the party and its ideas. Within weeks of the party being formed, Michael Viney, writing in his 'Another Life' column in *The Irish Times*, eloquently dismissed the concept.

'The reference to unearned income stirred my hackles; nothing could be more at variance, surely, with the impulse of self-sufficiency. It will be time enough to talk about it when we have found alternative solutions to the generation of wealth – notoriously the weak spot of utopians.

It is one thing to deplore the planned obsolescence of consumer goods industry, the squandering of world resources, the desperate artifice of a world of Rubik's cubes and pot noodles – but another to find alternative jobs or substance and the margin that pays for hospital and schools.

It is possible to have a pastoral vision of a society in which the backbone is the small, diversified, labour – intensive farm, raising food next door to the consumer, but it is hard to picture any orderly transition to it. Perhaps, if the economic doomsayers are right, there won't be one.'

The same argument, it seems to me, still holds twenty-five years later, if you replace Rubik's cubes and pot noodles with X Box 3 and Pringles. Perhaps, a system of 'basic unearned income' would work. But unless somebody is able to explain to the nth degree exactly how such a utopian system could work in reality, it's a policy that would never ever wash with wider society.

The party's originality extended beyond its unique outlook. It also wanted to beat an entirely new path in how it organised itself and the manner in which it pursued its goals. Decisions would not be made by diktat or be delegated to the leadership but would be arrived at by the widest possible consensus. The greens, for two decade, also eschewed personality politics.

No matter how desirable it sounded, it was always going to flunk in practice. In practical terms, the party was without a leader until the turn of the millennium. To be very kind about it, this was unwise. In terms of appearances, as green parties in other European countries discovered, being leaderless also meant being rudderless. The election of Trevor Sargent as leader by 'preferendum' in 2001 was one of the factors that helped the party recover from its flatline performance in 1997 and its local election reverse in 2001, as did the emergence of candidates who were clearly identifiable from their work in local election wards or constituencies. It's all very well being self-deprecating but the importance of candidate-recognition cannot be underestimated when it comes to the business of getting your people elected – in a more cynical vein, you only need to look at the lengths to which other parties have gone to recruit 'name' candidates to add to their slates.

You cannot but agree with Boyle's analysis of the other idiosyncrasies that seemed good ideas at the time. He borrows a phrase from Karl Rove in relation to the adoption of the original name, the Ecology Party – 'if you are explaining, you are losing'.

It is intriguing to note that the famous seven point manifesto from 1982 was arrived at by consensus. But it's quite obvious that this process of decision-making became increasingly problematic as the movement expanded and the circle of consultation was widened. And clearly, it was always going to lead to stasis when there were deep divisions over policy or strategy – neatly illustrated in the divergent stances of the 'fundis' and 'realos'.

Boyle gives a graphic description of what it was like to hit those doldrums. He paints a picture of 'the often soul-destroying and hair-tearing reality of the practice of consensus decision, seeing the making of decisions becoming frequently prolonged and frustrating.'

Certain things had to be conceded to reality over the years. It happens with all parties, as they find that they need to change tack, or implement internal modernisation and reform to address flagging performances or impetus.

But it must be said that the party's motives have appeared to be consistently honest and transparent, a party doing its best to be as democratic as possible.

Fianna Fáil and Fine Gael have long surrendered all key decisions to its ruling elites and to powerful central committees chaired by senior ministers or advisers. With the Labour Party it is less so – Pat Rabbitte's plans to forge a pre-election alliance with Fine Gael had to get the imprimatur of delegates. But the greens remain the one party that still defers to its grass roots for major decisions.

That has meant that its TDs do not always get their own way, individually or collectively. At its national convention in 2005, the party delegates decided for an independent electoral platform unfettered by any arrangements. The party's leadership, though it hasn't baldly stated so, has always tended towards a Rainbow government with FG and Labour and might have preferred to have got backing for that strategy.

Equally, at the same conference, the party's membership (sensibly) decided not to make the ending of the Shannon military stopover a precondition for entering government. If that motion had been passed, the party would have been bound – and quite possibly hide-bound in coalition negotiations – by the wishes of its own membership.

It might not make for the most convenient approach, especially when compared with the sanguine and harsh strategy decisions of the hard chaws in the larger parties, for whom internal democracy has become a relative concept.

And it has been costly. The Green Party admirably turned its head against the dual mandate a decade before its counterparts. This undoubtedly cost the party electorally and the reluctance of realists like Sargent and Gormley to stand down – at such a critical building stage – reflected this reality.

It took a while for the party to find its feet electorally. Indeed during the 1980s, support for the party plateaued over three successive elections. That wasn't unusual for a smaller party struggling to get its voice heard nationally. But there is also strong evidence that there wasn't sufficient focus on the business of vote-getting and seat-winning. Things did change after the 1989 election of Roger Garland and especially after the 1991 local elections, with its 'bolt out of the blue' seat bonus. Now the party's vote share had climbed over the 2 per cent mark, a symbolically important figure when it came to viability. But the successes masked underlying weakness that came home to roost the following year.

In the run-up to the 1992 elections, most of the indications pointed to further green advances. The portents from the 1991 local elections seemed especially positive. Against all expectations, thirteen councillors were elected, most of them in the greater Dublin area. The success of Sadhbh O'Neill in Donaghmede was extraordinary, perhaps the only demonstration ever of the greens' issue-led and anti-personality philosophy in practice. O'Neill had allowed her name to go forward but had not canvassed at all as she was in the US on a student visa for the duration of the campaign. Some Green Party realists believe that the remarkable election of O'Neill (who incidentally became a very effective councillor) created false expectations that the hard graft of constituency work could be avoided; that the issues and policies in themselves would be enough.

The 1992 election remains difficult to analyse. It was no great surprise that Fianna Fáil and the PDs would take such a hit, partly because of the impetuosity displayed by Albert Reynolds and Des O'Malley in their growing rift over the Beef Tribunal, and their mutual distrust of each other. Fine Gael, with its own ongoing leadership problems, never looked like it would have the wherewithal to recover the support levels of 1982. But conversely, there was absolutely nothing to suggest that Labour would reap such a monumental seat bonanza.

I have always considered the Spring Tide to be a bit of a misnomer. Dick Spring and his parliamentary party had been impressive but certainly not astounding in opposition (though Spring had been the most effective haranguer of Charlie Haughey in the chamber). Much of the party's astonishing success could be ascribed, in my opinion, to the afterglow of the Mary Robinson presidential campaign and particularly to hopes that her enticing vision of a new, transformed Ireland could be achieved in the Oireachtas as well as in Áras an Uachtarain.

For once, an idea or vision, rather than personalities or traditional allegiance, predominated with the electorate. Mosajee Bhamjee's success in Clare (with its echoes of Sadhbh O'Neill) epitomised this. And Labour could have easily won 36/37 seats if it had run two candidates in some Dublin constituencies.

By corollary, why did the Green Party perform so poorly? Yes, it had been involved with the Robinson campaign but while she ran on an independent ticket, she was always strongly identified as a Labour Party candidate. Moreover, the greens sought floating support from the same vote pool as Labour, and all of that was annexed by the latter. To be sure, if Labour had run a second candidate in Dublin North, Trevor Sargent would have surely become a cropper and the party would have been completely shut out from the Oireacthas. If that had happened, with no presence in the Dáil, the consequences would have been, if not quite catastrophic, very damaging for the party in the long-term.

As the 1990s progressed, the debate about whether the Green Party was a political party or hybrid political vehicle began to peter out. A new generation of ambitious and impatient politicians came to prominence, all of whom emerged from ground-up campaigns in their own localities. All the valuable political lessons (i.e. dispiriting losses and disappointments) were duly learned, especially after the disappointments of 1997 and 1999.

The party began to analyse the conundrum whereby the electorate was almost treating the Green Party as a discretionary purchase. Why were people backing the party so strongly in Europe, but refusing to do so in parliamentary or local elections? Some of the reasons for this were complex and ultimately gave rise to false perceptions of where the greens were at their most effective politically. But some others were more prosaic. The first no-brainer was that the party needed to be seen as relevant at local and national levels. It needed to come up with policies and campaigns to buttress that perception. The second was that it also needed to establish a strong personalised presence in local election wards and in target constituencies; to come down from the ivory tower and campaign where it really mattered, on the streets.

To that end, over a relatively short period of time, the greens produced impressive and eye-catching papers on waste management, water quality, childcare, air pollution, decentralisation, public transport investment (including a light rail system for Dublin), cycle lanes, and recycling. Most were novel – like many of the Green Party's standpoints, they have become subsumed over time into the general political maw.

It also took a leading role in a number of high-profile campaigns that highlighted its own strong stances on nuclear power, incineration, planning abuses, the Iraq war, and its concerns about how the ceding of power to Brussels would impact on Irish neutrality and on the democratic process.

Sargent was almost a lone voice crying in the wilderness about the rampant graft of Dublin councillors on planning issues. When he waved the famous 'cheque' in the council chamber in the early 1990s, all he got for his troubles was to be disgracefully headlocked by Fianna Fáil senator Don Lydon. The party has consistently returned to this theme of political clientilism, most recently with Trevor Sargent's coruscating attack on junior minister Frank Fahey in the Dáil before the summer recess. Together, these campaigns conspired to give the party credibility and a profile.

But equally, the party has been validly criticised for relentless negativity in some of its very vocal campaigns. Europe, in particular, was to bring out something of a soft underbelly, with other parties pointing out the disparity between the positions on Europe of the Irish greens and their European counterparts. Yes, the party might argue that it too wanted a better, more democratic, more accountable EU. But if the party had been successful in raising awareness about the implications that Nice would have for Irish neutrality, then what were the big ticket issues that were, for example, driving its emerging opposition to the EU Constitution? The referendum results in France and the Netherlands have delayed the debate for now. But a conference of European greens held in Dublin exposed stark divergences of views between 'continental' activists and those from mainly Ireland and Britain. The 'pause for reflection' on the constitution has now allowed the party begin a detailed internal debate on where it stands on Europe.

Sometimes, too, there have been displays of over-zealousness on the purely political front and the party has not been found wanting in the brazen stunt department, sometimes to its detriment – the events that immediately spring to mind are its TDs chaining themselves to railings on O'Connell Street; Sargent's *Podge and Rodge* escapade; and the silly press release chastising George Galloway for appearing on *Celebrity Big Brother*.

But there have also been a raft of thoughtful new policies, including the crucial step-change on its tax policies. The importance of this cannot be underestimated. It will do much to silence the scaremongering adjectives – 'loony', 'wobbly', 'barmy', 'flaky' – that have been flung so often at the greens in the past. By undertaking not to alter current rates of corporation tax and income tax, it removes at a stroke any claim of an unbridgeable chasm between the party and others and signals a maturation of its approach, although, yes, it is without doubt a compromise.

That does not necessarily mean it is an abdication of principle. There has been no abandonment of its commitments to remove inequitable relief for the very rich or budge from the core policy of introducing a carbon tax system (on the 'polluter pays' principle) with balancing reliefs in other areas. Whether or not such initiatives will see the light of day in any coalition arrangement is another question entirely, though the greens will argue until they are blue in the face that they are essential.

With one or two of its new policies, you wonder if there is an element of wish-fulfilment about them – is its long-term policy of doubling the state pension to sixty per cent of the average industrial salary a realistic option, given that there will be only two workers to every pensioner by the middle of this century?

At the party conference earlier this year, Trevor Sargent said when he looked around the hall that he saw a 'Green Party fit for government'. He also gave a glimpse of what the shopping list might be: windfall taxes to guard against speculation, a major reform of the Environmental Protection Agency, improved insulation standards for buildings, paid parental leave, and free pre-school places for children.

The message – if somehow you haven't cottoned on by now – is that the Green Party leadership really wants to go into government. Twice in the past three years two former green ministers, Pekka Haavisto from Finland and Reinhard Bütikofer from Germany, have addressed the party's conference to prove that green participation in government can work smoothly.

The Green Party has survived its first twenty-five years. You sense it is going to emerge from next year's election as a stronger and more robust party. But if the dice falls as predicted and the Green Party steps into the breach of government, it will face its greatest test of all. It will be a rough ride.

The contribution of Finnish MP Haavisto, the environment minister in a highly successful government, was intriguing. He said archly that he had come to Ireland as the living embodiment of a Green Party MP who had survived government, in spite of constant attacks from critics.

'And who were the most outspoken critics of all?' he asked with a Cheshire cat grin on his face. 'None more outraged than those from within the Green Party ranks.' The comments evoked a ripple of laughter, but it was also the laughter of recognition.

After twenty-five years the party may be stronger, focused, and 'fit for government'. But the next Dáil period will be a rough ride for the party, especially if it is in government. And being a painfully democratic party, a lot of the most severe criticism will come from its own opposition within. Politics is a tough business. The pains of gestation never fully go away.

Harry McGee,
Political Editor, *Irish Examiner*

1981

1981 was a turbulent year in Irish politics. The decade had yet to define itself, but some portents of what was to come were already in the wind. Margaret Thatcher had served for two years as Prime Minister in Britain but she was far from secure in her position. She received some support with the election of Ronald Reagan as President of the United States. Their complementary vision of market-led economics – Thatcherism and Reaganomics – created the era of the 'yuppie', who lived by the dictum: 'greed is good'.

Change in the world at the time seemed slow and piecemeal. Leonid Brezhnev remained in charge of the Soviet Union. The revolt by Solidarity in Poland seemed destined to go the way of previous uprisings in Hungary (1956) and Czechoslovakia (1968). John Lennon had been assassinated and with his passing, the idealism that many of us hoped might continue from the 1960s, died.

In Ireland the 'two and half party, tweedle-dum tweedle-dee' arrangement of politics, which had served the state since 1921, showed no sign of changing. Charles Haughey was Taoiseach, since taking over from Jack Lynch in 1979. He had planned to call an election in February but the Stardust tragedy caused him to postpone his plans to go to the polls. He eventually called the election in June. Fianna Fáil failed to gain a majority in the Dáil and a Fine Gael/Labour coalition formed a government under Garret Fitzgerald as Taoiseach and Michael O'Leary as Tánaiste.

This election was the first time in decades that a significant number of independents and others were elected to the Dáil. Sinn Féin the Workers Party, won its first ever Dáil seat, while Provisional Sinn Féin, began their electoral strategy of 'an armalite in one hand and a ballot box in the other'. The H-Block hunger strike had become a major issue in Irish politics. Provisional Sinn Féin sought to take advantage of the emotion that followed the death of the first hunger striker Bobby Sands and ran eight candidates under the H-Block banner. Two of these were elected – Kieran Doherty in Cavan Monaghan and Paddy Agnew in Louth. Collectively the H-Block group won over 32,000 votes.

Noel Browne was elected under a Socialist Labour Party banner and staunchly independent Sean 'Dublin Bay Rockall' Loftus finally succeeded in being elected. Dr John O'Connell was also elected as an independent, as was Jim Kemmy, who broke through in Limerick East. Meanwhile Neil Blaney retained his seat for independent Fianna Fáil in Donegal.

Accepting the fact that these seats were essentially the result of personal popularity, there was an indication that a growing number of voters were prepared to consider changing their traditional pattern of voting. It was into this political context that a mild-mannered teacher, an Englishman, convened a meeting of people who might be interested in setting up a new political party in Ireland.

Christopher Fettes had been living and working in Ireland since 1958. He was frustrated by the narrow focus of Irish politics and the lack of any real political choice. He was active in the Vegetarian Society, the Esperanto movement and Friends of the Earth. He had read the writings of Jonathan Porritt, later to become Chief Environmental Advisor to the Prime Minister Tony Blair, and was interested in the philosophy of the emerging green movement in Europe.

Christopher wrote to the letters page of *The Irish Times* to enquire whether there were any like-minded people interested in establishing a branch of the UK Ecology Party in Ireland. A subsequent letter to the paper in November 1981 reacted to a report by the journalist John Cooney that four greens had been elected in Belgium indicating that moves were afoot to establish a similar party in Ireland. The editor of the letters page did not seem to take this particularly seriously as he gave it the heading 'Eco Freaks Unite'.

The positive feedback Christopher received from this correspondence encouraged him to convene a meeting at the Central Hotel, Exchequer Street, Dublin, on 3 December. Invitations were sent to those who responded to his letter, in which he explained his reasons for calling this meeting:

Dear Fellow-Thinkers,
Many thanks to all those who have responded in one way or another to my letter, and especially to those who had the confidence to send a founder's donation: an official receipt for all these will be sent in due course.

The reaction to my letter has been very encouraging. I am particularly grateful for the enthusiasm shown by Dervla Murphy, David Cabot, and the International Secretary of the Green Parties movement, Jonathon Porritt. But the support of every one of you is worth having, for our political aspirations concern not just the planet, but also the individuals upon it.

On a separate sheet, you will find on one side, a poster advertising our meeting on 3 December. On the other, some pertinent extracts from the European Green Manifesto. Further copies of the latter will be available at the meeting, so if you wish to put up the poster, you need not feel unmanifestoed!

You will see that at the bottom of the page some extracts from the EGM. I suggest that we might adopt these as a basis for our party.

I believe that we shall need to be more radical (which does not mean more leftwing, or indeed any wing at all) than the extracts suggest; but it is important that those whose heart is certainly in the right place, have time to come to terms with the concepts of land-value taxation, and a basic unearned income for all, before being asked to endorse them.

These last two ideas will be explained at our first meeting, and I hope shown to be inherently part of our political philosophy.

"Until there be correct thought, there cannot be right action; and when there is correct thought, right action will follow." – Henry George.

Since we are not likely to have a chance to stand for the Dáil in the next twelve months, we have time to think things out properly.

Now, some good news for those in the Cork area. Seán Dunne tells me that there is such enthusiasm for EPI in the south that he intends arranging a meeting in Cork city on Sunday 13 December. I shall be delighted to come to this with news of the Dublin meeting; but I hope that there will be some Cork (wo)men in Dublin too.

And what of the north of the island? I do hope that eco-minded people in the Six Counties will consider this party just as much theirs as that of the Twenty Six: not because we claim jurisdiction over them – heaven forbid! – but because ecological sanity demands decentralisation to a point where control from Dublin, London and Belfast – and therefore the border – becomes largely irrelevant. I believe that a more than amicable relationship with British ECO could ensure that inhabitants of Northern Ireland could be members of both our parties for the price of one!

On the other side of this letter, you will find the agenda for our first meeting: I hope it will please you. With gratitude and good wishes to you all.

Christopher Fettes,

Convener, E.P.I.

Eighty people turned up to the meeting. Christopher asked Máire Mullarney to chair the meeting so as to allow him to contribute more freely from the floor. Her brief was to steer the meeting through the following agenda:

Original Poster

The Convener will outline the purpose of the gathering.

Election of a person to chair the meeting.

Apologies and greetings.

The Convener and others will briefly explain the meaning and implications of the proposed philosophical basis for the party.

Questions and discussion. (Donations towards the cost of hiring the room will be sought at this time!)

The Convener will propose that the circulated extracts from the European Green Manifesto be accepted as a basis on which to build the E.P.I.'s own policy.

Election of a Steering Committee; Chairman, Secretary, Treasurer, Publicity Officer, plus maximum of six others.

Proposals for the venue of the March Convention.

Any other Business.

The Convener will propose that a meeting be held on a Saturday or Sunday in January, at which succinct papers on the philosophical basis of the party be presented. Proposals will be invited to produce, or co-produce, short papers on each of the following topics, with specific reference to this country:

Storehouse economics V steady-state economy.

Non-exploitive approach to nature.

Land reform and land value taxation.

Common ownership of natural resources.

Common ownership of the technological heritage.

Basic Unearned Income for all.

Satisfying work as an aim, rather than mere full employment.

Decentralisation of political power.

Separation of policy creation, from policy administration.

It is proposed, that if those attending the January conference find these papers reasonably satisfactory, they be provisionally adopted and published, and that members should then be invited to produce papers on more practical matters for discussion at a weekend Convention on March 20/21.

The discussion at the Central Hotel centred round the question as to whether the proposed organisation would be a political party or a campaigning organisation. A majority of those present seemed to favour forming a political party. It was clear from the tone of the meeting, that whatever emerged from the process it would be an Irish-based, Irish-directed organisation. The Convener inaugurated the meeting with the following address:

For longer than most of us can remember, an increasing number of talented and idealistic people have found themselves excluded from the political life of our country by a growing distrust of both capitalism and socialism. It is my conviction that the combined wisdom of all these people is the only thing that can save us from disaster, and that we therefore have a duty to lay the foundations of a political party which will allow us to tap their talents without compromising their integrity.

I believe that the basic political philosophy of all these people can be summed up in the saying: *We do not inherit the earth from our parents, we borrow it from our children.* The emphasis is firmly on stewardship; whereas the left and right (and the soft left of centre) argue endlessly about ownership.

To use the word "ecological" to describe this philosophy is to risk accusations of misusing the language, of un-Irishness, and of bourgeois sentimentality. As the word is already in international use to describe this heightened form of political awareness, I hope that the reader will accept it in this sense, and not think of an Ecology Party simply in terms of a group obsessed with saving the whale and the Amazonian forests; (though we would certainly be poorer without the one, and dead without the other).

The idea of stewardship can be given both a religious and a humanitarian dimension. Those with a profound religious belief and/or a deep concern for the appalling suffering which mankind inflicts on the animal world will find that the ecological approach to politics offers full scope for their convictions. I wish, however, to turn to issues which are more commonly thought of as political. I believe the most fundamental of these to be land reform.

The idea that the land can actually be owned is a convenient fiction: like the idea that the sun moves round the earth. The truth of the matter was clearly expressed by John Stuart Mill when he wrote: *No man made the land: it is the inheritance of the whole species.* This concept seems to have been inherent in Irish thinking (Brehon laws) before the conquest by the English began, and is of course far older than that of capitalism or socialism. Thus, if we are to talk of ownership at all, we should think of common ownership combined with individual stewardship. This idea is fundamentally different both from state collectivisation on the one hand and private ownership on the other.

Socialists believe that the land belongs to the state, and that the state alone has the supreme right to organise its use. Capitalists on the other hand believe that private ownership is justified because individuals will work the land better for themselves rather than for the state. Even communist party ideologists are now beginning to admit that this is indeed true.

What all countries could benefit from, and Ireland more than most, is the practice of Land Value Taxation. This was first conceptualised a century ago by the American philosopher Henry George and our own Dr Thomas Nulty, Bishop of Meath, who came to the same view independently. (That the latter's theories were called "communistic" in his London Times obituary should not disconcert us.)

Land Value Taxation guarantees security of tenure, and involves no tax on the produce of the land. It also disallows profit (and loss) on the sale of the land itself. It does not deny that some sites are more valuable than others, or that some will increase in value more rapidly. What it does emphasise however, is that any increase in land value due to society (as distinct from an individual's good stewardship) belongs to society itself, and should therefore be used to its benefit.

The idea of the land as a common inheritance logically implies also the common ownership of mineral resources: but once again, we must be careful to distinguish this from nationalisation. If it is decided by the people that a mineral be mined – an independent tribunal having taken fully into account all the implications of such a process – the profits should not go into the government coffers, but be distributed as unconditional dividends to all citizens. This applying no less to resources found in the sea than in the land.

Now, just as people are entitled to share in, and must accept responsibility for, the natural resources of the earth and the benefits resulting from their use: so too do they have a right to share in the benefits which result from the application of technical knowledge accumulated over the centuries. Sir Isaac Newton said, 'If I have seen farther than others, it is because I have stood on the shoulders of giants.'

How many more giants do our modern scientists and technologists stand upon? If those past geniuses are no less our ancestors than theirs, then surely the profits from all inventions must partly be ours also. For this reason, the price of each artifact, from a brick to a computer, should have built into it, not only its full cost to the planet, (as ecological thinking demands), but also a profit to be shared equally by all citizens, a profit which, like the profits from natural resources, should be given directly to the people as an 'unearned dividends', not (as at present) handed to the government as a tax to be spent just as it happens to think fit.

The concept of an unearned income can be upsetting to those who have a firm belief in the work ethic. I hope it will be seen that the idea of a basic unearned income for all, to which a person is as entitled; as a daughter is entitled to inherit her mother's wedding ring. This concept offers a solution – perhaps the only solution – to today's problem of rising unemployment. Such an income, it must be seen, is a right. It is neither a sop to prevent civil unrest, nor (as the dole is often considered to be), a payment to ease the conscience of the rich.

Far from discouraging work, a regular income of this kind would release people to work as they wish, they of course adding to their income; such work might well mean a personal involvement with alternative or intermediate technology, instead of the boring life as a fully employed serf in a large factory. (That such factories may be necessary, at least at present, I do not dispute; but it is common knowledge that they could be run far more efficiently if automated. Only the workers' fear of unemployment – by which they mean loss of income – prevents such a logical development.)

A steady unearned income would not only release people for work at less energy-consuming industries, it would also free them for a variety of other activities. Parents would be able to spend more time with their children.

Farmers (including many who have been forced to leave the land to seek an income in a less appealing urban environment) would be able to enjoy work on the land once more. Artists of all kinds would be free to follow their instincts more fully. Trade unions would become outdated. Their raison d'étre would have ceased to exist.

All this may seem merely idealistic to many people – just as the idea of abolishing the slave trade doubtless appeared to most of our ancestors. However, no less than the elimination of slavery, it is a highly realistic concept that could bring about a better way of life for all.

It is now more than fifty years since an eminent engineer, Major C.H. Douglas, first pointed out the advantages of an unearned income for every citizen. Its greatest advocates today include Dr Keith Roberts, Chief Theoretical Physicist of the U.K. Atomic Energy Authority (not my favourite institution, but one cannot deny Dr Robert's qualifications) and Dr James Albus, Director of the Artificial Intelligence Program at NASA. (Another unfavourite institution, I admit). I believe that it is only by spreading out the wealth of the nation in this way, instead of through either bureaucratic legislation or a struggle between employers and employees (with an increasing number of unemployed people and pensioners being left out in the cold); that freedom for everyone can be brought about without bloodshed. Freedom that will involve not only justice for all humans but also a reverence for the rest of creation.

You will have realised that, unlike other political philosophies, this one chooses to take power away from politicians. This would remove its appeal to many who normally choose to enter the political arena. I believe, however, that life is far too rich in pleasures – the pleasures of being, not merely of having – for a full human to want to waste energy on regimenting others. The urge to do so is surely a perversion of the creative instinct.

Yet it would be foolish to suggest that such a perverse desire does not exist. In any organised society, it is sensible to have a safeguard against the usurpation of power. For this reason it is essential that the administration of corporate decisions be separate from the decision-making process. All decisions in a sane society would be taken at the lowest effective level; but in so far as some decisions must be taken centrally, no government should have the right to claim that it 'has a mandate' to act in a particular way simply because its party represented the least objectionable choice at the previous election. Major Douglas claimed that freedom consisted of the right to 'accept or reject one thing at a time'. The role of politicians should thus be to persuade us, if they can, to elect certain courses of action, not to urge us to choose them to do our thinking for us. Only in this way can we become a fully responsible society.

It is popularly assumed that opposition to capitalism implies approval of socialism, and vice-versa. The result is that people of good will who recognise the absurdities of the one often find themselves forced to defend the absurdities of the other. For this reason I have avoided discussing the enormous environmental problems which each of these these two outworn ideologies can only tackle piecemeal (and largely create) in order to outline a political philosophy which I believe would allow us to attack these problems at their roots. I am of course not in a position to insist that those forming an Ecology Party adopt these radical ideas, but I do hope that none will be rejected out of hand. If we are to justify our existence as a separate political force, it will be through our willingness to keep our minds open to radical solutions to the problems of our country and our planet.

At the end of the meeting a steering committee of twelve people was formed. About forty of the people who attended the Central Hotel meeting, agreed with the decision to pursue a political route, and formally became members. Many of this core group remain active members of the party to this day.

One such original member was Tommy Simpson. A true Dub, Tommy has never been your stereotypical green. He would have looked, sounded, and probably felt out of place among the clipped tones of the largely émigré attendance at the Central Hotel that evening. He had come with an American friend, the late Rico Harris. Rico, observing the gathering crowd, turned to Tommy and asked if he was sure they had come to the right place, because there didn't seem to him to be too many Irish people in the crowd.

What Tommy brought to the meeting, and subsequently to the greens, was some degree of prior political experience gained from knocking on doors and seeking votes. Tommy had been actively involved in the 1974 Community Group Local Elections campaign that succeeded in electing six councillors to Dublin Corporation. These councillors would include later Lord Mayors of Dublin - Carmencita Hederman, Sean 'Dublin Bay' Loftus and Brendan Lynch.

An account of the discussion on what to call the party probably best illustrates the neophyte attitude that characterised many of the party's members. For some reason the title 'green' was not accepted for use in the party's title. Perhaps it was thought that the colour green was subject to too many different interpretations already in Irish politics. Some members openly expressed a fear of being associated with the IRA. In the end, the meeting agreed to use the title 'The Ecology Party of Ireland'. It was a choice that broke the old saying: 'If you are explaining yourself, you're losing.'

The formation of a political party in this manner and for the reasons stated above was a unique event in Irish politics. With the probable exception of the Labour Party, formed in 1912, and some parties that had been formed to represent farming interests, all other Irish political parties had arisen from the Irish Civil War of 1922/23. The Ecology Party was the first political party in Ireland since the foundation of the State to arise spontaneously without any previous political reference point.

Of course the roots of environmental politics had already existed prior to this meeting. In 1979, after widespread public protest, (including a music concert on the proposed site), plans to erect a nuclear power station at Carnsore Point were cancelled. Many of those who participated in this campaign continued to involve themselves in environmental politics, through organisations such as Greenpeace or Friends of the Earth. Others, encouraged by the successful application of public opinion, were now preparing to engage in the political arena.

1981 was also the year when the British nuclear industry conducted a public relations exercise in an effort to allay growing public concern over the management of its nuclear facility at Windscale. The name was changed to Sellafield.

Máire Mullarney, Dublin

The Green Party has its roots in *The Breakdown of Money* by Sheed and Ward, published in 1937. I was sixteen when I first read this book. I have since read many books with a similar theme, but this one made it clear that money is not like the seasons: part of the order of nature. Several books by James Robertson detail the potential for justice that could be released by a shift to the concept of 'a basic income' payment to all citizens.

When I was a young girl, I realised that were I to live to a ripe old age, I would need some help when I would be elderly. I concluded that I should do my share of helping while I could, so I decided to become a nurse. The Accident & Emergency ward was not the bedlam I read about now. I even had the opportunity to get to know a regular visitor whom I later had the good fortune to marry.

My husband and I found a basic cottage in which to start our married life. Fresh water from a spring in a nearby field; bread, baked in a pot-oven. To grow our vegetables we used the Indore method of making compost. The family flourished beyond the capacity of our cottage so we moved to a spacious and elegant house in Rathfarnham.

Despite being a young mother with a growing family, I was active in several different fields. My earliest public activity was a campaign to make it illegal to beat children in school. I had been a freelance journalist for several years and wrote mainly about education. This prompted me to publish a book, *Anything School can do, You can do Better*, which stayed on the bestseller list for several months.

It was in December 1981 that Christopher Fettes invited some like-minded people to a meeting in the Central Hotel. Christopher asked me to chair that meeting, so that he would be free to speak.

The Ecology Party, later to be called An Comhaontas Glas, was formed. Early in 1982, we all met for a weekend at the Glencree Reconciliation Centre. After hours and hours of intensive debate and patient discussion, the forty members present agreed by consensus on seven principles that would guide the party in its future course of action.

During the 1980s I represented the party at meetings of the European Co-ordination Committee of Green Parties. For various reasons I was a convenient delegate. I had spoken Spanish from childhood and had functional French. These international meetings reinforced the belief of Christopher Fettes in the need for an easily learnt language, spoken all over the world – Esperanto.

Máire Mullarney is a founding member of the Green Party/Comhaontas Glas. She has been an extremely influential and active member since. She was elected to South Dublin County Council in 1991.

1982

By the summer of 1981 there was a minority Fine Gael/Labour coalition government in office. The first test for the government, within six months of it being elected, was the budget to be presented by the Minister for Finance, John Bruton. His most controversial proposal was that Value Added Tax be introduced on clothes and footwear. No exemption was to be given, even for children's clothes or shoes. The independents supporting the government found this proposal particularly hard to take. Garret Fitzgerald frantically tried to keep his government together but failed. Eight months after the coalition came into office, the country was being asked to vote again.

This unexpected election presented a difficulty for the still largely aspirational Ecology Party of Ireland. With little more than a handful of meetings held, and no opportunity to register officially as a political party, it was decided to forego this contest. A booklet was printed entitled 'The Reckoning'. To all intents and purposes this publication was a manifesto for a political party. Policy positions were offered on employment, trade, natural resources, inflation, industrial policy, energy, pollution, agriculture and food, transport, social policy, women, education, minorities, health, foreign policy, defence, population growth, decentralisation and political reform. The document stated that the Ecology Party was on its way and would be contesting the next election.

The newly formed Ecology Party of Ireland has not put up candidates at this election, but you will certainly have the opportunity to vote for our radically sane policies on future occasions. This is because we believe that our country must be given the chance to work towards a more self-reliant, decentralised economy, with a more responsible use of scarce resources, and a fairer sharing of wealth. For this reason our policies will:

Recognise that economic growth cannot continue endlessly in a finite world.

Reduce our overall dependence on imported energy, and invest more in native renewable sources of energy from sun, wind and wave.

Encourage industries that use recycled materials and produce goods that are made to last.

Establish a totally new attitude towards work and income, making technology our servant rather than our master.

Introduce much tougher legislation to control pollution, and ban the use of lead in petrol.

Develop the skills that will make sense when energy and raw materials are no longer cheap.

Promote small, local businesses, cooperative ventures and community schemes.

Take responsibility for decisions back to where it belongs – with the people, in their own communities.

Encourage self-help organisations, and reduce people's dependence on state institutions.

Help to create self-reliant economies in Third World countries, so that their populations can satisfy their basic needs from their own resources.

Make ourselves much more self-sufficient in those areas where we are unnecessarily dependent on imports.

Establish a society in which cooperation counts for more than competition.

This was a reprint of a document that the British Ecology Party used in their 1981 General Election. It was a template that was to prove useful to the developing Ecology Party of Ireland.

On 13 February, *The Irish Times* columnist Michael Viney, devoted his 'Another Life' column to the election.

> I take the election down the field with me, propping the transistor inside a plastic box, to keep it safe from showers. It adds resonance to the inquisitions of John Bowman, Pat Kenny and the rest. Bruce the dog, comes too; to lie near me as I dig: nose on his paws, an audience for my own asides.
>
> We are, almost willy-nilly, part of a movement bent on social change, a movement slowly cohering from a hundred strands of thought bonded chiefly by belief in what has been called a 'voluntary frugality'.
>
> The self-sufficient rural homestead epitomises a lot of these ideas and tests them out in microcosm. The pressing need however is for 'urban solutions to urban crises'… Is it possible, for example, by sharing houses and skills, organising communal

craft work, finding land on which to grow food, experimenting with 'city farms', bartering within a like-minded network, to express the non-exploitative alternatives to big power systems and consumerism? ... The politics of alternatives cut across the established political divide of Right and Left. Their non-violence and abhorrence of the nuclear threat, their rejection of big business, exploitative employment and the rape of natural resources – all these tend to place them on the left, and the radical rhetoric of the alternative magazines is still predominantly socialist in tone... But the belief, with Fritz Schumacher, that 'small is beautiful', is incompatible with the state colossus. The rejection of consumerism, so immediately vital to employment, makes them no friend of the trade unions.

In Germany, Die Grünen's concern with the environment and the hazards of nuclear power has become a focus of alternative ideas and aspirations. In Britain, for example, the Ecology Party aims at a self-sufficient, decentralised society based on regional authority and localised industries.

The Ecology Party of Ireland, which will have its first convention next month, is shaping up along similar lines. Its inaugural meeting last December was presented as 'a radical alternative to both capitalism and socialism. It appealed to those who favour a storehouse economy, a non-exploitative approach to nature, land reform, human scale institutions, alternative technology, a basic unearned income for all and the decentralisation of political power'.

It is possible to have a pastoral vision, of a society in which the backbone is the small, diversified, labour-intensive farm, raising food next door to the consumer. But it is hard to picture any orderly transition to it. Perhaps, if the economic doomsayers are right, there won't be one.

It is ironic that the idea of voluntary frugality or simplicity – the acquisition of goods only to satisfy basic needs – should be as relevant to this election as it is to the wider arguments about the shape of a sustainable society. In western countries with a longer experience of affluence, changing values are leading more and more people to reject the materialism which confuses quality of life with an ever-expanding consumption of goods and services.

Voluntary frugality is not at all the same thing as Mr Bruton's budget. But this election must say something, nonetheless, about the balance of values in Ireland and its capacity for adapting to a national self-sufficiency. 'Isn't that right, Bruce, old fellow?'

The general election of February 1982 was not a particularly successful one from the point of view of independents and small parties. The most significant trend was the advance of Sinn Féin the Workers Party, who now had three seats. The H-Block campaign had ended. Noel Browne retired after a long and distinguished political career. Neil Blaney was re-elected in Donegal, as was Jim Kemmy in Limerick but Sean 'Dublin Bay Rockall' Loftus failed to retain his seat. John O'Connell had been Ceann Comhairle in the previous Dáil, and so was automatically returned. A new name in the chamber was that of Dublin inner city community activist, Tony Gregory.

The result of the election made it difficult for either the outgoing coalition government or Fianna Fáil to win a Dáil majority. Attention was turned to the new boy, Tony Gregory, who was wooed heavily by both sides. In the end Charles Haughey made a deal with Tony Gregory in return for his support in the Dáil and thus became Taoiseach. The nine months that were to follow were to be amongst the most controversial ever in Irish politics.

While the real political parties were going about the business of reconvening the Dáil and forming a new government, the Ecology Party was holding its first convention at the Glencree Reconciliation Centre in the mountains overlooking Dublin. This meeting reached agreement on the founding principles that would guide the future actions of the party:

- The impact of society on the environment should not be ecologically disruptive.
- Conservation of resources is vital to a sustainable society.
- All political, social and economic decisions should be taken at the lowest effective level.
- Society should be guided by self-reliance and co-operation at all levels.
- As caretakers of the Earth, we have the responsibility to pass it on in a fit and healthy state.
- The need for world peace overrides national and commercial interests.
- The poverty of two thirds of the world's family demands a redistribution of the world's resources.

These principles, and the political policies that would eventually emerge from these early meetings, owed much to written works. Books such as *Silent Spring* by Rachel Carson, *Small Is Beautiful* by EF Schumacher, *The Limits to Growth* (Club of Rome Report), *The Future of Work* by Charles Handy and *The Sane Alternative* by James Robertson, informed these early policy discussions.

A young nineteen-year-old came to the Glencree meetings out of curiosity. Ciarán Cuffe was prompted to go to the convention after reading Michael Viney's column in *The Irish Times*. Little did he know that day that he would later become a Dublin City Councillor and a Green Party TD for Dún Laoghaire.

A small report on the convention appeared in *The Irish Times* on Monday 22 March 1982. It explained the party's stance on Northern Ireland, which advocated a policy of self-reliance within a community of regions 'in these islands', leading eventually to political independence from Britain. The Ecology Party, which had members on both sides of the border, proposed that a multiple-choice preferendum (a logical extension of proportional representation) should be held to allow expression to every shade of opinion in the province.

Mr Raymond Crotty, who had been prominent in the campaign against Ireland joining the EEC said that only radical policies, based on land taxation, could avert economic collapse.

Mr Michael Crowson, representing the European Union of Green and Radical Parties, told the conference that membership of the green movement ran into many millions. He said that there was growing awareness that the human race was about to face a reckoning because of its exploitation of the earth.

Three months after the general election, a by-election was called when Dick Burke agreed to become a European Commissioner. This by-election gave the Ecology Party an opportunity to contest a Dáil seat. Unfortunately the party chose not to, for much the same reasons it chose not to contest the general election the previous February. They missed a golden opportunity to register a semi-respectable vote with which to compare their performance with those of other small parties operating on the fringes of Irish politics. The greens had yet to learn that it was necessary to go 'on the canvass' to contest votes, before votes could be won.

Back in the real world of politics the minority government that Haughey put together was teetering. His European Commissioner scam had backfired and now fate intervened to further undermine his Dáil position. The Fianna Fáil minority government was a precipitous arrangement that was plagued by a series of GUBU 'events', and leadership revolts.

When the Dáil reconvened in the first week of November 1982 to discuss a Fine Gael motion of confidence, there was to be no escape for Fianna Fáil. For the third time in seventeen months the Irish electorate went to the polls to choose a government.

Meanwhile, on the fringes of Irish political life, the Ecology Party was busy establishing itself as a new political party. A constitution was devised and formally adopted on 27 June 1982. A great deal of the work in bringing this constitution into being was undertaken by prominent Cork member Pat Madden.

In August agreement was reached on a party logo. The centrepiece of the logo, within a circular badge, was a tree, below which were a number of wavy lines that represented either earth or water. It was coloured green on a white background. The logo had been designed by a school colleague of Christopher Fettes, an art teacher named Chris Vis.

Leadership had always been an issue with the greens. Greens don't do leaders. They distrust any concept of 'a leader' that demands that members surrender part of their individuality, freedom and responsibility to another. The closest the greens were to get to a party leader was a 'first among equals' role as party representative. This concept of leadership continued to be the subject of debate over subsequent years at party conventions. Christopher himself felt that:

'I see myself as an initiator but not as a leader; if a leader is needed, a matter that many members question, (s)he must be sought elsewhere. We are not a party of the right, the left or the centre. We are an alternative to the political morass that exists and poses as democracy. With the adoption of policies we will be ready to go out into the world and proclaim our existence. We will be able to undertake the fight to bring about the changes so desperately needed to ensure the survival of the world'.

In October 1982, just before the election, the party held its second convention of that year, again at the Glencree Reconciliation Centre. Topics that were discussed included decentralisation, Northern Ireland, energy, transport, employment, land tenure, agriculture, women, education, Irish language and peace. Henceforth, the party would hold two conventions every year.

At this convention the party was now facing an important decision. The country was faced with a second general election that year. This presented the Ecology Party with another opportunity to put forward candidates for the first time. They decided this time to go ahead, despite the fact that the party was only eleven months old, had not registered, and had little organisation. Now was the time to participate in the grubby business of seeking votes.

Candidate selection in a party of reluctant politicians was relatively easy.

Whoever wanted to be a candidate was allowed to stand. Christopher Fettes was chosen as director of elections. Seven candidates was the minimum number required to get any access to the services of RTE. Seven brave souls entered the fray – three in Dublin constituencies; Roger Garland, Máire Mullarney and Aidan Meagher; two in Cork, Owen Casey and Elizabeth Ryder; one in Limerick, Richard Power; and one in Wicklow, Liam De Siun.

The total return from this first interaction with electoral politics was 3,676 votes, representing 0.2 per cent of the national poll. Of these votes, 1,307 were won in the Cork South Central constituency contested by Owen Casey. Owen, a teacher, was the son of Sean Casey, a former Lord Mayor and much-loved Labour Party TD. While his family background was a big factor in Owen's vote, it also indicated that a green vote existed in Cork that could be developed. Another interesting performance was that of Roger Garland, standing in Dublin South where he polled 950 votes.

The business of contesting an election brought the party and its members into contact with a process that they had not experienced before – registering candidates, producing election literature, drafting a manifesto, dealing with the media and ultimately knocking on doors to ask voters for their support.

An election leaflet common to all green candidates asked potential voters a series of questions:

- Would Ireland not be better run, and would people not have more control over their own lives, if responsibility was held chiefly by local communities, not by an overgrown central power?
- Is full employment as now understood, what we should be aiming at?
- Should work not be satisfying and useful?
- Is it not more so in local businesses, co-operatives and community schemes, than in vast companies?
- Is our present classification of people as employed or unemployed not itself unreal, unfair and divisive?
- Could it be that everyone whether 'employed' or not, has a right to a basic income?
- That such an income would allow greater freedom for serving the community?
- Could our greatest material source, the land, be used more pro-ductively and with more regard to conservation?
- Could it become a source of satisfying work for many more of our people?

- Since the world is a finite system, is it not foolish to assume that economic growth can continue indefinitely?
- Should we not produce goods to last rather than to be thrown away?
- What about recycling much of what is now being wasted?
- To what extent can economic growth justify pollution?
- For example, why do we permit lead in our petrol when it is known to cause brain damage in children?
- Are we over-dependent on energy and especially on imported oil and coal?
- Should we invest more in the harmless, renewable energy sources of sun, wind and wave?
- Is it satisfactory for anyone, even the motorist, that cities are choked with cars? Is it really impossible to make public transport cheap and efficient?
- Are women justly treated in our country? Should society not ensure that no person's potential is in any way restricted by virtue of his or her sex?
- To what extent is the present system of schooling really benefiting either society or the children themselves? What should schools be doing and for whom?
- Has the Republic been neglectful in making constructive suggestions towards a solution in the North? Should we not be pressing for some way of letting the people there implement their wish for compromise? Have we not an urgent duty to make the Republic more the sort of country others would wish to be associated with?
- Should the primary aim of our economic relationship with Third World countries not be to help them to become self-reliant?
- Should Ireland not be more courageous in promoting international peace and justice?

It is remarkable how many of the points outlined in this leaflet remain issues of importance to the greens. The presentation and the prioritisation of the issues may have changed over time, but the germ of the ideas formed in 1982 remains essentially the same.

Small victories, such as the removal of lead from petrol, the ban on burning bituminous coal, or the plastic bag levy, have been achieved in the interim; but most of these issues still remain unaddressed. Other political parties 'talk the talk' and claim that they are promoting environmentally friendly policies but they have no idea whatsoever of the shift that is required if Ireland is to become a sustainable society in the future.

An interesting feature of the election literature printed by the party is the use of the phrase 'Ireland's Green Movement'. This was printed quite prominently on the leaflets. A two-page press release issued in conjunction with the election campaign launch described the party as being neither left wing nor right wing. It could be described as internationalist, as it did not see Ireland as being any more important than any other country.

Media coverage for the Ecology Party in the November 1982 election was scant. Some of the reportage only served to confuse potential voters. In some reports, the Ecology Party was described as being 'Ireland's answer to the Green Peace Movement'. Party activists had to point out that while it was supportive of 'Greenpeace' and of the 'Peace Movement', it was not formally a part of either.

The *Cork Examiner* provided the best coverage of the active campaign conducted on behalf of Owen Casey. The paper reported on the launch of the two Cork candidates, Owen and Elizabeth Ryder. A small piece on green economics was printed in the *Evening Echo*. *Examiner* reporter Maureen Fox also wrote a profile piece on two of the Ecology Party candidates, Elizabeth Ryder and Richard Power. There was some paid advertising with the newspaper, and a creative use of the Letters to the Editors page. Here a series of letters, masquerading as public information, brought the existence of the Ecology Party and its candidates to the readers' attention.

Mentions in other media outlets were less than forthcoming. RTE seemed to acknowledge the presence of the Ecology Party and its candidates only once when Máire Mullarney was asked to make a small contribution on behalf of the party on the subject of women's issues on the RTE Radio 1 programme, *Women Today*.

The Irish Times did make some reference to the fledgling group. A small interview piece appeared with Máire Mullarney. She outlined the party's position on 'Basic Income', and took the opportunity to mention that the party had policy positions on the Third World, lead in petrol, public transport, the use of referenda, the conservation of resources, nuclear power and Northern Ireland.

The Irish Times was the only media organisation to send a reporter to the formal launch of the party's election campaign at Buswell's Hotel in Dublin. The reporter, Willy Clingan, seemed utterly charmed by the whole process. 'The Ecology Party' he noted 'introduced its seven election candidates at quite the nicest and most endearingly honest press conference of the whole campaign. The one reporter present was sat down to tea, sandwiches and cake, while the chairman opened the proceedings by acknowledging that the party did not expect to have anyone actually elected.'

Willy Clingan's report gave information about the numbers of people who were associated with the Ecology Party at the time. Twenty supporters attended the election launch. It was claimed that the party had between two and three hundred members. Given the level of exaggeration that often accompanies these events the truth was probably less than this.

The piece reported a statement from the travel writer Dervla Murphy: 'It wouldn't make any sense, at this early stage in the party's development, to take the Ecology Party seriously on a political level. Its present importance is on the moral / philosophical level – though I doubt if many of its members would use such a pompous phrase.'

The report concluded with a description of the seven Ecology Party candidates, who the greens were and where they had come from. They tended to be middle-class. Máire Mullarney was a journalist, Roger Garland a chartered accountant, Aiden Meagher was a teacher, Owen Casey a guidance counsellor. Liam De Siun from Wicklow was a salesman, Elizabeth Ryder a nurse, and Richard Power a farmer. These backgrounds show that the party exhibited a healthy balance between the urban, the suburban and the rural among its membership.

The following extract from the election literature of Richard Power shows the almost apologetic nature of what was green election campaigning.

There is an old proverb that states: Without a vision, the people will perish. I believe that the Ecology Party offers a new vision of a political future based on co-operation and compassion. We should aim for a universal right to work with dignity. There needs to be a serious questioning of the ruthless exploitation of our fellow creatures and of the land itself, for mere personal gain and so-called progress.

Because the Ecology Party is not yet registered, it will not appear on the ballot paper; so please remember my name and remember too that by giving me your first preference you need not deprive your own party of your traditional support. As soon as I am eliminated your vote will continue to your next preference just the same.

The campaign run in the Cork South Central constituency was the most successful. Even here reality had to be introduced to help bring about the real campaigning that was necessary.

Tommy Simpson worked for a semi-state agency, and was transferred to Cork for a two-week-period that happened to coincide with the general election campaign. He offered to help the Casey campaign and was asked to attend a meeting. This meeting went on for some time discussing the philosophical aspects of ecological politics. After a period of time Tommy asked when the group were going to go canvassing. This question was met with a shocked response. Apparently canvassing was something that other parties did. The Ecology Party was different. Eventually the penny dropped and the Casey campaign got going.

The election resulted in a coalition of Fine Gael and Labour, under Garret Fitzgerald and Dick Spring. When all the bunting from the campaign had finally been removed, director of elections Christopher Fettes returned to the letters page of *The Irish Times* to deliver one last riposte. The paper was taken to task in its election count coverage for not mentioning the Ecology Party as a separate entity. While it seems inconsistent that the paper had mentioned the party on a number of occasions during the campaign itself, it could be argued that the paper didn't have to mention the party at all because it had not yet registered as a political party.

Christopher Fettes, County Offaly

When first invited to contribute something to this book, I thought that I would write about all those marvellous people – many of them no longer active in our party – who helped establish green politics in Ireland in the early 1980s. But there seem to be two good reasons for not doing this: firstly, the risk of repeating much of what is presumably already included elsewhere in this volume (and whose omissions, if any, can be rectified in later editions); and secondly, a somewhat cowardly fear of forgetting to include anyone to whom I should nevertheless be grateful.

Instead, I shall write about two things which probably won't be mentioned elsewhere: the ten years of gestation which led up to the founding of the party, and some important aspects of green thinking which we should at the very least be discussing even if they cannot yet be part of our official policy statements.

According to *The Encyclopaedia of Ireland*, the Green Party was formed 'by the ecology movement and the Green Alliance of the 1970s': untrue. I have read elsewhere that it started as a branch of the UK Ecology Party: equally untrue. So let us start at the beginning. People generally get the birthday of the party right: 3 December 1981, but its conception took place eleven years earlier, in the form of a talk to the Irish Association for Natural Health on 'The Need for Biopolitics'. Some of those present felt that this need could best be satisfied by putting pressure on the traditional parties through independent groups, but a few of us could not see this having a radical enough effect. In any event, the number thinking along these lines in those days was very small indeed.

In the mid-seventies I was fortunate enough to be on sabbatical leave in New Zealand at the time when the Values Party stood for election with a splendidly ecology-minded manifesto entitled *Beyond Tomorrow*. It won no seats, but attracted enough attention among idealists with such a wide range of views that, alas, the party began to disintegrate – something we narrowly managed to avoid ourselves a decade later.

Returning to Ireland with renewed vigour, I joined the freshly formed Friends of the Earth and various animal welfare groups, refounded the Vegetarian Society, and became involved with people interested in the ideas – very different, but not incompatible – of Henry George and C.H.Douglas. More important for many were the feminist, anti-nuclear and peace movements, culminating in the successful gathering at Carnsore Point and the publication of the Alternative Ireland Directory.

But I remained convinced that, whatever the value of these pressure groups, there was definitely room, especially under our PR voting system, for a party based on specifically ecological principles. Two things finally prompted me to round people up for the inaugural meeting of the EPI. One thing were the admirable publications being produced by the new UK Ecology Party: largely written by Jonathon Porritt, these managed brilliantly to show that green thinking – not known as such in those days – was quite different from the nationalist-left-right-centre politics to which we had become accustomed. (Of course Die Grünen were already in action at this point, with their emphasis on being the 'anti-party party', but also with the shadow of Marx not absent.)

The other thing which allowed our party to come into being was of a quite different nature: the invention of the photocopier; this meant that we could, with permission, reproduce all kinds of stimulating material for sale at cost price. The fact that we sold over a £100s worth of pamphlets and small books at our very first meeting showed how eager people were to deepen their knowledge of truly radical ideas.

I now turn briefly to three of these ideas which I think we have neglected: all of them involve overcoming forms of injustice. The first of these is the concept of Site Value Taxation, so beautifully expounded, if only people would take the time to read even parts of *Progress and Poverty* by the American philosopher, Henry George. His basic message, which nothing could be greener than, is that although we can own a house or a farm or a restaurant or an office, we can claim mere possession, not ownership, of the land they stand on. We did not create that land, and in so far as we need to exclude others from it in order to carry out our aims, we should be compensating others for their exclusion. The greater the demand for the patch of land in question, the higher the tax to be paid; and the total accumulated in this way should be equally redistributed among all citizens. Yes, even the owners of small farms would pay the tax, but they would get a lot more back than they paid.

Of course there would be administrative problems, as there are in all worthwhile activities; the point is, however, would it promote justice? Interestingly, no less a person that the president of the Royal Institute of Architects recently commended this idea in a letter to *The Irish Times*. Here in Ireland it could put an end to property speculation; applied in a country like Brazil, where wealthy land-owners would soon realise that they did not after all need such huge estates, the millions of acres that would become available to desperately poor people would take the pressure off the rain forest.

A second idea that we do not discuss nearly enough is the meaning of money; yet money can have only two worthwhile purposes: providing the means for the fair redistribution of the nation's wealth, and facilitating the exchange of goods and services. The first of these I have dealt with above. The second demands that the money supply be increased as the goods and services themselves increase; but at present this does not happen, which inevitably both limits the availability of genuinely desirable things (such as suitable housing, bicycles for all and safe pathways for them to travel on) and increases the national debt.

All new inventions, whether physical or social, are the result of centuries of thinking and working by our ancestors, all our ancestors; and when, as is usually the case, they involve basic materials which – like the land – existed before the appearance of the human race, they too have an aspect to which we may all lay claim. It is thus perfectly sound, and indeed only equitable, for the increase of goods and services to be accompanied by an increase in the money supply, taking the form of a basic income distributed to everyone from the richest (who could give it away if they wished) to the poorest. As with Site Value Taxation, there would be problems, but they need not be insuperable. And once again, if the idea is just, we need to talk about it.

My final niggle, if that is the appropriate word, is our failure to consider the injustice of language discrimination. There are good reasons for deploring the disappearance (fortunately not total) of the Irish language, but I have never heard anyone regretting their knowledge of a language whose widespread use is the result of cultural and financial imperialism. We cannot unknow English, and who would want to forgo the pleasure which this wonderful creation provides? But we are surely duty-bound to be aware of the injustice of expecting everyone else to speak it, especially when we are abroad. And here at least each individual can make a personal effort to overcome this inequality, and enjoy doing so. The international language Esperanto may be spoken by only a few million people in the world, but every time you use it rather than English to communicate with a 'foreigner', you are implying, 'I want to help bear the linguistic burden which history has placed upon you'. Isn't that justice in action?

Christopher Fettes is the founder of the Green Party/Comhaontas Glas. He served as Convener in the early '80s. He ran in the European elections in 1984.

1983

This was to be a significant year for greens in Europe. Die Grünen, the German Green Party, succeeded in winning twenty-seven seats in the Bundestag, making them the first green parliamentary group in the world.

The success of Die Grünen gave great heart and encouragement to the Irish greens. Among the newly elected MPs was Petra Kelly, who was to become an international political celebrity. Petra was a regular visitor to Ireland, and took a particular interest in Irish affairs.

During 1983, politics in Ireland sank into the quagmire of the abortion referendum. Divisions on this issue among the greens were the same as those in other political parties. The liberal wing of green thinking argued strongly for a woman's right to be in full control of her body in all circumstances. Conservative greens maintained that life in all its forms is precious. It was felt among the greens that the issue was best left to individual conscience and therefore the Ecology Party decided not to become involved in this referendum.

The party was more concerned with drawing up its own constitution than that of the nation. The initial proposal for its organisation was hierarchical, in order to meet the requirements necessary to register as a political party. Members expressed their unhappiness with the name of the Ecology Party. Some felt that the use of the word 'ecology' was too complicated and difficult to explain. Others, in their wish to distance themselves from conventional politics, objected to the use of the word 'party' in the title.

An office for party administration was established at 15 Upper Stephen Street. This was funded partially by Christopher and partially by donations to an office fund. Party members in fulltime jobs were exhorted to give a portion of their monthly income by standing order to fund the office. Janice Spalding (*née* McNair) and Tim Torsney, two AnCO trainees, worked for three months full time in the office for free.

Four permanent national committees were established to look after co-ordination, finance and fundraising, information and elections, and conventions credentials.

Branches existed in Cork, Kerry, Wicklow, Rathfarnham, Dublin 8, Dublin North, Tallaght, and at UCD. The smallest unit of the party was the branch. The geographical area of each branch tended to be no smaller than a county administrative area. A complicated formula existed to elect the National Executive. Each branch was to elect a representative who in turn would elect the executive. Finding twelve people willing to be involved on the executive was difficult in these early days. Whoever was willing and able found themselves on the National Executive.

It was decided at the outset that all decisions within the party would be reached by consensus. This form of decision-making seeks the agreement of everyone within a group to a particular course of action. No vote is called and the discussion continues until a compromise is reached. The successful operation of consensus requires a high level of awareness and personal discipline of those involved, the use of periods of silence for reflection, and a willingness not to engage in delaying or in destructive tactics. This form of decision-making has a long and honourable tradition within the Quaker community, where forebearance, patience and tolerance characterise the decision-making process.

Among the greens however, the practice of consensus frequently descended into fractious and petty argument as a minority (or single individual) could block decisions and prolong meetings to a point of frustration and despair. Experience showed that the bigger the grouping, the more difficult it became to achieve consensus.

A week after the abortion referendum George Colley, Fianna Fáil TD for Dublin Central, died. The subsequent by-election was to be held in November. This was a by-election that couldn't be avoided by the greens. It was a constituency in which a large number of the membership of the party lived and where some semblance of a party machine could be organised. Tony Ryan was chosen by the party to contest the by-election. John Gormley, who had only recently joined the party, tells what that experience was like for the party and the candidate:

Tony Ryan took a back seat but was persuaded by the fledgling party to put his name forward for the by-election in Dublin Central in 1984. This was my first experience of canvassing. The response of inner city Dubliners to our message was one of bewilderment and bemusement. I recall canvassing a gentleman standing in his vest at the door of his inner city corporation flat looking at me with a puzzled expression as I tried to explain how substances from his fridge, known as CFCs, were escaping up into the stratosphere, eroding a layer of molecules known as the ozone layer, which protected him from UV radiation from the sun, which would increase skin cancers.

Getting the Green Message across in those early days was not easy, and the audience, generally, was uninformed and not receptive. At least now in 2006, most people know that the problems exist though many may choose to ignore them, as is their democratic right. Later on in that campaign RTE agreed to give us a party political broadcast. This very nearly turned into a complete disaster. Poor Tony Ryan was inundated with ideas at a specially convened meeting at head office, where everyone was throwing in their tuppence halfpenny worth. At one stage one of our Buddhist members suggested, in all seriousness, to Tony that he should look at the camera and say absolutely nothing. "Silence", this man said, "is our strongest response to what is happening currently". I quickly intervened and pointed out that I didn't think that RTE would appreciate a party political broadcast which ended with 'this two minutes of silence were brought to you by the Green Alliance,' an echo of a Guinness ad popular at the time. Anyway, it all passed off without major incident and a nervous Tony did the broadcast. His mother was very proud of him and we didn't do too badly in the election. We were allocated ten tickets to the count, which took place in Kevin Street, DIT. As we didn't have ten people who wished to avail of the tickets, we gave our surplus to some Fianna Fáil guys who were looking for them.

The by-election was won by Tom Leonard, the Fianna Fáil candidate, with Fine Gael candidate Mary Banotti trailing in his wake. The Workers Party and Sinn Féin candidates performed well. Tony Ryan won 453 votes for the Ecology Party.

In 1983 links were established with the European Federation of Green Parties that were to prove a valuable source of support for the party. The first representative was Pol Breannach. Despite financial difficulties it was decided that this link should be maintained and that someone should travel to meetings in Brussels. Máire Mullarney became the regular delegate as she was free to travel more frequently and less expensively. In later years these roles were performed by Tommy Simpson and Dr Lucille O'Shea.

Tommy Simpson, Dublin

It was my friend, the late Rico Ross, (a left-wing Bostonian), who rang to tell me of the inaugural meeting of The Ecology Party of Ireland in the Central Hotel in December 1981. He and I were on the committee of the Dublin City Association of An Taisce. We were also members of an organisation called the Community Government Movement, which had been set up in 1974 to try to break the control of the big parties at local government level. We had success in '74 with six council-lors elected to Dublin City Council, three of whom topped the poll. These 'Community Councillors' were not just independents, but were selected by their communities to contest the elections. Others community councillors were elected in different parts of the country.

I had been a committed environmentalist since the early seventies. I worked as a maintenance fitter on night shift in a tyre factory in Ballyfermot. I spent my time in between, repairing machine breakdowns and reading about the threat to the planet from the excesses of industrialisation. Even back then, writers such as Gordon Rattray Taylor were predicting such things as sea level rises due to global warming. I was deeply shocked by what I read. My electrician mates advised me stop reading that stuff, as it would 'do my head in'.

Sitting beside Rico, I listened to the speeches and felt this was a new beginning. The various activists brought together could be an 'anti-party party'. A mixture of environmentalists, community and anti-nuclear activists, anarchists, solar energy enthusiasts, Esperantists, animal welfare campaigners, vegetarians, all with strong views, were about to embark on the political road. Some present were not convinced of the need for a 'party'.

The organisers seemed to be sincere, if somewhat politically 'green'.
Early in the meeting, Rico commented to me, in his Boston accent, that we might be in the wrong place. We were listening to cultivated south Dublin accents talk about how they were about to take on the (not so civilised)

political machines of Fianna Fáil and the other Irish political parties. I became a member.

Tommy Simpson is a founding member of the Green Party/Comhaontas Glas. He was a candidate for Dublin Central in the 2002 General Election. He is currently a committee member of the European Greens.

1984

From the experience gained in fighting the elections in 1982 and 1983, it was clear that the title 'Ecology Party of Ireland' was inaccessible to most people and was difficult to explain. It was decided to change the name of the party to something more user-friendly.

The debate on the change of name coincided with the adoption of a revised party structure. The party was composed of autonomous local groups working in co-operation with one another to achieve a national political goal. This arrangement represented the party's belief in decentralisation, and in the making of decisions at the lowest effective level.

It was accepted that if the party was to promote green politics then the word 'green' should appear in the party's title. After much debate and a certain amount of rancour, it was eventually agreed that the party in future would be known as 'An Comhaontas Glas / The Green Alliance'. The 'An Comhaontas Glas' part of the name, the Irish translation of 'Green Alliance', was suggested by Bert Walsh, an Irish teacher at the same school where Christopher Fettes worked.

Thus on 12 April 1984 'The Green Alliance / An Comhaontas Glas' formally applied to the Clerk of Dáil Éireann to be registered as a political party. The title had been used in the Dublin Central by-election but this was the first occasion that a green environmental party was officially recognised.

The next challenge that faced the Green Alliance was whether it should contest the European elections due to be held in June of 1984. It was agreed that the party should contest the election and that the Dublin Euro-constituency offered the best prospect of making an impact. Christopher Fettes, the party's founder, was considered the person most capable of representing the Alliance.

A press release of this period illustrates the beginnings of a pan-European approach being adopted by greens of various national organisations across Europe.

> …it is the aim of the greens to work towards a democratic Europe of self-deter-
> mined regions. While the Irish people have the prime responsibility to work for
> their own development, they cannot bring this about in isolation. In Europe
> the greens will seek to change and influence the EEC by opening ways for

regular participation of all citizens in the political life of Europe. The greens will also seek the democratisation of the present European Parliament such that any decision that comes into force at community level would require an endorsement by the majority of the elected members.

The election gave Dublin voters an opportunity of voting green for the first time. Christopher Fettes won 5,242 votes (1.9 per cent).

The Green Alliance had been looking forward to contesting the local elections to city, county and town councils in 1984. These elections were postponed. This was a serious disappointment to the greens, who knew that their future development as a new political party was dependent on them winning seats on local city and county councils.

The year 1984 was the year that the party sought a permanent base. The lease on its first office at Stephen's Street had not been renewed after a fire at the building. Tommy Simpson was delegated the task of finding suitable office accommodation. The first property he was shown was on South Frederick Street. The office size was sufficient, but the rent, at £80 a week, was beyond the capacity of the party. This premises was later to become the headquarters for another political party – the Progressive Democrats.

Fownes Street was the next property that was seen. At £20 a week, the rent was affordable. However, the deposit to secure the lease was not readily available. As had happened so often before, Christopher Fettes came to the rescue and provided the financial backing required.

Having secured the lease to Fownes Street, Christopher saw that this office could also be of use to other groups, such as the Vegetarian Society and the Esperanto Society, as well as for the partial use of the Green Alliance. Other party officers were not happy with this arrangement and so interest in the lease was transferred from Christopher's name to a group of party nominees. The Fownes Street office then became available for the exclusive use of the Green Alliance.

These were difficult economic times. Emigration was at levels that the country had last experienced in the 1950s and successive governments seemed impotent in the face of the prevailing economic conditions. Being unable to do anything with the economy, Garret Fitzgerald as Taoiseach turned his attention to promoting his 'constitutional crusade' to turn Ireland into a more liberal country. Part of this crusade consisted of trying to make some progress in relation to Northern Ireland. To this end the government established the New Ireland Forum in May 1983. Unionists chose not to participate in the forum. Sinn Féin wasn't invited because of its ambivalence towards violence, and the Workers Party wasn't considered large enough or important enough to be involved. The Green Alliance wasn't even considered. The party did however make a written submission to the forum.

The submission stated that it was only the people of Northern Ireland who could decide their own future. It urged the British and Irish governments to replace the British army with an international body (to include not only soldiers, but jurists, solicitors, prison officers, policemen, political scientists, and constitutional experts). The submission also sought the provision of integrated or secular co-educational community schools, a change in both the republic's constitution and in the British guarantee to the Unionists, and the establishment of a public enquiry into the constitutional position of Northern Ireland, with a view to holding a multiple choice preferendum with at least six options.

An Ecology Party had existed in Northern Ireland for some time before the formation of the Green Alliance in the Republic. In 1981 they had contested the local elections. Three candidates had put themselves forward for that election. One of them, Peter Emerson, was later to establish the De Borda Institute that promotes multi-option preferenda. In the sectarian atmosphere of Northern Ireland these intrepid three barely mustered 350 votes between them.

Sean O' Flynn, Cork

The following is a personal reflection on what I consider to be a remarkable group of people who came together during the 1980s to establish, in Ireland, a new political party now known as 'An Comhaontas Glas / The Green Party'. A review of the personal characteristics of these founding members, would include marginality, tolerance of public ridicule, 'transgenerational' thinking, emotional sensitivity, political homelessness, courage, tenacity and perseverance. The greens' expression of these qualities in the political arena provides an insight into the spirit of the party and legitimates its claim to a significant role in the future governance of the Irish Republic.

Marginality

Those who initiated this political movement were idealistic, thoughtful, generally quiet people, who had little or no previous political experience. Many were middle-aged or elderly. A disproportionate (to the general population) number were non-Catholic or agnostic. A surprising number were fluent Irish speakers who could conduct meetings 'as Gaeilge' with ease. Many had lived or worked abroad. Only four had any family background in politics. Some pursued a low energy lifestyle, cycled to work and grew organic vegetables in the back garden.

Though disparate in values, they shared certain commonalities. Most felt marginalized in Irish society, and had no affinity with the mainstream parties and the rigidity of conventional political thinking. This quality of marginality gave the pioneering greens a different perspective from which to reflect upon the transformation that was taking place in Ireland towards the end of the twentieth century. Because they had a different set of values, they were able to offer an alternative political interpretation of the future.

During the 1970s authoritative scientific reports, such as 'Limits to Growth' (Club of Rome Report 1972), indicated that the exponential growth in postwar 'western' economies was unsustainable; and would eventually decline in the twenty-first century, due to limited availability of oil, water, and mineral deposits.

Other reports indicated that the capitalist market-driven system of human development was beginning to 'spoil the nest'. The exponential growth in the human population (with its insatiable appetite for fossil fuels), uncontrolled urban expansion and habitat destruction, and the burning of fossil fuels had begun to contribute to climate change, global warming, ozone depletion, and a visible decline in biodiversity.

Throughout the 1970s successive governments in Ireland had engaged in programmes of economic expansion based on imported multinational industry, native construction and global financial services. By the early 1980s however, it was becoming clear that this model of development was vulnerable (to global trends and the whims of transnational companies). This is unsustainable in the long term. Some people were concerned and felt the need to do something.

Tolerance of Public Ridicule

New political or social ideas are often greeted with suspicion, and then subjected to ridicule, before being accepted as 'normal'. In Ireland, the development in awareness of ecological and environmental concerns has followed this predictable pattern of resistance, followed by ridicule and later assimilation.

Historically, (because of poverty, colonialisation, insecurity in tenancy of land holdings, emigration and low population density), care for the countryside, wildlife habitat, and the environment generally, were not viewed as issues worthy of political consideration.

During the 1960s, '70s and '80s, concern for the health of the planet or indeed the local environment, were regarded in much the same light as French cheese, Georgian houses, abstract art, or cricket; of interest to the well-off, the middle classes, or the effete *Irish Times* reader who went hill-walking on Sundays, but not the stuff of common discourse. 'Denvironment' was dismissed as being of sectional interest to members of An Taisce or the committees of tidy towns. In the popular mind, it could only be jus-tified in terms of promoting tourism. But it was definitely *not* an election issue.

From the beginning, the Ecology Party was subjected to a campaign of mockery and vilification. Established politicians resented the entry of the greens into the political arena. The 'brown-rice, beads and sandals' caricature was compounded by the cynicism of media commentators unable to place the greens on the left/right axis of Irish politics.

The orthodox view throughout the 1980s was that green policies did not belong to 'the real world'. Members and spokespersons for the green move-ment were dismissed as elitist, aging hippies, idealistic, foreign, and worst of all, intellectual! Fortunately many of the greens had previously worked with environmental organisations, peace groups, third world development groups, tidy town committees etc., and had become skilled in dealing with the igno-rant incredulity that a new idea encounters when first introduced to the smug conservative world of the Irish establishment.

The party is indebted to those candidates who, during the 1980s and early 1990s, allowed their names to go forward to seek public acceptance for the party and its policies. They stood in elections to public office and contested seats they clearly had no hope of winning.

Transgenerational Thinking

The greens realise, as do most people who apply their minds to the logic of the situation, that the present economic paradigm, based on capitalism, and dependent on constant growth in GDP, is unsustainable in the long-term. In support of their conclusions they point to depleting, finite stocks of available oil, water and raw materials.

Greens claim that the pollution and waste of industrial and commercial capitalism is now of such a magnitude that it poses a threat to the wellbe-ing of this planet and its dependent plant and animal life. They favour an economic model that would prioritise a longer-term, slower, smaller-scale sustainable model of human development. They believe that for human soci-ety to achieve long-term sustainability, and not destroy the planet, it will be necessary to curtail personal consumption and slow-down short-term economic growth.

These ideas are not readily understood or accepted by a culture that glorifies and promises immediate gratification. Consequently, they were in direct contrast to the mood that prevailed in Ireland during the 1970s and '80s.

The founding members were aware that green economic ideas would be unpopular with an Irish electorate whose instinct was to get away from poverty as quickly as possible. During this time, the 'transgenerational' vision of green spokespersons contrasted sharply with the orthodoxy of capitalistic economic thinking among the Irish electorate. In a culture where politicians think exclusively of the next election, the greens were speaking of future generations and a more long-term strategy. Not surprisingly, they seemed out of touch.

Emotional Sensitivity

> *The destiny of machines is the making of roads.*
> *The destiny of man is the losing of all.*
> Michael Hartnett, *The Grove.*

Many of those involved in establishing An Comhaontas Glas recall that as children they were fortunate to have had a 'significant other' as a grandparent, parent, teacher or neighbour. A figure the child admired, who was perhaps a gardener, or had an interest in birds or simply walked the dog. These significant others, by their personal example, inspired in the child a love of nature and a respect for justice.

Sensitivity to natural phenomena, and an appreciation of the intricate web of the natural systems that supports life on the planet, is a common attribute among those active in the green movement. Such people are naturally shocked and saddened when they witness first-hand, incidents of pollution or habitat destruction. In fact most children are 'greens' before they grow up. For some greens, this childhood awareness provides the passion that fuels their commitment to continue as active members of the party.

Have Ye No Homes To Go To?

By the mid-1980s green activists had become accustomed to the anarchic energy, spontaneity and direct action of local environmental/community/anti-dump campaigns. Some had taken part in the successful campaign to stop the building of a nuclear power plant at Carnsore, County Wexford, in 1978-1979. Others had opposed the inappropriate siting of pharmaceutical plants in rural areas and around Cork harbour. Most were members of organisations such as CND, Friends of the Earth, Greenpeace, Amnesty International, Concern, Afri, animal welfare groups, women's groups, returned development workers in Comhlamh, etc. Yet, despite all this political action, until 1982 there was no political party these citizens could support when an election was called. Many did not vote at all, or if they did, it was usually a 'protest' vote for an independent candidate.

In this milieu, what held the early greens together (despite all the internal rancour) was the fact that they had nowhere else to go.

Courage

It takes courage for anyone to stand up and put themselves forward as a candidate in an election, particularly when there is a likelihood of facing a humiliating defeat. For some greens, the courage to take cases as far as the Supreme Court, was far in excess of what would be normally required to engage in politics. It took courage for Raymond Crotty and later Patricia Mc Kenna to enter the high stakes arena of Irish law. Stiofán Nutty describes the financial implications of the action the Green Party took against RTE regarding convention coverage. Even when Trevor Sargent refused to pay his TV license (on the grounds that the provision for Irish language programming was inadequate) It required courage to go to court and later jail in order to make the point. Any contact with the courts is stressful even when you know you are right, but fear you might not win.

Tenacity

The sheer doggedness required by those in public life is beyond what most of us can readily imagine. They are on constant call and always in the public eye. The strain is even greater when one is operating without the support structure that the mainstream party candidates can take for granted. To be an elected representative at any level requires a special dedication to 'the cause'!

I remember canvassing with Dan Boyle in 1991 in the local elections. It was a lovely sunny Saturday. We had worked our way down along the Blackrock road. When we got near the end, I lay down with exhaustion, in the shade on the grass at Janemount and looked on as Dan continued like a driven machine, leafleting the remaining estates on his own. Later I accompanied him when he drove all over Munster seeking out unsuspecting independent county councillors, in order to canvass their vote for some obscure vocational panel seat in the senate.

Trevor Sargent demonstrated the same determination in the early days, when he would regularly travel the round trip from Drimoleague to Cork, in mid-winter, on a small motorbike, to attend meetings in the city.

Perseverance

In the early days when a member agreed to stand as a candidate in an election they invariably had to rely on their own personal resources, friends and family to fund the campaign. Most candidates in the early years had to take out loans and spend their own money on campaigns. Homes became offices. Phone bills shot up. Families made big sacrifices. The sheer physical demand of canvassing with no funds, no replacements for posters ripped down or removed. Not enough leaflets, areas not canvassed, too few people, too little time left until polling day. And that is only one campaign.

'It takes, on average, ten years from the time you are elected as a councillor to the time you might make it to the Dáil.' John Dennehy, TD.

What of the Future?

In a healthy green movement, (of which the Green Party would be the political expression,) a balance has to be found, between the polemic polarities of the 'fundis' and the 'realos'.

The task that faced the original group who succeeded in getting elected on behalf of the greens was to present a reliable, solid image to the public. In this, they have succeeded very well. You do not hear much talk of brown rice, sandals or aging hippies these days. The Green Party has adapted to the Irish stage very well and has found its place. However, in its assimilation to the demands of protocol and those of the media, there is a danger that the 'realo' hand might be overplayed. If the greens are to appeal to younger voters, and forge ahead, they will need to keep their radical cutting edge sharp, and ready.

Sean O'Flynn is a founding member of the Green Party/Comhaontas Glas. He has been an active member of the party since its inception.

1985

The coalition government arranged to hold local elections in June 1985. The greens put forward thirty-nine candidates, with little expectation of any being elected. This was an exercise to see how many green votes were out there.

Twenty-nine candidates contested local authority wards in the Dublin city and county area. There was some degree of geographical spread throughout the country with the remaining candidates standing in Cork, Limerick, Wicklow, Louth, Monaghan and Kerry. What these candidates had in common was a sense of isolation and a lack of support. In Dublin, at least there existed some critical mass of membership.

Despite the fact that the majority of greens lived in Dublin, it was in Kerry that the first green electoral breakthrough occurred. Marcus Counihan had acquired a reputation for his campaigning in relation to the National Park in Killarney. He was encouraged to contest the Urban District Council election for the town. To the surprise of many he received 244 first preferences (7 per cent of the vote) and thus became the first Green Alliance elected representative in Ireland.

While the Killarney success could be attributed to campaigning on the part of the candidate, it was still unanticipated at a local level. A young reporter for the *Kerryman* newspaper, John Downing, later to become a respected member of the Dáil press gallery, wrote in his weekly column that the greens hadn't a hope of winning a seat in Killarney.

Only two of the seven candidates who had stood for the Ecology Party in the November 1982 election contested these local elections. This lack of consistency in candidate presentation was another inhibiting factor during the early years of green politics in Ireland.

The benefits of operating as a party however were beginning to become apparent. There were economies of scale to be achieved with the pooling of resources, particularly in the printing of election literature. Common election leaflets were printed with a space left on each leaflet where candidates could stamp their names and contact details.

In total, Green Alliance candidates won 8284 votes in the local elections. This represented 0.5 per cent of the national vote, or 2.3 per cent of the vote where the party contested. Trevor Sargent contested the Balbriggan ward of Dublin County Council on behalf of the Alliance, winning a total of 227 votes. The performance of women candidates standing on behalf of the greens was an encouraging feature of this election. Betty Reeves in Blackrock and Fiona Garland in Rathfarnham each won around 6 per cent of the vote. Ingrid Masterson dipped just under this percentage.

During this period the coalition government signed the Anglo-Irish Agreement and introduced legislation to liberalise the laws on contraception. In the course of the passage of the bills through the Dáil, Dessie O'Malley, the Fianna Fáil TD for Limerick East, voted with the coalition and was subsequently expelled from the party.

O'Malley had long expressed his dissatisfaction with the leadership of Charles Haughey and just before Christmas 1985 he formed a new political party – the Progressive Democrats (PDs). Within a few weeks O'Malley was joined by Fianna Fáil TDs Mary Harney, Pearse Wyse, and Bobby Molloy, and others, notably Michael Keating from Fine Gael, were also to join.

Marcus Counihan, Killarney

Nobody gave us a chance in 1985. Even some of our own crowd gave us no chance. When you have been written off as a no-hoper it makes it more difficult to get people to vote for you. At the same time, it gives you the advantage of the underdog, the element of surprise. I remember the day after the election well: the feeling of shock and disbelief on hearing the news that the greens in Killarney had made history by having the first and only green candidate elected in the entire country. Then the realization slowly set in that I actually was this candidate.

In the early 1980s a public meeting was advertised in the Killarney Library on the topic of Sellafield. It was an issue that I found frightening then and still do now, so I went along and that is how I became involved in politics. The Kerry greens were a small group of committed people, mainly from Killarney, who wanted to make a difference and felt their outlook was not reflected by the traditional parties, which were still trying to shake off their civil war legacy.

The Green Party was known then as the Green Alliance. It suffered from a bit of an identity problem. The electorate did not know who we were or what we stood for and if they did, they were usually wrong. The media largely ignored us and we were not taken too seriously. We were seen at best as an environmental pressure group and at worst as some sort of an extension of the Republican movement.

We might have been small, but we were well organised and 'ready to go' the minute the elections were announced. The *Irish Star*'s political correspondent John Downing was a young reporter working with the *Kerryman* newspaper in Killarney at the time. In his column that week he wrote that the greens had no chance of being elected. I must admit to a wry smile every time I hear John being introduced by Pat Kenny as part of his 'expert panel' to discuss issues of the week.

Polling day was 21 June 1985, midsummer's day and possibly the wettest day I can remember. Considering that this is Killarney, that is really saying something. Up to that morning I had been confident that we could cause an upset. With the incessant rain my confidence waned. I had hoped to motivate people who did not normally vote, the youth and the disaffected, but would they brave the rain?

They did. The green candidate got elected, and that was not the only thing that was green. Most of our members at that time had little or no experience of active politics. I had to learn everything from scratch but some of the councillors were decent enough to help me out until I got the hang of things. In the years after I left the council I went to work in theatre, where I came across an interesting paradox: there is more politics involved in the theatre than in the council chamber, and more acting in the chamber than on stage – well, at least in local politics anyway. I witnessed some very serious disagreements between councillors in my time. Ten minutes later the protagonists would be down in the pub buying each other drinks, each hoping their performance would merit the headline in tomorrow's local paper.

One particular motion I put to my council colleagues was for bottle banks to be provided for recycling. I failed to have it passed and was informed that it would be completely uneconomical. Economics have changed in the meantime. It is no longer economical to dig a big hole in the ground and dump everything into it. Many of the issues we brought up back then were seen as 'way out' but have become mainstream today.

I did not see out my full term for a number of different reasons. The darker side to Irish politics at that time had a part to play in my decision to retire politically. Officially things were done one way, but unofficially things were done another. The tribunals of recent years have shed some light on how politics were carried out in the '80s. To be a politician one needs the hide of a rhinoceros and I must admit that it is an attribute that I do not possess.

Many of the same issues that motivated me to get involved in Green politics are still major issues today: Sellafield, the impending energy crisis and human rights being the major ones. Another issue which greatly troubles me is the lack of rights given to pedestrians and cyclists in this country. Ireland used to be rated as having a good quality of life, a place where children could walk and cycle to school, where people had time. Economics are important but a lot of what is important cannot be measured in monetary terms and we have to start giving more recognition to this fact.

The Kerry greens gave the party its first electoral victory twenty-one years ago. It was a small step but small steps are crucial, especially when they mark the beginning of a journey as important as the one the greens are on today. In the near future I hope to see another step on that journey when green ministers take their place at the cabinet table.

Marcus Counihan joined the Green Party/Comhaontas Glas in the early eighties and became the first Green Party councillor in 1985. He served as a member of Killarney Urban District Council until 1988. He was a candidate in the 1987 General Election for South Kerry.

1. The Waterboys playing a fundraising concert for the Green Party in 1987.

2. The Green Party acquired an office in an old Georgian house on Fownes Street, Temple Bar, in 1984. The small office served the party for twenty years.

3. John Gormley addressing the Environmental Emergency Conference organised by the Green Party in 1987.

4. Sean McBride, Grattan Healy and Emer Colleran at the Environmental Emergency Conference in 1987.

5. At the Environmental Emergency Conference in 1987. From right: Michael Keating, John Boland, Frank Convery, Eamon Gilmore, Alison Batten.

6. Petra Kelly visiting Ireland on Hiroshima Day, City Hall, 1989. Patricia McKenna, John Gormley, Steve Rawson and Carol Fox.

7. Opening of the National Ecology Centre, Sonairte, in 1989. Left to right: Anna Doran, Tommy Simpson, Edmund Fitzgerald Selby, Dr David Cabot, Kathy Marsh, Trevor Sargent.

Right: 8. A young European election candidate –Trevor Sargent in 1989.

Below: 9. Canvassing in Dublin during the 1994 European election campaign. From left: Trevor Sargent, Roderic O'Gorman, Patricia McKenna.

10. European election candidates Nuala Ahern and Patricia McKenna, Dan Boyle and Richard Doubtwaite with Trevor Sargent during the 1994 campaign.

11. Former MEP Nuala Ahern with former European Commission President Romano Prodi.

12. John Gormley, Lord Mayor of Dublin, with Prince Charles during his visit in 1994.

13. John Gormley TD meeting Joschka Fischer, German Green Party Foreign Minister, during a visit to Ireland in 1998.

14. Front: Former MEP Nuala Ahern and Trevor Sargent TD. Back: Fintan McCarthy and John Gormley TD celebrate as the Nice referendum votes are announced for Dublin at the 2001 count in the RDS. **(courtesy Photocall Ireland).**

15. Paul Gogarty and Ciarán Cuffe at the 2002 Green Party General Election campaign launch outside Dublin Castle. (courtesy Photocall Ireland).

16. Dan Boyle with daughter Saoirse campaigning during the 1997 General Election.

Right: 17. Harry Sargent demonstrating at a large anti-war march at Parnell Square Dublin 2003 **(courtesy Photocall Ireland)**.

Below: 18. From left to right: Cllr Chris O'Leary, Thomas Connole, Ann Glynn, Graham Lightfoot, Anne Marie Flanagan, Colm O'Brien, Reinhard Bütikofer (German Greens), Cllr Donal O Bearra and Trevor Sargent TD at the annual convention in Galway 2004.

Above: 19. Daniel Cohn Bendit (President of the European Greens) and Cllr Deirdre de Burca at the European Green Conference hosted by the Irish Green Party in 2004 in Dublin Castle.

Below: 20. Members from Dublin South East Greens (Anita Curtis and Eunice McKeown) demonstrating against the proposed incinerator at Ringsend, Dublin. **(Courtesy Photocall Ireland)**

Right: 21. Former Green Party MEP Patricia McKenna placing a campaign poster against the Citizenship Referendum in 2004 outside the Minister for Justice Michael McDowell's constituency office in Dublin **(courtesy Photocall Ireland).**

Below: 22. The Green Party 'Save Our Salmon' campaign that travelled around the country to end the practice of drift netting and to save Irish salmon stocks in 2005.

23. On Car Free Day in 2005 the Green Party launched its 2010 vision for Dublin city centre. From left: John Gormley TD, Trevor Sargent TD, Ciarán Cuffe TD, Cllr Bronwen Maher.

24. Deputy Green Party Leader and Spokesperson for Agriculture Cllr Mary White at the National Ploughing Championships in 2005.

25. In 2005 the Green Party organised a Civic Forum on Climate Change in the Mansion House, Dublin. The forum was addressed by scientific, civic, economic and political leaders and had a live link to the United Nations Climate Change Conference in Montreal, Canada. At the forum the Dublin Declaration on Climate Change was agreed unanimously by the participants. From left: Ciarán Cuffe TD, Eamon Ryan TD, Trevor Sargent TD, John Gormley TD.

26. The fight against GMOs continues to be a major campaign issue for the Green Party. From left: Cllr Caroline Burrell, Cllr Deirdre de Burca, Cllr Tom Kivlehan.

Above: 27. The Green Party supporting the Rossport Five in 2005 during the Corrib gas pipeline controversy.

Below: 28. The Young Greens highlighting Ireland's Kyoto protocol commitments. From left: former Chair of the Young Greens, Pat Barrett and Deputy Chair Molly Walsh.

Right: 29. The late Dermot Hamilton, a long-standing Green Party member who was made General Secretary of the party in 2004.

Below: 30. The Kinsale Greens' launch in 2005. Back row, from left: Cllr Chris O'Leary, Cllr Dominick Donnelly, Andrew Dillon. Front row, from left: Dan Boyle TD, Rossie Corrigan, Cllr Isabel Sutton. (**Courtesy Howard Crowley**).

31. Trevor Sargent TD being interviewed by Sean O'Rourke for the RTE show *The Week in Politics* during the 2006 National Convention.

32. Cllr Niall Ó'Brolcháin, who was made Mayor of Galway city in 2006, with members of the Young Greens.

33. The six elected TDs outside Leinster House. Left to right: Paul Gogarty, Eamon Ryan, Trevor Sargent, John Gormley, Dan Boyle, Ciarán Cuffe. **(courtesy Photocall Ireland)**.

34. Members of the enlarged staff team in 2006.

1986

An opinion poll in January 1986 recorded that the PDs had 19 per cent support among the electorate. O'Malley embarked on a series of nation-wide tours of public meetings in small halls, all of which were very well attended.

The PDs held one such public meeting at the Metropole Hotel in Cork. People were everywhere. There was such an overspill from the main meeting room that a public address system had to be rigged up all over the hotel so that everyone could hear what was going on. Most people were there out of curiosity. Many were attracted to the PDs because they wanted something new in Irish politics.

On 25 April an explosion occurred at a nuclear power plant at Chernobyl in the Ukraine. Fallout from the explosion dispersed over a wide area of Europe. As a result, higher than normal levels of radiation were recorded in County Wicklow. The accident at Chernobyl caused many people in Ireland to look nervously across the Irish Sea at what was happening at the Sellafield nuclear installation on the Cumbrian coast. This installation had been in commission since the 1950s, but concern increased significantly after the Chernobyl explosion. It became a major campaign for the greens in Ireland.

Two years before, in 1984, a major disaster had occurred at the Union Carbide plant in Bhopal, India. Around this time a number of other incidents involving industrial and nuclear safety alerted public opinion to the fact that conventional political parties were not addressing environmental concerns. Many in Ireland wondered at the long term environmental impact of an industrial policy that encouraged multi-national chemical plants to locate on green field sites throughout rural Ireland without proper safety or environmental safeguards. Campaigning organisations, particularly in the Cork harbour area, began to ask questions and seek assurances on health, safety and environmental concerns. The oil tanker *Kowloon Bridge* broke up off the coast of Cork, inflicting considerable ecological damage to the adjacent coastline. This accident drew further attention to the fact that the Irish political system had neither the technical expertise nor the conviction to deal with environmental accidents.

During 1986 it was proposed to hold a referendum to remove the prohibition on divorce contained within the constitution. Opinion polls indicated this proposition might be successful. However, the government campaign was a disaster. An overwhelming majority voted against the amendment. As had happened previously during the referendum on abortion in 1983, and for the same reasons of personal belief, the greens stayed neutral.

Within the greens the long-running debate on whether it was a political party or a campaigning organisation resurfaced. Many members were frustrated by the lack of any real political achievement to date. The political realists within the Alliance argued for a more reformist long-term strategy. Those who despaired of electoral politics formed a group within the party that was, to all intents and purposes, a party within a party. They titled themselves the GANG, (Green Action Now Group). So intense was the distaste of this group for politics that it stamped, '…the policies in this leaflet are not necessarily shared by all groups in the Green Alliance' on leaflets.

The branch structure of the Alliance mirrored these anarchist tendencies. There were no uniform titles for Green Alliance branches. The names of these autonomous groups varied widely from 'The Fingal Greens' and 'The Cork Green Movement' to 'The Rathmines Radicals'.

Matters came to a head when a decision was taken by the National Council of the Green Alliance to pursue green ideals exclusively by electoral means. This resulted in a significant number of members leaving the Alliance. The split rejuvenated the remaining members of the Alliance who were now free to focus on the task of winning political office. They examined their structures to see what changes might be needed to enable the party to become an efficient electoral machine.

During 1986, the Irish government agreed to ratify the Single European Act. This act was to be the template for the future development of the European Union. The Irish government assumed that the 1972 referendum, which had given public approval to Ireland joining the European Economic Community in 1973, was sufficient and that there was no need to hold any further referendum to decide on how the EEC itself might change.

On Christmas Eve of 1986 a High Court injunction restraining the government from signing the act was initiated by the agricultural economist Raymond Crotty. This action was to have a significant impact on Ireland's future relationship with the European Union. Mr Crotty made his court challenge on constitutional grounds. He argued that any change in the relationship between Ireland (as a nation) and the European Union had implications for our national sovereignty and consequently would require a change in the Irish constitution. This change, he claimed, required public agreement through the holding of a special referendum.

Everyone involved in Irish politics had a nervous Christmas in 1986.

Ciarán Cuffe, Dún Laoghaire

One of my earliest memories is watching the moon landing at home in 1969. Neighbours and family were gathered around a small black and white television. The reception was blurred and grainy. We watched enthralled as Neil Armstrong stepped on to the surface of the moon. Those magical images of the earth from space made us realise for the first time that our planet is a delicate, precious and beautiful home. These images raised awareness of how fragile the earth is, and that the natural resources of the earth must be safeguarded for the benefit of future generations.

There were always lively conversations at mealtimes in our house. I naturally became interested in current affairs. I remember my dad presenting a paper on Irish Travellers to the United Nations Conference on the Human Environment at Stockholm in 1972. My parents were interested in education and with someone like Máire Mullarney as a neighbour in Shankill, lengthy discussions ensued.

I remember being angry at the destruction of Viking Dublin at Wood Quay, and taking my 'Save Wood Quay' placard into town from Shankill, on the Number 45 bus, to join a march through central Dublin in the late 1970s. In particular I recall listening to Mary Robinson's fiery speech under the shadow of Christchurch Cathedral.

Michael Viney was the catalyst in my actually joining the Green Party. He wrote the article 'Alternative Votes', in *The Irish Times* of 13 February 1982. In his article he stated that the Ecology Party of Ireland was 'presented as a radical alternative to both capitalism and socialism. … [of interest to] those who favour a storehouse economy, non-exploitative approach to nature, land reform, human-scale institutions, alternative technology, a basic unearned income for all, and the decentralization of political power.'

It struck a chord, and within days I had joined the fledgling party as member number sixty-three. Máire Mullarney tried to persuade me to run for election back then but having only just turned eighteen, I told her that I wanted a few more years experience of politics before I'd consider running.

Charlie Haughey won the election that was held a few days later. As the new Taoiseach he told the nation to tighten its belt. While this was going on, a few of us gathered at the Glencree Reconciliation Centre in Wicklow and after the obligatory minute's silence proceeded to discuss the state of the world. The founding principles of the party were adopted at those Glencree meetings, and have underpinned the party's actions ever since.

The early days of the greens weren't all peace and love. I remember Ubi Dwyer storming out of an early convention. He felt that we were compromising our beliefs by actually running candidates for election. Ubi had run for election himself though, in Dún Laoghaire in the 1981 election. His main platform was to decriminalise and reclassify certain illicit drugs. He generated a small cult following among the youth of Dún Laoghaire. Ubi never ran for the greens and died tragically after a bike accident in Wicklow.

Liam de Siuin ran for the Green Alliance in Wicklow in 1982 and 1987. He received 1.1 per cent of the vote first time out and 1.4 per cent five years later. There were debates as to whether candidates should have posters or not. Eventually Liam was allowed put up small cardboard posters with his name, the words 'Green Alliance' and the party's logo (of a tree with mountains behind). I remember canvassing for him in Bray. Back then every door had the key left in the latch outside, a rare thing to see nowadays. John Gormley eventually broke the taboo of placing his photograph on a poster. He was only allowed do so because he had a photo of planet earth behind him. His slogan was – 'Other parties promise you the sun, moon and stars; only the greens guarantee the earth'. It contrasted sharply with 'Fast forward with Fianna Fáil', or 'Rise and follow Charlie'.

Ann McGoldrick was our first Green Party candidate in Dún Laoghaire. She ran a no-nonsense campaign to clean up dog litter, and tackle bad planning in the town. She received 929 votes in the 1987 election and joined the Progressive Democrats soon afterwards. She still writes to me with ideas on planning enforcement in Dalkey, where she lives.

I myself went along to the first meeting of the PDs in the Royal Marine

Hotel in Dún Laoghaire. I will always remember a question from the audience about live hare-coursing. Dessie O'Malley said he wouldn't allow any city-dweller interfere with a countryman's 'innocent day out'. That confirmed my decision that I had joined the right party.

The party went through various name changes in the 1980s and for a while had offices over Banana's vegetarian restaurant on Stephen Street in Dublin. There was a particularly gory butcher's shop next door which couldn't have been great for the restaurant's business. It must have been fairly off-putting for our members who were also in the Vegetarian Society.

Eventually we moved to premises in an ancient building on Fownes Street in Temple Bar. I manned the office as a volunteer over the course of a cold winter, and I have vivid memories of freezing there. The few visitors that did call were usually looking for the tailor who did alterations next door. I was able to concentrate on reading through the extensive library that Christopher Fettes had donated to the party.

Back in the late 1980s, the greens were active in the debate about the future of Dublin city. Mike Curtis, Gerry Boland and others wrote submissions looking for alternatives to knocking down buildings and displacing communities. By this stage I was at UCD studying architecture. A group of us formed Students Against the Destruction of Dublin, and put forward alternatives to Dublin Corporation's madcap proposals for motorways through the heart of the city. Within the greens I wanted to tackle transport and planning, and was much more comfortable working on these kinds of issues than promoting Esperanto and basic income. We used megaphone diplomacy to fight City Hall, and it worked. We marched to the City Hall on Dame Street and harangued councillors such as Ben Briscoe and Alice Glen for neglecting the heart of Dublin. We got widespread publicity for our efforts. The 'Dublin City in Crisis' conference acted as a catalyst for the recognition of the rights of inner city communities. Our marches to save Clanbrassil Street from destruction, and to stop the Georgian buildings being knocked down were (at least partially) successful.

John Gormley, Clare Wheeler, Sadhbh O'Neill and I were elected to Dublin City Council for the Green Party in June of 1991. Sadhbh was in the United States on a J1 student working visa when she was elected. I remember waiting anxiously for her return. John Stafford, the leader of the Fianna Fáil group on the council, engaged her in conversation the moment she arrived back in Ireland, at a reception for the Dublin and Meath teams in the Mansion House. We were terrified that she would be taken in by his charm. We negotiated a Civic Charter for Dublin. It undertook to tackle dereliction, improve public transport, and build more housing. Those negotiations also led to John becoming Lord Mayor of Dublin a few years later. We had a fantastic meeting a few days after the election in Taylor's Hall in Dublin. I remember someone suggesting that we move the meeting outside to the Peace Park beside Christchurch. There we sat in a circle, and worked out how to 'green' the city of Dublin. Frank Feeley was the City Manager back then. He and his press officer Noel Carroll tended to oppose every idea that the greens put forward. It wasn't until the late nineties, when officials like Owen Keegan and Dick Gleeson were appointed to senior positions in the executive, that green ideas slowly began to penetrate the 'politburo' that was Dublin Corporation back then.

Looking back we were both far-seeing and at the same time naïve, in what we were trying to achieve. Very often we were simply out of touch with what weighed heavily on the voters' minds. Even in 1997, when we made the issues of food and waste management a central theme in our campaign, these issues were only really of interest to a narrow segment of society. Both John Gormley and Trevor Sargent presented a professional image of the party following their success in the 1997 election. Patricia McKenna and Nuala Ahern's presence at the European Parliament for ten years connected us to environmental issues on the European stage.

We are well-placed for the next election. Articles on global issues of energy price hikes and climate change appear in every Sunday supplement with increasing frequency. Poor planning and public transport are issues that will sway voters. People are looking for change. We may yet have more influence over the future of this country than we currently appreciate. I feel the greens can do well in the next election, provided that we are fully engaged with social justice, and economic issues as well as environmental concerns.

Ciarán Cuffe joined the Green Party/Comhaontas Glas in 1982. He was elected to Dublin City Council in 1991 and 1999. He is a TD for the Dún Laoghaire Dáil Constituency and is party Spokesperson on the Environment, Heritage and Local Government and Justice, Equality and Law Reform.

1987

With the coming of the New Year it seemed unlikely that the coalition government of Fine Gael and Labour would last for much longer. The two partners in government failed to agree on a budget. Hardened positions were adopted and the government duly fell apart on 20 January when the Labour Party ministers resigned. An election was called for 17 February.

The Green Alliance put forward nine candidates. Three of the nine, (Roger Garland, Máire Mullarney and Liam De Siun), had previous Dáil election experience. Other candidates such as Trevor Sargent (Dublin North), Alison Larkin (Dublin North West), Bridín O'Connor (Dublin West), Anne McGoldrick (Dún Laoghaire), Declan Lehane (Limerick East) and Councillor Marcus Counihan (Kerry South), had been candidates in the 1985 local elections.

The 1987 manifesto illustrates the party's prescience:

> The energy crises; incurable unemployment, mounting incidences of corporate fraud and corruption; chronic economic dislocation; increasing degradation of the quality of urban life; the relentless assault on non-human species and the environment in general; the ruthless exploitation of the Third World, leading to political, economic and social disintegration; institutionalised terrorism and criminality; the notion that violence solves problems; the growing list of disasters attributable to technological giantism ('Torrey Canyon', Seveso, Flixboro, Three Mile Island, Bhopal, Chernoby...); and finally the escalating balance of terror, euphemistically called "peace", arising from failure to conduct meaningful disarmament negotiations: All these signals are finally beginning to convince people that you cannot trust existing power structures.
>
> The policies of traditional left, right and centre have been abject failures. The promise of unlimited growth, a technological 'fix' for all our problems, and universal affluence is a lie. The system is running out of control. The unbridled consumerism of the developed countries is the root cause of the poverty of two-thirds of the world's human family.
>
> Conventional politics cannot supply an adequate answer to our dilemma; if

planet Earth is to have a future, a totally new, radical, spiritual approach will have to be adopted.

The following pages include outlines of policies which you will find, are a recipe for forms of growth far more worth having than the merely economic kind with which contemporary politicians are obsessed. For if we are to achieve a sane, humane and ecological society, we must accept that, the finite resources of our planet will not allow conventional economic growth to continue indefinitely.

The new frontiers of growth are not technical and economic, but social and psychological. Further growth must meet the criteria of providing satisfying and rewarding occupation (good work), and of meeting people's higher-level needs for belongingness and love, esteem and self-actualisation. In short, what we need is politics of personal growth.

The nine green candidates collected 7159 votes between them. This represented 1.8 per cent of the contested vote, or 0.4 per cent of the national poll. They were very disappointed, as this was the third successive election in which the greens had posted nearly identical results. It hardly represented progress.

Especially frustrating was the electoral benefit the Progressive Democrats reaped from of the growing public discontent. They had won 11 per cent of the vote and gained fourteen seats, which made them the third-largest party in the Dáil. They polled less than their previous opinion poll ratings had indicated but still won a significant vote. They had by now defined their political philosophy and had produced their policies, all of which showed an advocacy of right-wing economic thinking.

The Labour Party had a poor election result. They gained only 6.5 per cent of the national poll, but thanks to the quirks of proportional representation,they managed to hold on to twelve seats. It was clear from the 1987 election result that growing numbers of the electorate wanted to vote differently. The Workers Party had resumed their upwards trend by winning four seats in this Dáil. Jim Kemmy was returned to the Dáil, this time as a representative of a party that he himself had established – the Democratic Socialist Party.

After this election, questions were being asked by greens of themselves, as to why not enough voters were looking to them as an acceptable alternative.

The pendulum had swung from Fine Gael to Fianna Fáil but not sufficiently to give Charlie Haughey a Dáil majority. However, he still managed to form a government and was to receive help from an unexpected source. Alan Dukes, the new leader of Fine Gael, proposed the 'Tallaght Strategy', which offered the minority Fianna Fáil government Fine Gael support, as long as that government followed the policies they felt were necessary to get the country back on the road to economic recovery.

Meanwhile, Raymond Crotty had his hearing in the High Court on his claim that the government was obliged to hold a new referendum on any proposed change to the structures of the European Economic Community. In April the Supreme Court decided in favour of Mr Crotty and so a referendum had to be held to ascertain whether Ireland would agree to the Single European Act.

The referendum date was 24 May. The greens became actively involved in the 'No' campaign. They feared that Ireland's neutrality was under threat and that Ireland was being 'trenched progressively' towards involvement in a European military alliance. Some of the posters used by the No campaign juxtaposed growing environmental awareness with the perceived threat to Irish neutrality. The most striking image carried the legend 'Sellafield – Sell A Nation'. The four largest political parties advocated a Yes vote and the referendum was carried by a large majority. Only 30 per cent voted No.

By 1987 Die Grünen, the German Green Party, had been re-elected to the German parliament. Their political success highlighted some of the contradictions that bedevilled the green movement. Petra Kelly was very much in the limelight and at the heart of this debate. Some of the German greens reminded their parliamentary representatives of the party's policy on the rotation of seats. Greens eschewed personality based politics. They preferred a procedure whereby each elected representative would resign their seat on completion of a term of office. This issue was part of a wider debate within green politics; between the fundis, who believed that policy should be guided by 'deep-green' principles, and the realos, who argued that policies had to adapt to the prevailing political conditions in order that green objectives might be achieved. This conflict was to plague green parties in many countries for years to come.

In the summer of 1987 the Green Party office on Fownes Street had some unexpected visitors. Mike Scott and Steve Wickham of the Waterboys, called to express their concern about the unprecedented number of fish kills in Irish rivers that year. They wanted to help out in some way. The party member manning the office that day was founding member Tommy Simpson, who unfortunately was not familiar with the who's who of the rock world. Tommy later contacted John Gormley and told him that a guy who looked like Mick Jagger, from a group called the 'Waterbabies' had been in the office. Tommy had given him a membership form and sent him on his way – without getting any contact details. John Gormley was incredulous on hearing this news.

At the time, the Waterboys were huge. It looked like the greens had missed an amazing opportunity. One week later however, John spotted Mike Scott through the window of a cafe in Ranelagh. He went in, introduced himself and asked if the Waterboys would do a concert for the greens. Mike Scott agreed immediately. The concerts, which were organised by John along with Grattan Healy and a young promoter called Denis Desmond of MCD, were an enormous success. They took place in the Olympic Ballroom and those who were there say that they were the best concerts ever given by the Waterboys.

Other prominent people were also associated with these concerts. The well-known artist Pauline Bewick designed a very fetching poster that was sold at the concerts. The posters that actually promoted the events were placed on billboards all over Dublin and were designed by the well-known graphic artist, Steve Avril, famous for his designs of the early U2 album covers.

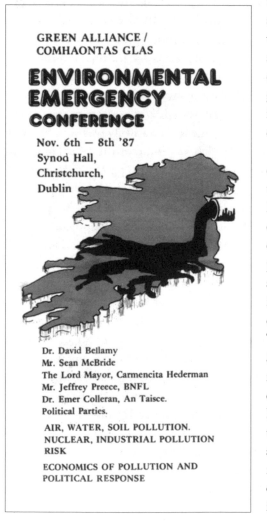

The proceeds of these concerts were used by the party to host an Environmental Emergency Conference as part of the party's commitment to encourage wider debate and promote greater public understanding of environmental issues. It was held in the hall of Christ Church Cathedral. The conference was opened by Sean McBride and featured a number of well-known speakers, including David Bellamy. He was well known at the time for his regular television appearances. A number of requests came into the party office for interviews and meetings, one of which was from the Taoiseach's office. They met and Bellamy was clearly impressed: 'Your Prime Minister is a remarkable conservationist', he told Green Party members on his return.

A special poster was commissioned for this event. On this occasion a new party member, who was an art teacher, offered to provide the necessary graphics. That person was Patricia McKenna.

John Gormley, Dublin

I'm not the nostalgic type. I don't look back to the early history of the greens, thinking those were the days. I would have been happy to forget and move on, but I was asked to cast my mind back for this account.

My green journey began in Germany, where I was studying in 1982 in what was said to be the greenest city in Europe, the university town of Freiburg. The greens had begun in Germany in 1979 and found a natural home in this student town. I attended a number of meetings of an unusual political party, an anti-party party, as Petra Kelly of Die Grünen used to call it. The greens didn't look, act or sound like politicians and that was their immediate attraction for me. On my return to UCD I noticed a stand in the university concourse during Freshers' Week. It contained a number of leaflets outlining the dangers of the Sellafield nuclear power plant. A student called Tony Ryan, who would later stand for us in the Dublin Central by-election, was at the stand. After a brief conversation, he told me he had to go to lunch, and would I mind looking after the stand. I agreed, and that's really how it started.

A feature of Green Party life in those days was the tedium and circularity of our debates. We operated by consensus which led to what I called the 'tyranny of the minority'. A small number of unreasonable people quickly cottoned on to the fact that they could easily block every decision. After about a year of this paralysis, I had had enough. I suggested that we introduce voting. This was the first of a number of 'heretical' proposals I was to make. It was agreed very reluctantly, but only after a new procedure was introduced. We first had to hold a procedural vote in order to decide if we would vote! I also proposed that troublemakers be thrown out of the party. The problem was that we had no constitutional means of doing this. So a convoluted expulsion clause was agreed. The fact that we now had such a procedure in place to deal with disruption encouraged some of the disagreeable types to leave voluntarily.

My next constitutional amendment – to change the name of the party – met with stiffer opposition and was defeated at two separate conventions. I believed we needed clarity. We needed to tell people that we were a political party. I was accused of being 'very political' – a serious charge and a grave insult in an organization that prided itself on being different from other political organisations. On the third attempt I was successful, but again it involved a compromise, which has been retained to this day. The official registered name of our party is Green Party/Comhaontas Glas. 'Comhaontas Glas' is a direct translation of the title 'Green Alliance'. This was the amendment suggested by Trevor in order to satisfy those, who felt that we might lose our identity as an alliance of autonomous green groups. These were difficult years for the party. Not only was there a continuing tension between the 'realos' and the fundis – to use the German greens' expression – but we were also finding it difficult to make ends meet.

I worked hard on Maura Mullarney's campaign in Dublin South East in 1987. When the next general election was called in 1989, Maura was unable to stand; neither could Enid O'Dowd, who had stood in the local elections in 1985. The party couldn't find a candidate, so I reluctantly stepped into the breach.

On a shoestring budget and with very little canvassing, I did very well in the 1989 general election. I even outpolled Roger Garland (who was elected) in percentage terms. During this campaign, there was a departure from previous electoral practice. We used posters! Some believed that we were heading down the slippery slope of personality politics. We ought to be about saving the planet, not promoting individuals, it was argued. It was agreed that there would be a small poster that would have my picture and a picture of planet earth of equal size side by side. The pictures were black and white and our slogan was 'Others promise the sun, moon and stars. Only the greens guarantee the Earth'. The real problem was that our black and white picture of the earth actually looked like the moon. One day during the campaign, I overheard two fellows on Morehampton Road who were looking up at the poster. One of the guys told his mate that he would definitely be voting for 'the man in the moon'.

Having come so close I was encouraged to continue with politics. I had been happy to be a backroom person and a campaigner. We focused mainly on the serious smog problem in Dublin at the time. I organised demonstrations outside of Coal Distributors Limited, and the offices of Dublin Corporation. The Corporation officials had refused to release the previous winter's pollution figures until the following summer. Following our success, Mary Harney quickly introduced a ban on bituminous coal. This had been one of our key demands during the election and was proof that the electoral path could work. The 1991 local elections saw that promise fulfilled. I was among four greens elected to Dublin Corporation.

Things were running our way until the tragic death of Petra Kelly, the charismatic German green who had been a regular visitor to Ireland. Only a year previously she and Gerd Bastian, her partner, had enjoyed tea and scones at my parents' house near Drogheda, following a visit to the nearby Sonairte Ecological Centre. The violence of their deaths shocked many people – especially my mother. The media saw this as an omen for the demise of the Green Party. *The Irish Times* ran a feature entitled 'The end of the Greens'. It very nearly was.

The General Election of 1992 caught many of us by surprise. We didn't have enough money, having spent our meagre resources on the local elections. I could not afford posters, except for hand-made ones. Just when I thought things couldn't get worse, my leaflets came back from the printers with my photograph upside down! To this day, the memories of that election defeat hurt. We were routed. If Trevor had not been elected to the Dáil it would have been a total wipe out.

A year earlier, I had proposed Trevor as Chief Spokesperson for the party, a move which greatly displeased Roger Garland, our only elected TD. Now that I have served two terms in the Dáil myself, I can appreciate just how difficult a task Roger faced as our first TD.

The consolation for my election defeat in '92 was my elevation in 1994 to the position of Lord Mayor of Dublin. Not only did I need a majority of councillors on the city council to vote for me, but more importantly, I first required the support of the Green Party membership in the Dublin City Council area. There were three candidates: Ciarán Cuffe, Sadhbh O'Neill and myself. On the day of the selection convention, having canvassed long and hard, I was unusually nervous when I got up to give my speech. Fortunately, I got sufficient votes to be elected Mayor.

There followed a very memorable and happy year, a year in which I married Penny Stuart, a year in which I met Prince Charles on his first visit to Ireland; a year in which I visited the United States with the Lord Mayor of Belfast, Hugh Smyth, of the PUP to promote the peace process. It was the year that REM came to dinner in the Mansion House. So many events packed into twelve intense, exciting, adrenalin-filled months. When it ended, I literally suffered withdrawal symptoms. It was back to the unglamorous, hard grind of council work in preparation for the next general election. This would be my third and perhaps final attempt to attain a Dáil seat. The pundits gave me little hope. Realistically, whose seat would I take? By 1997, when the election was called, my stint as Lord Mayor had, as Pat Cox put it to me one evening, become a dwindling asset. He believed Michael McDowell's seat was vulnerable. It was a tall order. Michael McDowell was one of the most high profile and vocal TDs. It was a highly charged campaign with the intense rivalry between the PDs and ourselves. This tension became even more acute when we discovered that a new independent candidate by the name of Gorman had been a member of the PDs right up until a few hours before nominations closed. I suspected immediately he was what is known in the business as a 'spoiler' candidate; voter confusion about Gorman and Gormley nearly made all the difference. Quite a few preferences, which logically would have gone to me, did go astray. I was informed about this on the telephone, as I had decided on this occasion not to go down to the RDS. I was slightly ahead of Michael McDowell on first preferences and had done well on transfers from the lower placed candidates, but then a major transfer came from Eoin Ryan to Michael McDowell. The word from the RDS was that the Fine Gael transfer would see Michael McDowell through. This assessment was shared by all of the TV pundits on a TV election special. I went to bed utterly depressed. At about half two in the morning I got a call from Colm Ó Caomhánaigh, a close colleague. Things were panning out differently than expected, Colm even suggested I might think of coming up to the RDS just in case I did snatch it. It was going to be very tight. I decided to go up, but waited outside in the car park. I really could not stomach the thought of another defeat. About five minutes after I had arrived, I was told to get inside quickly – the announcement was going to be made. I got in just in time to hear that I had won by twenty-seven votes. Our jubilation was short-lived. The PDs were demanding a recount. I had to be back in the RDS for eight o'clock the next morning. I was met there by a triumvirate of Ireland's best legal brains from the PDs. The message was clear – they were not giving up. They even hinted that they would go to court to challenge the arbitrary way in which transfers were taken from the top of the pile and then distributed. This had been standard practice in all Irish Elections, but who were we to question these great legal minds. My own legal advisors recommended a barrister who had expertise in electoral law and who had assisted Dick Spring in his famous recount in Kerry. Early on, in the recount, Michael McDowell wanted to throw in the towel but was persuaded to continue by Fianna Fáil. During the weeklong recount, we actually discovered more votes for me. I won by thirty-four votes, but the originally figure of twenty-seven votes was retained.

There were now two green TDs in the Dáil. Trevor and I agreed that if the party was to realise its true potential, reforms would be needed. At our convention back in 1995, I had suggested that the party needed a position of 'leader' but the idea was not well received. I suggested to Trevor that we needed to try again, so new proposals to create the positions of Leader, Deputy Leader, and Chairman were put to the members. This time the reforms were accepted.

I look back on the early days of the party as a period of self-indulgence, delusion and wasted opportunity. The process of reform within the party continues. Our task now is to deliver on our political agenda, which can best be done when our hands are on the levers of power. There will be many challenges facing us in the future, but the best days of this party are still to come.

John Gormley joined of the Green Party/Comhaontas Glas in 1983. He was elected to Dublin City Council in 1991 and was Lord Mayor of Dublin from 1994-1995. He was elected to Dáil Eireann in 1997. He is the party's Cathaoirleach since 2002. He is spokesperson on Foreign Affairs, Defence and Health & Children.

1988

I joined the party in 1988 with some difficulty. I had heard that a vibrant group had existed in Cork during the early 1980s but I could find no trace of them. By the late '80s no meetings were being held, and no mechanism was available to attract people like me into the party.

In time I was to learn that the Cork group had been particularly badly affected by the 1986 split within the party. Much of this strife locally had been instigated by a group of radical anarchists known as 'Revolutionary Struggle'. Their modus operandi was to infiltrate community/environmental or fringe political groups that might be involved in public protest or agitation. There were only a handful of these manipulative people involved, but in a small group of little more than a dozen, such as the Cork Green Movement, they could be very effective at dominating the meetings and frustrating the will of the majority.

Revolutionary Struggle was facilitated by the open decision-making procedures of the greens and the tenet that decisions would be made by consensus. During the early life of the party, with the goodwill that the founding members had towards each other, many decisions were indeed reached by consensus. However the goodwill that is integral to consensus decision-making can be abused to manipulate meetings.

The Cork Green Movement had, at one time, been one of the most active elements in the Green Alliance in the country. It was composed almost entirely of people who had been involved in Friends of the Earth and the anti-nuclear movement. Hugely influential in all those organizations were a husband and wife from Kinsale, Keith Haight and Maureen Kim Sing, who have sadly both passed away within the last twelve months. Locally the group involved itself in several campaigns – river clean-ups; maintaining green space; planting trees and organising a series of public lectures which brought the Cork Green Movement to greater public attention. Enthusiastic members helped to define in the public eye what it meant to be green. Owen Casey's vote in the November 1982 election indicated a potential green vote in Cork. An office was established in the city centre years before any Dublin equivalent was considered.

It was in fact through the Cork group that Trevor Sargent first became a member of the greens. He was teaching at the time at the Model National School in Dunmanway and became aware that the Cork group held weekly meetings in the city. He regularly made the seventy-six mile round-trip to Cork on his motorcyle, often in atrocious weather conditions.

By 1988 all traces of any group that had existed previously had dissipated. Trevor had long since moved to Dublin and what remained of the Cork group had fallen out with each other.

Not being able to identify a green presence in Cork, I tried to make contact with the greens in Dublin. This wasn't an easy task either. I was eventually to learn that the party was operating out of a small office in an upstairs room at 5a Upper Fownes Street, next to the Central Bank building, in the Temple Bar district. I wrote a letter to the Fownes Street address, stating my interest in becoming a member of the greens. The co-ordinator responded to my letter. Paul O'Brien, a philosophy lecturer at Trinity College, held this position at the time. A series of letters passed between us, after which I became a member of the Green Party.

I was sent a list of the greens in the Cork area and it was left up to me to make contact. It was not until the following year that I succeeded in locating the elusive party members in Cork.

One of the people on the list was Sean O'Flynn. Sean epitomized counter-culture among the greens in Cork. He had been my science teacher at secondary school during the 1970s, where he was very popular during his time there. He set up a cycling club at school, and regularly gave up his Sundays to take large groups of his students on fifty-mile cycle trips around County Cork.

During 1988 in Dublin, a clear commitment to the political process encouraged the Green Party to participate more in identifiable environmental campaigns such as the aim to reduce the dangerous levels of smog in Dublin. The consultant Dr Luke Clancy had led the medical campaign to deal with this hazard. The greens recognised that this was a campaign worth supporting. The party highlighted the hazards of smog and campaigned for the introduction of smoke-free coal to the capital.

The party was becoming better organized. It had an administrative base. It had a committed party membership. Policy development was proceeding well. The party was not afraid to engage in the wider philosophical debates, which narrow politics often avoid. John Goodwillie represented such a strand when he published his pamphlet 'Colours in the Rainbow: Ecology, Socialism and Ireland'.

The party continued to reform its organisation. The most pressing reform that signified the commitment to electoral politics was to change the name from Alliance to Party. John Gormley formally proposed that from now on the movement be called 'The Green Party'.

There followed a series of meetings, including two national conventions, in which party members took up strong positions on this issue. Tommy Simpson was strongly opposed to the use of the word 'party' in the title. He was afraid that the greens would be perceived as being the same as the other parties. The debate was conducted with intensity. Eventually John Gormley's motion was accepted, but only after a significant compromise had been reached. Trevor Sargent proposed that the party retain the Irish part of the title and thus the official name was changed to: 'An Comhaontas Glas/The Green Party'.

John Gormley recalls the confusion that accompanied these meetings.

> The debate on the name change took place in Buswells Hotel in 1988. I recall a well-groomed American lady with a speech impediment, making many long and insightful interventions during the debate. I had never seen her before, so afterwards I asked her to which local group she belonged? "None", she replied. She was in Ireland on vacation, saw the sign for the green meeting and decided to take a look!

With little expectation of another election being held soon, some party members used this time to further green ideals through practical effort. Trevor and Tommy Simpson, along with others, developed a National Ecology Centre called Sonaírte. The centre located near Laytown in County Meath was modelled on a similar centre that had been operating successfully in Wales. Sonaírte, a registered educational charity, was established to increase public awareness and interest in the environment. The centre encourages the use of appropriate technology, organic horticulture, energy conservation techniques and renewable energy sources. Particular emphasis is placed on encouraging visiting school groups.

Original Green Party logo designed by Chris Vis. It was adapted in 1988 to accommodate the name change to the Green Party/ Comhaontas Glas.

Eamon Ryan, Dublin

People become aware of green thinking in a variety of different ways. For some, it was the first pictures of planet earth beamed back from space, or watching television programmes on the natural world that opened their hearts and minds to an awareness of green issues. For others it was reading books such as *Small is Beautiful* or *Limits to Growth* that got them thinking. Some came to an awareness through their engagement with civil rights, the women's movement, or CND. However, my own green awakening began in a classroom.

In 1979 I was fortunate to be included in an educational experiment undertaken by a far-sighted headmaster and an inspirational biology teacher at my secondary school. They decided that, rather than studying the prescribed Intercert biology syllabus, my class would instead, complete the GCE O level in Ecology, specialising in parkland ecology.

We exchanged an exam that tested your memory for a new course that exposed us to the latest thinking in the earth sciences. This syllabus allowed us the freedom to approach the subject in whatever manner our teacher saw fit. For the first time in my life I discovered that education could involve real discovery. I started to thrive with the excitement that comes from a real sense of learning.

It took us a while to adapt to the new system. I remember our hilarity when, as part of the field studies, we went to the Glen of the Downs armed with a tape recorder and camera, to record whatever wildlife we could find. We all dashed from our minibus to take cover in the woods, in order to have a cigarette. We had been given balls of putty in case we happened across any animal tracks along the way. We returned to the lab with nothing but casts of human paw marks in the putty, hoots of laughter on the tape recorder and a collection of bedraggled weeds pulled from our pockets. Despite it being a laugh, deep down I think we sensed that this newly-found freedom should be treated with respect.

For the first time I walked home from school noticing every small bird along the way. The mundane creatures in my own back garden suddenly told the story of life's interconnections, which was a central thread of the course. We were enthralled by the depiction of the life and death struggles in the food chain. We climbed a tall larch tree next to the school football pitch, to rob three eggs from the nest of what we now understood to be an 'invading Norman' magpie. The sharp admonition we received from our normally gentle teacher, when we returned to the lab with the eggs was a lesson in itself. The course lasted for one year and ended in an exam that included questions, which I am sure would still be cutting edge today, almost thirty years later.

I went on to get my highest mark in the Leaving Certificate in biology. I was not offered my first CAO choice of Architecture, which in a roundabout way I thought might involve a career developing our own local environment. Instead, I found myself accepting my second choice of Commerce at UCD, as recommended by a career guidance teacher less known for inspirational flights of fancy! I enjoyed studying and working in the business world, but never lost the instincts that were born in that year of exciting discovery in school.

After a period of emigration, I returned home in 1988 and I decided that the best expression of my true identity was to join the Green Party. That decision was facilitated by the tide of global green consciousness that was rising at the time. The party attracted various people with different individual motives for joining, but there was a sufficient sense of shared values and common understanding between us to enable us to work together towards a common goal.

In those years, decisions on who would stand for election were decided on a 'go on, go on, you will, you will' basis. Despite or perhaps because of that, six of the members in our small local group have since gone on to elected office either on local councils, the Dáil or the European Parliament. We were all in our twenties when we joined and are all in our forties now.

Because there was no rule book or precedent to follow for the type of political party we were establishing, there were endless procedural wrangles over what could or should be done. My recollection is that our attempts to achieve consensus helped rather than hindered our efforts to grow as a party. Having to learn and decide things for ourselves gave us valuable confidence in trusting our own instincts, judgement and ability. You don't need to inherit a seat from your father or employ expensive spin doctors to make a good politician.

The green tide ebbed a little after the high water mark of the Earth Summit in Rio in 1991. In the new millennium there are clear signs that people across the world are again turning to green thinking. The difference now is that the imbalance between our use of the planet's resources and their availability has become ever starker. Issues such as climate change and the peak in global oil production are now at critical junctures. They are no longer matters for further conjecture. They require urgent action now.

To face those challenges will require the involvement of a new, younger group of people in our party. It may be harder for them to find a role in an organisation which is being run by a group of experienced politicians supported by a professional backroom staff. It is hard to take up the reins when someone else is holding on to them. If we recognise that the aim of our party now is to become one of the largest political parties in the state, then the task becomes easier. We need sufficient members who are willing to become the green representative in every council ward and Dáil constituency in this country.

We will need a younger perspective on all issues because our own formative experience of growing up in the Ireland of the 1960s, '70s and '80s is becoming less relevant to the children of the last two decades. The capacity of the greens to tackle crucial issues in the future will depend on our ability to engage with a younger electorate, and to encourage them to become interested in politics. We must speak to them in a way that makes sense to them.

At a time when only a handful of people are publicly active on vital environmental issues such as climate change, the opportunities for a younger generation to effect change for the better are limitless.

One would expect that the educational system would help to achieve this. However, twenty years on from when I was at school the newly revised Junior Certificate Science paper still has no meaningful questions on the subject of ecology. Admittedly, the Leaving Certificate Biology course does include some of the concepts that I was learning at the age of sixteen, however the emphasis appears to remain on learning off and regurgitating scientific terms rather than taking a real look at the natural world around us.

The An Taisce Green Flag Programme in primary schools is hugely popular. However, there is a danger that environmental studies will go the same way as the learning of Irish. It could become something a student has to 'do' in school but has little relevance to everyday adult life. A subconscious understanding may develop amongst students that once they leave school, the important decisions about which car, holiday or clothes they will buy, are made without any regard to the environmental and social consequences of their purchase.

If future generations are to meet the social and environmental challenges facing them, they will have to leave school eager to learn more about what is happening in our world and how they can change things for the better. We need to move away from the points race, towards an educational system that engenders a real sense of learning, awareness and discovery. When the greens get into government perhaps that should be the first thing we try to change.

Fianna Fáil is known for its close connections with land developers; Fine Gael for its links to big farmers and Labour for their association with the trade unions. Perhaps we in the Green Party might become known for our bond with the young minds of the future.

Eamon Ryan joined the Green Party/Comhaontas Glas in 1988. He was a member of Dublin City Council from 1998 until he was elected to Dáil Éireann as TD for Dublin South in 2002. He served as Director of Elections for the 2004 European and Local Elections. He is the party spokesperson on Transport, Enterprise, Trade and Employment and Communications, Marine and Natural Resources.

1989

1989 was to prove a watershed year for the greens in Ireland. The Green Party continued to hold its biannual gatherings, in spring and autumn. The spring convention of '89 was held at Crannagh Castle, near Templemore, County Tipperary. The castle was the home of Gillies McBain, a long-standing party member who regularly made his facilities available to the party. A photo of Gillies with Mick Jagger, taken on the steps outside Crannagh Castle, sat proudly on the mantelpiece in the main room of the house. It was a reminder that this was a man who took pride in standing apart from the conventional.

The minority Fianna Fáil government under Taoiseach Charlie Haughey, was increasingly unhappy with its position, especially with having to be supported in the Dáil chamber by Fine Gael. Haughey sought any opportunity that would help improve his situation. He decided that since the voters would be going to the polls anyway, he would take the opportunity to call a general election to coincide with the European Elections and seek a stronger Dáil mandate. A pretext to disband the Dáil was created when the government lost a vote on the funding of haemophiliacs, and so for the fifth time in eight years Irish voters were asked to select a new Dáil.

This was the first election the greens contested under the banner of the Green Party. They now had to contest two sets of election at once. What meagre resources it had were directed towards the general election. Eleven candidates were chosen. All the candidates, with the exception of Sean English, in Kildare, were located in Dublin.

The 1989 manifesto highlighted the green's holistic approach to politics:

> Many politicians from the established parties have tried to give their own interpretation of green politics. They believe they can capture 'the green vote' by making statements on 'denvironment'. This approach to our present pollution problems deals merely with the symptoms. Green politics goes much deeper than that. The green philosophy is an ecological one – it goes back to the root causes.

The Green Party's policies acknowledge the vital importance of ecology, that is, our whole environment. Our future is vitally dependent on that environment. We depend upon a network of links with the rest of creation. Green politics acknowledges the reality and importance of that web of life.

Over the years, human beings have dominated and exploited the planet. Many of the problems which the greens have long predicted (they were called 'alarmist' for doing so) are now coming to pass. It is now clear that if our warnings are ignored much longer humankind will destroy the planet.

The potential catastrophes which we face are finally beginning to convince people that the existing power structures cannot be trusted. The policies of traditional Left, Right and Centre parties have been abject failures. Their promises of unlimited growth, a technological 'fix' for all our problems and universal affluence are false. The unbridled consumerism of the developed countries is the root cause of the poverty of two thirds of the world's human family. Conventional politics cannot supply an adequate answer to our dilemma. If planet Earth is to have a future, a totally new, radical, spiritual approach will have to be adopted – an approach which recognises that the fundamental problem is our materialistic society itself. We can no longer ignore the spiritual dimension of our lives in the interests of selfish consumerism.

In this manifesto you will find well-thought-out policies on the environment, agriculture and urban conservation. These policies are fundamentally linked – in a truly ecological sense – to our policies on employment and economics.

When you have studied our manifesto we hope you will agree that the green approach provides the best hope of achieving the sort of future you really want for yourself and your children.'

As the campaign progressed it was clear that there had been an increase in green awareness nationally since the last election. The party's candidates looked forward to an improved voting performance, but nobody was prepared for what was to happen.

The party received just under 25,000 votes – a 350 per cent increase from the 1987 election. The lowest vote received by any Green Party candidate in this election was greater than the highest vote the party had ever received in any constituency previously.

There were some excellent performances. Trevor Sargent won close on 3,000 votes in the Dublin North constituency. The high profile that John Gormley had gained from the Dublin Smog campaign stood him in good stead when he won close on 3,500 votes in Dublin South East, and just missed winning the fourth seat, by a margin of no more than 300 votes.

The big surprise however was when Roger Garland, on his third attempt, succeeded in becoming the first Green Party TD to be elected to Dáil Éireann. He polled more than 4,700 first preference votes and was well placed after the first count. Transfers came to him from all parties and independent candidates and soon he was elected. Roger had placed great store on seeking transfers. The experience learned from previous campaigns had taught him that if first preference votes were not forthcoming for the greens, then they should seek the next highest available preference vote. It was a tactic that was to serve the Green Party well in future elections.

Collectively the eleven candidates had done the party proud. Aside from Roger's election and the strong performance of John Gormley and Trevor Sargent, Mary Bowers in Dublin South Central, Enda Connolly in Dublin Central, Conor Delaney in Dublin South West, Sean English in Kildare, Patricia Griffin in Dún Laoghaire, Alison Larkin in Dublin North West, Máire Mullarney in Dublin North East and Bridín O'Connor in Dublin West, achieved votes that would have been undreamt of at the beginning of this campaign.

If the general election results were stunning for the party, the strength of the performance of the party's candidates in the European Elections was truly amazing. The party had decided to contest only two of the four Euro-constituencies – Dublin and Leinster. The candidate for Dublin was Trevor Sargent, who also contested the Dublin North Dáil constituency on the same day. Trevor had first stood for the party in the local elections in 1985. His aim was to build on the 5,000 or so votes that Christopher Fettes had gained in the 1984 European election. In the event, Trevor won almost 40,000 votes. He even outpolled Mary Harney of the Progressive Democrats. This indignity was something that may have fuelled her dislike and distaste for the greens, which she was to reveal on several occasions in subsequent years.

Another candidate Trevor succeeded in outpolling was Raymond Crotty. The fact that the Green Party was standing against Crotty caused great difficulties for Patricia McKenna. Patricia strongly supported Raymond Crotty and shared his Euro-sceptic views. She also believed he was more electable than Trevor Sargent. She resigned her membership of the party in protest and in order to support Crotty's campaign. She rejoined the party once the elections were over.

Trevor learned that he had another admirer when he was approached by the Taoiseach at the election count. Mr Haughey shook hands with Trevor and confided in him. 'I'm a bit of a "green" myself.'

The green candidate for the Leinster constituency was a Naas publican, Sean English. Sean also contested the Kildare Dáil constituency. Neither he nor the Green Party could have anticipated his winning over 23,000 votes.

Together both Trevor and Sean polled over 60,000 votes. This was 3.7 per cent of the valid poll and indicated that the Green Party had arrived.

A point worth noting is that the Green Party polled more than twice the number of votes in the Euro election than they did in the one for the Dáil. This indicated for the first time that voters were exercising the franchise in a discerning and strategic manner. This phenomenon was concentrated on the eastern seaboard of Ireland and a contributory factor may have been the access to British television stations by these voters. The British Green Party won 15 per cent of the vote in the same European elections. Their success was due to the confluence of an increasing awareness by the public of environmental issues, coupled with a number of very effective party political broadcasts, which were seen by those voters in Ireland who had access to multi-channel television stations from the UK.

In the January/February 1989 edition of *Nuacht Ghlas*, the party's internal newsletter, Margie Bach eulogised the qualities that Trevor Sargent possessed that would help make him an MEP:

> Trevor Sargent is my friend; but any honest observer would attest to the validity of my opinions. I think the fact those who know him best withdrew their candidacies as soon as they heard he was willing to run is some measure of their esteem.
>
> His first quality is what the Romans called 'gravitas'. He has authority. I remember especially a disagreement about consensus at a convention. Although he spoke quietly, his opinion seemed naturally to carry weight.
>
> Second, Trevor is a born teacher. He sees his subject clearly. His preparation is meticulous; his enthusiasm, infectious. The press launch of Sonairte demonstrated his skill to me. Photographs of the orchard and of greens working in it, were mounted and labelled. He had slides and diagrams of what he planned to with the various buildings and land. His press handouts contained graphics and clear exposition. He answered all questions easily, with assurance.
>
> Third, Trevor plans and organises well. He is relaxed and flexible. He arranged a week in the Gaeltacht for us at Inverin. This included rooms, meals, lessons at all levels, side trips, entertainment and opportunities to chat informally with native speakers. He kept the group together; and the ripples he started seem to spread out infinitely.

Fourth, Trevor is not just an intellectual green. I've watched him working at Sonairte, bringing apple trees back to blooming life and planting an organic garden. He attended the Clonmel Hare-Coursing Meet to demonstrate and protest against cruelty. He is a builder and a creator, a musician and singer.

Fifth, he can work well with anyone. He is not a one-man-band. He is no "great man", the master who has the complete truth. As a woman, I've never seen the slightest inattention to or dismissal of my opinions.

Finally, he has great courage. He faced prison for not paying his TV license as a protest against the death of Irish programmes on RTE. He has taken on this thankless, arduous campaign and fights on, despite media indifference and office inadequacies.

In short, if the best man wins, we'll have Trevor Sargent, M.E.P.

Margie and her husband Richard, now both sadly deceased, were retired US citizens who had settled in west Dublin. At this time in late eighties/early nineties not much was happening electorally for the party in Dublin west. Margie and Dick were involved intensely in national Green Party activities. They frequently made their home available for meetings, and policy formation never proceeded without lengthy written contributions from either. Margie was at one time co-ordinator of the party. Her effusiveness and commitment was typical of those members who worked behind the scenes and never think of putting themselves forward for elected office.

The 'eastern seaboard effect' contrasted with the European election in Munster, where environmental issues did not feature at all during the campaign. In Cork, the various splits within the green movement in the 1986-1987 period, had resulted in many activists leaving the party. A new political movement, 'Meitheal/People First,' was formed to contest the Munster constituency in the Euro election. Joe Noonan, a Cork solicitor, was chosen to be the Meitheal candidate. Joe, (along with his wife Mary Linehan), had been instrumental in conducting Raymond Crotty's constitutional case. He was later to establish a national reputation as an environmental rights lawyer.

Petra Kelly continued to be the most renowned green in Europe. Her strongest ties in Ireland were with the anti-nuclear lobby, in particular with the Campaign for Nuclear Disarmament (CND), which was run largely from the home of Adi Roche and Sean Dunne. Adi had continued to maintain a strong friendship with Petra Kelly and invited her to come to Ireland to support the candidacy of Joe Noonan.

Arrangements were made to fly Petra into Dublin Airport, meet her there and take her to Cork. When Green Party activists in Dublin learned of this they saw this as a golden opportunity to promote Trevor Sargent's Dublin European election campaign. At the appointed time a number of greens, including John Gormley and Tommy Simpson, arrived at Dublin Airport with flowers for Ms Kelly. A presentation was made, and photographs were taken. This annoyed members of the Noonan/Meitheal campaign who were waiting for their guest. They felt aggrieved at the Dublin greens 'running off with their woman'. An almighty row broke out between the two groups and as a result, many of the people involved have not spoken to each other since.

The Green Party chose not to contest the European election in Munster. The 15,000 votes won by Joe Noonan in Munster constituted a very respectable total. But it paled in comparison to what the greens were achieving in Dublin and Leinster.

In Northern Ireland the greens contested the Euro election as the Ecology Party. Malcolm Samuel won 6,500 votes. This was insignificant when compared to the other green candidates on the island, but, in the context of Northern Irish politics, it was a surprising vote.

The success of Roger Garland's election and the votes received by the Green Party in the European elections was the impetus that was needed to resurrect the Green Party in Cork. The party's skeletal presence in the city had been maintained with difficulty by Pat Madden and Sean O'Flynn. In East Cork, the 1985 local election candidates, Chris Lordan and Sean Bell, still maintained an interest. Those who became involved were either like me, and had joined prior to the election, or had expressed their interest immediately after the election success. The new members such as Jane Power, Brendan Burke and Donogh MacCarthy Morrogh brought the group from shell-like status to something approaching a functioning group. To solidify this commitment it was decided that the newly re-constituted Cork group would organise and host the next national party convention. The Metropole Hotel in Cork city was the chosen venue. The slogan 'The Nineties Will Be Green', (a play on the unfulfilled Labour Party slogan 'The Seventies Will Be Socialist') though a cheeky theme, was a sign of the growing confidence within the party.

The convention was the first green convention that attracted any serious reporting by the media. In organising the convention, the Cork group had to straddle the expectations of the media with the peculiar traditions that had come to surround green gatherings. The conference room was arranged in a series of round tables at which sat between eight to ten delegates. Each table was garnished with flowers and bowls of organic apples. No specific press table was provided. Instead journalists and reporters were invited to sit where they wished among the delegates.

This typified the greens naïve transparency to the media at the time.

Roger Garland, Dublin

Before joining the Ecology Party in 1981 I had never been involved in party politics though I always took a keen interest in current economic and social issues. I had a great interest in the basic principles of democracy – do we need a constitution, electoral systems and the way parliament works.

I regularly communicated with the late John Kelly, one of my local TDs, but was never tempted to join Fine Gael. I was attracted by the idea of a basic income and attended many meeting of the Natural Rights Society where I met such pioneers as Raymond Hannegan, Harvey Boxwell, Michael Horsman, Christopher Fettes and Máire Mullarney.

In those days the environment simply wasn't on the agenda. The only significant issue that had arisen was the proposal to build a nuclear power station at Carnsore.

I joined the party at the beginning, and took early retirement shortly afterwards. This enabled me to become a full-time volunteer for the Party. Prior to my election as a TD, I served on the Co-ordinating Committee. I also represented my local group on the National Council for many years throughout the 1980s.

Before joining the party, I had never taken any particular interest in the environment, but on being exposed to the thoughts of people like Joe Dunne, Rosemary Rowley and John Gormley, I soon became aware of the disaster facing the planet if we didn't mend our ways.

I stood as a candidate in my constituency of Dublin South in 1982 and the three subsequent elections. I was elected in 1989 getting the fourth seat, but failed to retain my seat in 1992.

I am still a member of the party though I am not active in it now, preferring to be involved in environmental organisations such as Friends of the Irish Environment, An Taisce, and Keep Ireland Open.

The future of the party? Well, if we get things even half right, we can't lose! I would advise caution on the question of being involved in government; unless it is as part of a national government. We could perhaps follow the example of the Tasmanian Greens where, some years ago, the greens held the balance of power between the right wing Liberal Party and the Labour Party. The Labour Party had to accept a long 'shopping list' of environmental requirements from the greens as part of a deal to enable a Labour prime minister be elected. A further part of the deal was a broad agreement on budgetary matters and the promise that the greens wouldn't support any vote of no confidence proposed by the Liberals. The Greens quite deliberately didn't seek any Cabinet seats. They reserved the right to oppose government bills or to support opposition amendments thereto. It must be realised that in any formal coalition, the smaller party is liable to be ground down by the larger party(or parties) and blamed for everything that goes wrong. As a result the smaller party is often rejected by the electorate at the following election.

Roger Garland joined The Green Party/An Comhaontas Glas in the early '80s. He served on the Co-ordinating Committee and the National Council. He was the first Green Party member to be elected to Dáil Éireann. He was TD for Dublin South from 1989-1992.

1990

Becoming familiar with the surroundings and working operations of Leinster House occupied Roger Garland's mind as the 27th Dáil began its life. The Workers Party had gained seven seats, a critical number which allowed them to claim full party status. Roger found himself outside the established political circle and it was difficult for him to make an impact. He was ostensibly an independent. He had to take what he was given in terms of the facilities and resources of the Dáil, and more particularly in terms of speaking time and his participation rate within it.

His office was on Molesworth Street in one of the buildings then rented by the Leinster House authorities. Roger's secretary, Anne Halliday, had been the secretary to Michael Keating, a Progressive Democrat TD, who had once been a Fine Gael TD for Dublin Central.

Speaking time in the Dáil had to be begged and scratched for. Roger Garland's contributions, while frequent, were rarely more than one or two minutes long. As the only Green Party representative he felt obliged to contribute as much as possible to as many debates as he could. While he had a reputation for being hard-working and diligent, he was also seen as eccentric by other members of the Dáil.

Inaugural Speech of Roger Garland to Dáil Éireann

A Cheann Comhairle and Members of the Dáil, as already indicated at the Green Party Conference last week, I shall be voting against the nomination of Deputy Haughey as Taoiseach. Indeed, I propose to vote against the nomination of Deputies Dukes and Spring, also… Lest people feel this is a negative attitude I should like to point out that the right-wing parties control 80 per cent of the Dáil and that a clear responsibility rests with them to elect a Taoiseach and form a Government. I made clear my position on this matter at the earliest possible moment, to remove uncertainty.

Everybody in this country knows there is not a tittle of a difference between the policies of the three parties of the right. It is all about personalities and style and not about issues. The electorate are sick and tired of party games. I appeal once again to the leaders of these parties to sink their historic differences and come together to elect a Taoiseach. Ideally, we would like to see a green government. However, none of the other parties will provide us with anything approaching a green-type government, as they all pursue consumerist policies which cause many of the world's most serious environmental problems, due to the resultant increase in the consumption of scarce resources. I must, therefore, vote against all the nominations for Taoiseach coming from these parties.

There has been surprise expressed by some political commentators that I shall not be voting with the left on this occasion. I want to make it quite clear that my party are not a left-wing party; neither are they a right-wing party nor a centrist party. The greens want the security of socialism, combined with the freedom of capitalism. At the moment, we have the bureaucracy of socialism combined with the inequality of capitalism. Thus, in their endeavours to find common ground in the centre, both right and left take the worst from both ideologies and try to combine them, whereas we in the greens take the best.

Much of the struggle between left and right in the First World countries is the struggle over the spoils of exploitation of the Third World. It seems, from speeches made so far, that we are heading for a constitutional crisis, as it seems unlikely that any nominee for Taoiseach will have the support of the majority of the House. Clearly, this is a very serious situation in which we find ourselves and it is the responsibility of one person, Deputy Charles J. Haughey, Leader of Fianna Fáil and the Taoiseach. It was he who called this election in an effort to gain total power for himself and his party. Fortunately, the electorate are mature enough to have seen through this ploy and they rejected it decisively.

In the event of the House failing to elect a Taoiseach this afternoon, there appears to be two alternatives. One is to seek the adjournment of the House for a short period of time, perhaps a week, to facilitate further negotiations to be carried out between the party leaders or, secondly, the Taoiseach could request the President to dissolve the Dáil and hold another general election. I would very much favour the former. The latter option — another general election — is clearly against the wishes of the people. Not that we in the greens would have anything to fear from another general election because I am convinced that not only would I hold my seat but that the greens would be elected in other constituencies as well. However, apart from that, another general election would have the undoubted effect of leaving the parliamentary arithmetic basically unchanged.

Another alternative worthy of consideration would be a national all-party government. The great advantage of this would be that the best talent of the House could be utilised in the selection of a Cabinet. This could be done by extending our PR voting system to the Dáil for its selection.

This country faces very serious environmental, social and economic problems and it needs a constructive government of consensus, not another disruptive general election.

Roger Garland's election in the notoriously fickle constituency of Dublin South, was said by many established political commentators to be little more than an accident. They claimed that the Green Party was nothing more than an apparition that would disappear in time, as had other small parties in Irish political history.

State funding of political parties was still some years off in 1990. After the 1989 election however, with someone elected to the Dáil, the Green Party could finally look forward to receiving some income. There was an expectation that a proportion of Roger's Dáil salary might come to the party. Roger's involvement with the party had been on a full-time basis in the period prior to his election. He was in effect semi-retired from his profession as a chartered accountant and had become independently wealthy through acquiring a significant property portfolio. This allowed him to donate his entire Dáil salary to the Green Party.

Having some bit of an income flow allowed the party to invest in literature and even compensate some members for their time and effort. Steve Rawson was the co-ordinator for the party at the time. Roger's donation of his salary allowed for expenses to be given to the co-ordinator. While this was not a wage as such, it is the first record of a remuneration given to anyone working on behalf of the Green Party in Ireland.

When Ireland assumed the Presidency of the European Union in 1990, a great deal of effort went into packaging the event as being a Green/Environmental Presidency. However, it amounted to little more than lip service.

One successful initiative of the new government, however, was the appointment of the Progressive Democrat TD Mary Harney, as a Junior Minister at the Department of the Environment with responsibility for environmental protection. Having been out-polled by Trevor Sargent in the previous year's European Elections she was motivated to respond to the existence of a green agenda, and wished to be associated with some of its more positive aspects.

Mary Harney sought a flagship project that would enhance her reputation and curry favour with environmentalists. Her choice was to introduce regulations to ban the sale of bituminous coal in the greater Dublin area. This was an issue which the Green Party had been closely associated with since the middle of the 1980s. The introduction of these regulations should have been credited to the Green Party. However the reality of politics and of being in power meant that it would be Mary Harney of the Progressive Democrats who was to get the benefit for finally doing the correct thing.

Mary Harney's achievement in introducing a ban on bituminous coal in Dublin was to be a valuable learning experience for those in the greens. They could now see the difference between being in power and not being in power. For many members this experience, strengthened their resolve to challenge the political establishment at every opportunity and to make sure that the correct decisions were taken and implemented.

The political system slowly began to identify green issues and to respond. The judicial system indicated that environmental protection would in future be seen as a valid right for all citizens.

A case in point was the positive High Court decision in 1990, made in favour of John Hanrahan of Clonmel, County Tipperary. For years he and his family and his farm animals had suffered ill health as a result of emissions from the nearby Merck Sharp & Dohme Factory. The fact that cases of this type were being taken, and that positive decisions were being made on behalf of the plaintiffs indicated that the environment was becoming appreciated as an important issue in Irish life.

Many other environmental issues were also prominent at this time. A controversy arose regarding proposals to construct a number of interpretative centres around the country. The most controversial was a proposal to build one at Mullaghmore in the Burren, County Clare. Green Party members worked closely with local activists to ensure that this ill-thought-out proposal was abandoned several years later.

The year 1990 was also the year of the first presidential election in seventeen years. An election was needed as the office of the President had become more and more distant from the people. The Labour Party chose to contest the Presidential election to help in its recovery from the depths of its 1987 election performance. They persuaded Mary Robinson, former Senator and respected barrister, to become their election candidate. She insisted on campaigning as an independent, but to all intents and purposes her campaign was sponsored by the Labour Party. She was the first candidate to declare for the election and launched her campaign over a year in advance, from the unlikely surroundings of Allihies on the tip of the Beara Peninsula, County Cork.

There was support for her candidacy from the Workers Party, and the Green Party also decided to endorse her as a candidate. There was some unease within the greens around this decision. Roger Garland in particular, expressed reservations about the party making such an endorsement. Nevertheless, a large number of green activists participated in the Robinson campaign. It was a campaign that would leave a considerable historic imprint on Irish politics.

Fianna Fáil, who believed that they owned the office of the Presidency, put forward one of its most prominent members, Brian Lenihan, as its candidate. The Fine Gael candidate was Austin Currie. He had become a Fine Gael TD, having spent most of his political life as an SDLP elected representative in Northern Ireland.

The early declaration by Mary Robinson placed her as the challenger to Fianna Fáil's Brian Lenihan. It was still expected that Brian Lenihan would be successful in the November election, but a number of factors intervened that ensured that this was not to be.

While the Green Party's involvement in the successful Robinson campaign was peripheral, they did make one request of her, that on becoming President she would appoint an environmentalist to the Council of State. She responded positively to this request, stating that it always had been her intention to do so, and she fulfilled her promise when at the suggestion of the party she appointed Dr Emer Colleran of University College Galway.

The Robinson victory celebrations took place in the Olympic Ballroom in Dublin. Formal speeches were made by Dick Spring on behalf of the Labour Party, and Prionsias De Rossa on behalf of the Workers Party. At this point Mary Robinson and her party were about to leave the stage when Green Party activists who were present asked if they could mark the occasion. Mary Robinson seemed anxious that they would. Breda Simpson was chosen as the Green Party speaker. She went on stage and instead of making a speech proceeded to read a poem, in a particularly green fashion.

Some of the more enthusiastic Green Party activists who participated in the Robinson campaign have pointed out that the margin of her victory, at 2.5 per cent of the electorate, was precisely the level of support the Green Party was receiving at that time in opinion polls.

After the success of the 1989 election, 1990 was a year of consolidation for the Green Party. Much effort was put into trying to revamp the party's constitution to make it a more streamlined, professional organisation. Some members took the opportunity to promote the green message in other ways. John Gormley produced a useful reference book, *A Green Guide to Ireland* published by the Wolfhound Press. It sold well and helped to maintain and enhance his profile and that of the Green Party.

Attention was also paid to the development of party policy. A key policy discussed and approved of at this time was the party's Women's Policy. Elements of this policy were based on the following key statement from the policy document.

All ecologists, women and men have a responsibility to recognise the connections between the debasement of women and that of nature. We also have a responsibility to replace the patriarchal values of competition, exploitation and control, with values associated traditionally with women: co-operation, caring, nurturance and respect.

The proposals put forward included:

- An end to all legislation which deliberately reinforces and fosters the traditional family unit which gives low status to the at home housewife and mother.
- Abolition of the constitutional ban on divorce.
- Promotion of women's economic independence.
- Men to share home-making and childcare, parental leave.
- The setting up of a government department for Women's Affairs.
- Positive alternative vocabulary to replace 'maleness' of language.
- Equal training and educational opportunities.

1990 was also a time of tragedy for the party. Active member Mike Curtis died when knocked down in Dublin while riding his bicycle. As well as the grief expressed by Mike's family and friends, the shock caused by his death inspired many green members to organise rallies on cycle safety and cyclists' rights in Dublin and Cork.

Steve Rawson, Dublin

Winning hearts and minds to implement green policies is at the core of what we attempt to achieve within the Green Party.

I've been a party member now for seventeen years, since early '89, and I remember clearly the day I noticed a sign in our local newsagent in Killester, Dublin, advertising a Green Party public meeting in the old Hollybrook Hotel, Clontarf.

It was a cold February night and I was reluctant to venture out.

Something got the better of me and I found myself in a tiny dimly lit room being addressed by Trevor Sargent and Tommy Simpson. Initially I found the meeting a bit hard going, but because it was such a small room, it was impossible to leave without appearing rude. I'm glad I stayed. The longer Trevor talked the more interesting he became and he finally won over my heart and mind that evening.

I joined shortly afterwards and immediately volunteered my time. Within a couple of months, I was working out of the Green Party office in Fownes Street supporting Trevor's campaign as the Green's Dublin candidate for the European elections. Quite unexpectedly, Charlie Haughey called a general election for the same date and we found ourselves fighting a European *and* a general election.

If people complain about resources now, they were absolutely non-existent then. We worked out of a tiny office with volunteers, using a clapped out typewriter – no fax, email or mobiles. There was even an ideological reluctance to use posters. Greens would campaign on policy – not personality. To everyone's surprise, and despite being ignored by the media, we made a significant breakthrough when the first green TD, Roger Garland, was elected for Dublin South.

Trevor did extremely well in the European elections, outpolling Mary Harney. Frank McDonald called around and interviewed the backroom team for *The Irish Times*. I recall a photo of us all standing beside the side wall of the office at Fownes Street. If memory serves me correctly the photo included Margie Bach, Paul O'Brien, Colm Ó Caomhánaigh, Roger Garland, John Gormley, Mary Bowers, Gerry Boland and myself.

At this point it is only fair to recall some of the old names with whom I worked around 1989. Margie and her husband Dick Bach, Mike Curtis, Sheila Hussey: all now deceased. Trevor, John Gormley, Gerry Boland, Mary Bowers, Phil Kearney, Larry Gordon, Cecilia Armelin, Paul O'Brien, Máire Mullarney, Sean O'Flynn, Patricia McKenna, Tommy Simpson, Aidan Meagher and of course the late Dermot Hamilton. Around this time, we began to receive enthusiastic phone calls into the office from an unknown Cork city member, Dan Boyle.

We celebrated our 1989 success by purchasing an Amstrad word processor and a fax machine. While we may have won the hearts and minds of the electorate we still had not convinced ourselves of the right direction to move in. I recall tension-filled Saturday afternoons spent upstairs in Mother Redcaps (Christchurch, Dublin) attending National Council meetings. The arguments were endless, revolving around issues such as: are we a campaigning organisation or an electoral machine? Were we promoting personality over policy?

By 1991 however we had made a significant breakthrough at the local elections. In Dublin the greens formed a Civic Alliance with Fine Gael and Labour in a deal that would see John Gormley elected Lord Mayor in 1994. Trevor Sargent was elected to Dublin County Council and caused uproar in the chamber when he produced a cheque he had received from a developer. The following year he was elected to Dáil Eireann.

The successes continued. In 1994, Nuala Ahern and Patricia McKenna were elected to the European Parliament. In 1997, John joined Trevor in Leinster House following a marathon count at the RDS. He beat Michael McDowell by a mere twenty-seven votes. In 1999, Patricia and Nuala were returned to the European Parliament.

Our greatest success to date has been the election of our six TDs in 2002. I will always remember that day. For me it was the culmination of years of commitment by ordinary members, volunteers, the small staff and our elected representatives, all pulling together to win the hearts and minds of voters. We have spent the last twenty-five years becoming an overnight success. Long may it continue.

Steve Rawson joined the Green Party/Comhaontas Glas in 1989. He served on the party's National Co-ordinating Committee in the early and mid-'90s. He organised Patricia McKenna's 1994 European election poster campaign for the Dublin area. He was Director of Elections for Dan Boyle in 1998. He was employed by the Green Party as Press Officer from 1998 – 2006.

1991

When the Fianna Fáil/PD government agreed to hold local elections in 1991, the Green Party was afforded an opportunity of building on their success in the 1989 Dáil and European Elections.

Contesting these elections would require the continued growth of the party. Unlike the Progressive Democrats, there were no elected public representatives seeking to become members of the Green Party.

The party selected sixty candidates. There was some degree of balance in the distribution of candidates. Thirty-four stood in the Dublin area and the rest throughout the country. The party hoped to make a breakthrough, though there were serious reservations as to the likely outcome.

Manifesto commitments concentrated on 'bread and butter' issues for local government, such as waste management, air and water quality, public transport, parks and playgrounds, issues that had a direct green connection. There were also commitments to a different type of local democracy, particularly the idea of decentralisation. Within the election literature there was reference made to the need to introduce a light rail system to Dublin, the first such mention by any Irish political party.

The party was still learning its way; it continued to be somewhat less than professional and was still considered to be amateur. An account in the *Irish Press* on the launch of the party's Dublin manifesto, by the journalist Gerard Ryle, is an example of reporting on the greens at the time.

'Think Locally – Vote Locally' urged the huge billboard at the press conference to launch the Green Party's Dublin Manifesto. It was held together by pieces of adhesive tape, like the conference itself. The function at Buswells Hotel seemed destined for chaos from the moment the main speaker failed to arrive.

When the conference got underway at midday the party spokesperson, the Balbriggan candidate Trevor Sargent, was already fifteen minutes late and the quips of 'he must have got a puncture or something' were beginning to wear thin. The Drumcondra candidate Dermot Hamilton, took the chair and dutifully read the statements that were supposed to be delivered by Mr Sargent. However, when the first question was asked Mr. Hamilton passed it to the party's chair, pollution spokesperson John Gormley. Mr Gormley was in the wrong place for the RTE camera, so had to swap chairs with Mr Hamilton before speaking.

When Mr Gormley had finished, some greens felt he had not said enough. Other green candidates who were gathered at the billboard began adding their offering; 'organic farming, tourism and wind energy would solve our unemployment problem.

This report was typical of the bias displayed by the Irish media when reporting on matters relating to the Green Party. It implied that this was a party that could not be taken seriously and demonstrated a certain impatience with the 'shambolic' structures of the party.

Expectations for these elections were low. The various spokespersons talked about winning between six and twenty seats on councils throughout the country. After the votes were counted the party had won thirteen seats, establishing its first presence on city and county councils throughout the country. The vast majority of those seats and votes had been won in the greater Dublin area.

The party had achieved a small but significant presence in local government. It had secured the election of key people who would be involved in future electoral success for the party. The names of these newly-elected councillors would come up again and again in future elections. Trevor Sargent was elected in Balbriggan, John Gormley in Rathmines, Ciarán Cuffe gained a seat in the South Inner City ward, Nuala Ahern was elected in Greystones and I was elected in Cork.

The most remarkable story in this election was that of Sadhbh O'Neill in the Donaghmede Ward to Dublin Corporation. Sadhbh was twenty years old, and had allowed her name to go forward with no expectation of being elected. She did not conduct any campaign and throughout most of the period of the election she was in the United States on a working holiday. Her election was to prove a mixed blessing. Sadhbh herself was an excellent councillor, but the manner of her election deceived many others into thinking that it would be enough to be a green candidate, without putting in the necessary legwork to ensure to ensure success.

In these elections other Green Party candidates, though unsuccessful this time around, had started the journey that would eventually lead them to electoral success. The most prominent of these was Patricia McKenna, who won 400 or so votes when contesting the North City Ward for Dublin Corporation.

Overall the party improved its performance from the 1989 Dáil elections, winning 32,799 votes or 2.4 per cent of the National Poll compared to the 1.5 per cent received in the 1989 Dáil Election.

The success of the party in the Dublin area opened up the possibility of being involved in alliances with other political parties. The scope of such agreements offered the possibility of green policies being implemented at local level, and to have party members included on the structures associated with local authorities, such as Health Boards and Vocational Education Committees.

Dublin Corporation was the local authority where such an agreement was most likely to be reached. Fianna Fáil had been dominant on Dublin Corporation during its previous term of office and now found itself in a minority position. All other parties and most of the independent councillors began negotiations to reach a common agreement.

Ciarán Cuffe, one of the newly elected Green Councillors, and long-time party activist Tommy Simpson represented the Green Party. The negotiations were a learning process in itself. For reluctant politicians and neophyte negotiators to be exposed to the bluff and counter-bluff that is part and parcel of such negotiations was disconcerting, but very illuminating. Despite its inexperience the party prided itself on plain speaking and on having a direct approach to politics. An agreement was reached on Dublin Corporation that involved the Labour Party, Fine Gael, the Green Party, Independent Community Councillors and the Workers Party. Each grouping would hold the office of Lord Mayor for one year in the lifetime of that Council.

The agreement was extended so representatives could claim representation on bodies like the Eastern Health Board and the City of Dublin VEC. The most significant part of this agreement was the establishment of a Civic Alliance with a policy platform of issues which were to be addressed during the lifetime of the city council.

A similar agreement on Dublin County Council resulted in Trevor Sargent being made chair of the Fingal Area Committee of the Council for the first year of the new council. This committee was the prototype of what was later to become Fingal County Council.

Roger Garland, the party's TD, did not contest these elections. This was due to a party policy that opposed the existence of a dual mandate, i.e. being elected as a member of a Local Authority and being a member of Dáil Éireann at the same time.

There was very little linkage between those who had stood as candidates in 1985 and those who stood in 1991.The only exception was Betty Reeves, who won a seat in 1991 and had stood in 1985 in the Blackrock area.

The party was beginning to attract people who had been politically involved in other political parties. One of these was Richard Greene, who was elected a Green Party Councillor in the three-seat Clonskeagh Ward of Dublin County Council. Mr Greene had attracted some notoriety opposing Fianna Fáil policy in relation to extradition and had also been associated with anti-abortion campaigns. He was accepted as a member and a candidate at the behest of Roger Garland a short time before the local elections were called. This proved to be a mistake. It showed the lack of an effective system to question the suitability and policy compatibility of those who applied to join the Green Party, having previously been involved with other political groupings.

In the Dáil, in another effort by Mary Harney to be seen to be addressing the environmental agenda, the Environmental Protection Agency Act was about to become law. The Green Party, while seeking a strong and effective environmental agency, rigorously opposed this bill on the grounds that what was being proposed was an 'industry-led', and thereby also a 'polluter protecting', agency. On RTE Radio John Gormley debated the merits of the bill with Mary Harney pointing out that even her own advisor seemed to have difficulties with what the bill was proposing.

The local elections in 1991 were to be the last national elections in which Charles Haughey led the Fianna Fáil party. Later in that year the former Minister for Justice Sean Doherty revealed on the Night Hawks Programme on RTE television that as far as he was concerned, Charles Haughey had been aware of phone taping of political journalists, had received and had read the transcripts that had been taken of those phone tapings. The result of Sean Doherty's revelation was that he paid a price for his involvement with these phone tapings, but that Charles Haughey did not. Haughey resigned as Taoiseach and leader of Fianna Fáil. He was replaced by Albert Reynolds TD.

Sadhbh O' Neill, Dublin

In June 1991, at 1.35 a.m. local time in Santa Barbara California, I got the call. When my mother told me I had been elected to Dublin City Council, narrowly defeating a Fine Gael candidate by eight votes, I was devastated.

I was a third-year student attending Trinity College at the time and had gone to the US on a student holiday with no expectation that I would be elected. I had not canvassed at all. Earlier that year, Roger Garland, the Green Party's first TD, had persuaded me to stand in the 1991 local elections. The only reason I allowed my name to go forward as a 'paper candidate' in the Donaghmede electoral area was on the basis that it would be impossible for me to win. Roger argued that the party needed to flush out the green voters in the area, in order to test the ground for the next general election, for which of course they would need a 'real' candidate.

I had joined the Green Party after reading Jonathan Porritt's book *Seeing Green*. I was very enthusiastic about green politics but was very naïve and inexperienced in the ways of *realpolitik*. In practice, I found student marches and occupations much more fun than canvassing the vast housing estates of Dublin's suburbs.

After I got over the shock of my mother's call, I spent the next few hours in the middle of the Californian night whispering down the phone to broadcasters in RTE while doing my best not to wake my American hosts. My surprise election was something of a media sensation. Despite all the attention that was directed at me personally, the real significance of my victory was largely overlooked.

I was elected with a mere 5.6 per cent of the first preference vote. Many green candidates in other Dublin constituencies had twice that percentage vote and yet failed to win seats. I returned to Dublin to a hugely positive reception from other greens. It was an exciting time for the party, its first widespread electoral breakthrough. We had won fourteen seats across the country and ten of these were in the Dublin region. This gave us a strong and un-ignorable mandate in the public debate on issues such as rezoning, transport and waste.

The four greens elected to Dublin City Council along with Labour Party, Fine Gael and Independent councillors formed a Civic Alliance. We were determined to wrest political control from Fianna Fáil. Our objective was also to take back policy control from the officials of the local authority. These officials, (under the aegis of the previous, lethargic and non-confrontational Fianna Fáil administration), had become accustomed to minimal political involvement in their decision-making, particularly at a policy level.

The Civic Alliance drew up a sweeping programme of reform and the greens had a big impact on the new council's agenda. Initially the focus was on the City Development Plan, where our aim was to scrap any further undesirable road widening plans. I found the focus on city centre/urban issues very exciting, and was inspired by my colleague Ciarán Cuffe's campaigns to promote city centre renewal through conservation and public transport.

During the years I served as a city councillor I found myself increasingly drawn to green policy issues generally, and inner city centre issues in particular. This was my political Achilles heel. Despite the best efforts of greens in the constituency and the support of Cllr David Healy in Howth, I had no political base in Donaghmede. What is worse, I didn't want one. Something in me resisted building one. I couldn't stand the image of the local politician going around begging to do favours for people. I probably did much more door-to-door canvassing for the 1992 Maastricht Treaty referendum, the European elections of 1994, and the Divorce referendum, than I did on my own behalf when I stood in the 1992 general election!

David for his part, with great skill and creativity, managed to avoid parish-pump politics and develop his own political style. He showed courage in standing up to corrupt councillors, and forged strong alliances with community groups across Fingal.

For my part I became involved in a number of campaigns over the years, particularly in relation to waste management and the plans to establish a large landfill site at Kill, County Kildare, to take all of Dublin city's waste.

Naturally, the Kill dump campaign was led by the local community who did not want a superdump adjacent to their village. But it was a key battle in the waste management crisis that was beginning to unfold across the country. For the first time, *political* resistance, on top of community objections, was beginning to bite.

I learned a lot about campaigning from the Kill experience, despite being a bit player myself. First, in a campaign such as this, putting the waste management authorities under constant pressure – using media and political resources – is key. Second, it does not matter – to a campaign group, whatever about a political party which might harbour more strategic policy goals – if the campaign is won eventually because of road safety concerns or obscure legal argument. Any tactic that is likely to be successful is worth pursuing.

It was inevitable however, that tensions would arise between a 'wing' of campaigning environmentalists and those who wanted to see the party become more professional, more prepared for elections, and less tied to environmental campaigns as its source of political strength. Also, it was the case in the party at the time that many of the rows had less to do with principle and a lot more to do with difficult personalities who, for whatever reason, had alighted on the Greens as a means of pursuing other political or personal agendas, or who simply couldn't work as part of a team.

However, there is an obvious tension between the style of campaigning I have just described and one's role as an elected representative. It makes sense to work from the inside as well as the outside, especially when you have a voice on the inside. This means using structures and procedures carefully to amend policy and push for changes, without alienating key staff of the local authority. The task of persuading other decision-makers is the ultimate challenge for all politicians. Making decisions as such is important but there you only have one vote – your own.

Over the years I spent on Dublin City Council, I began to appreciate that politics is a learned art. Power and political authority come from the skill of listening to different opinions, putting a shape to them, and then reaching an agreement. Leading that process is exercising *real* power.

I spent nearly five years on Dublin City Council. I loved politics but I felt stuck. I was devoting between ten and twenty hours a week to my work as an elected city councillor. I had no time left to either complete my studies properly, or develop any career options, as well as work. I was unhappy that I was not fulfilling (to my satisfaction), the responsibilities I felt I owed to my own electorate. At the end of 1995, it was announced that the next local elections were to be postponed for a further two/three years. I decided that I should retire at that point, in order to allow a new candidate time for a run-in to the next election.

When I did 'retire' from politics at the mature age of twenty-five, I found myself missing the policy work and the campaigning. I took on a project working for Earthwatch – Friends of the Earth Ireland, and eventually became a campaigner with that organisation. Later I worked for Genetic Concern and An Taisce, before moving to Kilkenny to take up a post as Environmental Awareness Officer with Kilkenny County Council to work on recycling and public education programmes. After ten years of political and environmental activism, I had come full circle!

In hindsight, I wish I had done more and worried less. Throughout my political involvement, I had few detractors and a huge amount of support and encouragement from greens, other elected representatives, council officials and members of the public. I attribute this support to the fact that people like the idea that an almost unsuspecting member of the public can be thrown into political life. Having made no promises, I was 'clean', so to speak, of political baggage and rhetoric.

It is inspirational to see a new wave of green candidates coming on the scene with enthusiasm and determination, despite the fact that it is difficult at present to engage young people in politics, never mind persuade them to stand in elections. Despite all the progressive changes in Irish society and the presence of high profile women in public life, it is even harder to persuade *young* women to get involved and run for election. Politics is still mostly a man's domain. It can be an aggressive and competitive activity that is neither family-friendly nor particularly appealing to many women.

Now that I am working at home rearing my children, I believe that addressing the gender imbalance in public life is more urgent than ever. After all, decision-making ought to be a shared responsibility in a democratic society. We cannot leave it up to electoral 'accidents' to get women into politics!

Sadhbh O' Neill was elected to Dublin City Council in 1991 and served as Green Party Councillor until December 1995. After leaving politics she went on to work for various environmental organisations, including Earthwatch, Genetic Concern and An Taisce.

1992

Albert Reynolds TD began his term of office by making significant changes to his cabinet. One of the rising stars in this new cabinet, Brian Cowen, began to refer to the coalition with the Progressive Democrats as being a 'temporary arrangement'. He made the comment 'if in doubt leave them out' at that year's Fianna Fáil Ard Fheis.

In July a referendum was called to ratify the Maastricht Treaty. Taoiseach Albert Reynolds turned this referendum into something of a Dutch auction. He brandished a promise that eight billion punts would come in the form of EU structural funds. The implication was made that if the right vote was not forthcoming then there would be no money at all. The government succeeded in getting the referendum passed, but the Euro-sceptic vote was beginning to creep in slowly.

In October an event occurred that caused shock waves in the green movement throughout the world. News of the violent death of Petra Kelly, believed to have been killed in Germany by her lover, Gert Bastien, who was suspected of being an East German spy, reached the public.

The Beef Inquiry, chaired by Justice Liam Hamilton, was taking place at Dublin Castle. This inquiry began to investigate political decisions into 'export credit refunds' that supported the beef industry. Tensions were high and a public confrontation between Albert Reynolds and the leader of the Progressive Democrats, Des O'Malley, seemed unavoidable. Both men felt that their competency and integrity was being undermined by the evidence being given by the other to the inquiry. At the end of October a general election that few were prepared for was called. It proved to be an election that would mix the unpredictable mess that Irish politics had become.

The 1992 manifesto demonstrated the need for a radical move towards positive change:

> Green politics is not simply a matter of protecting the environment. The environmental policies put forward by other parties can only deal with such symptoms as pollution. A new, radical approach is necessary to deal with the

root causes of the potential catastrophe that is facing the planet.

Over the years human beings have set themselves up to dominate and exploit the Earth. But our whole future is vitally dependent on the environment. We depend upon a network of links with the rest of creation. Green politics acknowledges the reality and importance of that web of life.

The policies of traditional Left, Right and Centre have been abject failures. They promise unlimited growth, a technological 'fix' for all our problems, and universal affluence. But this materialistic approach is the fundamental problem. We can no longer ignore the spiritual dimension in the interests of selfish consumerism.

There is a strong link between our economic and ecological problems: both are due to the excesses of the system of industrialism. It is the system of large-scale, industrial factory organisation that has helped to despoil the planet of its mineral and energy resources, is at the root of widespread pollution and ecological destruction. It has caused us to feel we are not at home in the world. It has led to the widespread regimentation of social life, and it currently threatens the Earth with destruction. While we condemn the excesses of industrialism as a "wrong turn" in human development we do not condemn technology itself – merely inappropriate technology and its wasteful and dehumanising use.

We are therefore fundamentally opposed to the following: growth economics; worship of technique; and the state of mind which holds work, regardless of its quality in practice of product, to be an end in itself. Growth economics values growth in the quantity of goods produced over growth in the quality of life. Consumerism places "having" over being. The unthinking worship of technology means that no thought is given to the bad effects of technological development. Lastly, the "work ethic" in the negative forms it takes in our society means that, for example, a nine-to-five job helping to produce nerve gas is valued more highly than the unpaid work of a child-minder. Clearly there is something wrong with a society which has its values in such a mess. Only a society organised according to spiritual rather than material values can offer a real alternative.

We live in a society where the values of quantitative, material growth hold sway over the values of qualitative, personal growth. We want a basic change of direction; away from consumerist values towards a society where the values of nurturing, caring, sharing, simplicity and respect for nature are foremost.

Earlier in 1992 the party had published a major policy document on economics entitled 'Communism and Capitalism – One Down and One to Go'. The document was published with the help of yet another donation from Christopher Fettes. It represented a fundamentalist view of green economics but continued to serve as the main template for green economic views until further refinements were made with the publication of *Economics As If People Mattered* (1997) and *A Greenprint For a Green Economy* (2000).

There was concern about whether Roger Garland would be able to hold his seat. Dublin South had always been a notoriously fickle constituency. Surprises and changes in personnel were the norm for the constituency. A number of factors were combining to make Roger's re-election to the Dáil difficult. One such factor was the residue of bad feeling created against Roger in the wake of Mary Harney's attack on him, for the stance he took on the Dessie Ellis extradition case.

Roger had unnecessarily protested about the proposed extradition of Dessie Ellis (later to be a Sinn Féin councillor) to Northern Ireland. His protest was on clear legal grounds, as the extradition eventually failed in the courts. However, it gave Mary Harney the opportunity she had been waiting for to portray Roger and greens in the most sinister way possible.

The decision by Richard Greene to also contest the general election in the Dublin South constituency as an independent candidate did not help Roger's situation. (Greene was a former Green Party Councillor who had resigned before he was expelled from the party).

Expectations were high that John Gormley might win a seat in Dublin South East. Unfortunately, his vote in 1992 was not sufficient and this time the constituency elected Michael McDowell of the Progressive Democrats instead.

The sole hope for the Green Party in maintaining its presence in Dáil Éireann and in winning a seat in any constituency fell upon the shoulders of Trevor Sargent. Trevor had performed very well in the Dublin North constituency in the 1989 general election, as well as a phenomenal vote in the European Elections on the same day. The Dublin North constituency, because of population changes, had now become a four-seat constituency. Trevor had been identified as the person most likely to fill the new space. He just managed to win the seat.

The 1992 election was the Labour Party's election. The party recorded its highest ever vote and ended up winning thirty-three Dáil seats. The late surge of support surprised even the Labour Party itself. They missed out on other potential seats as they did not choose more than one candidate in certain constituencies. Dublin North was one of those constituencies. The strong performance by Sean Ryan, the Labour Party candidate, would have seen a second Labour Party TD being elected in the constituency, had a second candidate been chosen. In the end, it was Sean Ryan's transfers that helped bring Trevor Sargent into Dáil Éireann.

It is no exaggeration to say that if the Labour Party had run a second candidate in Dublin North and if Trevor Sargent failed to be elected to that Dáil, then the efforts of the Green Party to maintain a presence in Dáil Éireann would have been dealt an irreversible blow.

The Labour Party surge might have deflected media attention away from the green's result but it could not hide the disappointment of the Green Party itself in what had been a very disappointing election. The party managed to win the same number of votes and percentage of votes that it had in 1989 but it had now run nine additional candidates and so the average vote per constituency had actually fallen.

The best that could be said for this election campaign was that more lessons were learnt by candidates who were subsequently to achieve electoral success. Nuala Ahern, Patricia McKenna and myself, despite the modest vote returns that we received, indicated that a lot more work needed to be done. Even with these disappointing returns there was some hope that the potential which the party had shown in 1989 could be revived and built upon again in the future.

Take for example the experience of Roger Garland in the 1992 election. While he polled a very poor first count total, the level of transfers he subsequently received kept him in the race until the very end. This indicated that the seat won in Dublin South in 1989 could be won back again.

On the same day as the general election the government decided to hold a three-pronged referendum on abortion, thought necessary as a result of the controversial 'X' Supreme Court decision. The Green Party had stayed deliberately neutral on this issue in the 1983 referendum. By 1992 divisions still remained in the party. The Women's Group, led by Mary Bowers, sought to achieve a coherent position for the party on what remained a contentious issue. The party agreed to support two of the amendments being proposed – those aimed at protecting the rights of travel and information. The party opposed the third as it saw this as an attempt to row back the effect of the 'X' decision. This was also the choice made by the Irish voters when determining these amendments.

After the 1992 election all political parties now had a lot of soul-searching to do in relation to the formation of the next government. The Labour Party was obviously 'cock a hoop' and wanted to have the maximum influence in any government they might be a part of. Initially Labour showed some inclination for forming a government with Fine Gael, their traditional coalition partners, with the addition this time of the Democratic Left. DL had been formed earlier in 1992 after a dispute within the Workers Party in the previous Dáil, which saw six of their seven TDs leaving the party with only Tomas MacGiolla left to fly the Workers Party banner. The Workers Party narrowly lost this precarious presence in the Dáil when MacGiolla failed to retain his seat, losing out to Liam Lawlor of Fianna Fáil.

Such was the strength and confidence of the Labour Party after the election that the party approached negotiations with Fine Gael on the basis of what they wanted and expected. Chief among these expectations was the idea of a rotating Taoiseach. These ideas and this type of approach were not to the satisfaction of John Bruton who had just completed his first Dáil Election as Fine Gael leader, having taken over from Alan Dukes after the presidential election in 1990. John Bruton also had difficulty being in any government with Democratic Left because its Workers' Party roots had originally sprung from their involvement with the Official IRA.

Bruton's preference was to form a government with the Progressive Democrats, who had bounced back in the election and won ten seats. Being in coalition with two right-wing parties was not to the Labour Party's liking, however. Meanwhile, Albert Reynolds continued to cling to power as Taoiseach by harbouring the hope of forming a coalition government with the Labour Party. Fianna Fáil and Albert's negotiating tactics seemed to centre around giving Labour whatever it wanted in policy terms. It was the option the Labour Party decided to choose.

When formed, the Fianna Fáil/Labour government had a huge majority. It was the largest government majority in the history of the State. The very formation of this government caused difficulties for the Labour Party. As Labour leader, Dick Spring had led his party into the election campaign opposed to Fianna Fáil, and for several months before the election Spring had lacerated the Albert Reynolds government. Now, after being given his political prize in additional votes and seats, he used that reward to return to office the very person and party he had criticised over the previous number of years. It was a decision that the Labour Party would regret.

When Trevor Sargent entered the Dáil he at least had the advantage of learning from the experience of Roger Garland. The particular arithmetic of this Dáil also made it somewhat easier for Trevor. The Dáil rule states that seven TDs are needed to form a recognised political party grouping. A number of deputies found themselves outside that particular definition, and needed to organise themselves effectively, in order to get some access to Dáil speaking time and facilities.

Democratic Left had succeeded in having four TDs elected. Tony Gregory had continued a remarkable run of electoral successes. Other independents elected to this Dáil included the Roscommon Hospital candidate Tom Foxe, a Wicklow independent Johnny Fox (who had broken away from Fianna Fáil over a row on candidate selection) and the Community Television candidate

Thomas Gildea who was returned for Donegal South West. Collectively, along with Trevor Sargent, these TDs joined forces to form a 'Technical Group'. This group was largely dominated by the Democratic Left who used their previous experience and knowledge of Dáil procedures to their best advantage. This arrangement however offered Trevor opportunities that had never existed for Roger Garland in the previous Dáil.

Internally debate within the Green Party centred on how the party could best support its elected representatives both in strategic and practical terms. A ten-person support team began to evolve around Trevor Sargent. This team was divided between constituency activists and senior party members. It reflected Trevor's own sense of priorities. He wanted to remain elected by making sure first and foremost that the needs of his constituencies were met.

This prioritisation highlighted the most significant difference in style between Roger Garland and Trevor Sargent as TDs. Roger Garland had never held a constituency clinic. He referred any constituents who had enquiries about rights and entitlements to the Citizens Information Bureau. In Dublin South this was not out of the ordinary. Fine Gael TD John Kelly, a predecessor of Roger in the same constituency, had followed a similar policy. However, Roger's attitude cannot have helped in his attempt to be re-elected in 1992. Trevor was a more political animal. He recognised the importance of personal contact and constituency service with the voters. By following this philosophy his Fingal Green Group developed into the most effective political machine in the Green Party.

A further internal party development was the creation of the function of Chief Spokesperson. Trevor Sargent's position as the only TD and de facto 'leader' was enhanced that year when he was unanimously appointed to that role.

Inaugural Speech of Trevor Sargent to Dáil Éireann

Déanaim comhghairdeas leat, a Cheann Comhairle as ucht an post seo a fháil. Tá a fhios agam nach post nua duit é. Mar chomhalta nua sa teach, gabhaim buíochas leat as do chomhairle go nuige seo. Is cinnte go mbeidh mé ag caint leat ó am go chéile.

Is fíor go bhfuil daoine fiosrach conas a votálfaidh an Comhaontas Glas i gceist an Taoisigh sa seachtú Dáil is fiche. De bharr nach mbeidh rialtas againn, de réir cosúlachta, inniu, d'fhéadfaimis gan votáil do dhuine ar bith.

Nonetheless, the Green Party is determined to be constructive and responsive to the urgent socio-economic and ecological needs which face society, Ireland, and the earth, in the formation of a Government even though parties of both left and right are still seriously flawed from a green point of view, in that neither side has come to terms yet, with the reality and needs of the post-industrialist society, which is developing all around us. The job of the Green Party is to show that it is possible for Ireland to be more self sufficient in energy and food. We do not need, nor is it doing our children's future any good, to drain the world's oil reserves. Unemployment, oppression of people in work, social inequality and environmental degradation all need to be addressed in a holistic and realistic way.

The Green Party provides the only realistic form of economics for Ireland and the future of the earth, by allowing us all to live within the means of the planet on which we all depend. The economics of both left and right believe that growth in general investment creates jobs, but this is a dangerous and outdated assumption as shown by German research where the effects of investment have been closely measured. This research shows that investment of one billion Deutsche Marks created two million jobs between 1955 and 1960; 400,000 jobs between 1960 and 1965, a loss of 100,000 jobs between 1965 and 1970 and a further loss of 500,000 jobs between 1970 and 1975.

Similarly, given that farming has been turned into more a business than a way of life, (as one leading farming commentator said) it is not surprising that so few are involved in agriculture compared to even ten years ago. It is clear that both left and right wing policies have not met the needs of people in order to have a reasonable quality of life. In desperation, a forum has been set up to address this failure.

The report of the Industrial Policy Review Group published last January was expected to be something of a handbook for many of those who are participants in the jobs forum. Interestingly, this report contains a section entitled 'Green Issues' which concludes with the supposed pearl of wisdom:

"We need to ensure that a balanced concern for environmental protection is not distorted by thoughtless anti industrial and anti-employment attitudes. Such attitudes sometimes appear to emerge in the area of planning approvals and the licensing of industrial activities".

To suggest, as the above quotation appears to do, that the greens and other passionate advocates of environmental protection are anti-employment is a blatant falsehood. The Green Party is in fact the party with the most radical approach to the question of unemployment and anyone with an ounce of sense would realise that a truly radical approach is urgently required.

Unfortunately, the aforementioned report is way off the mark. It swears by the principle that increasing industrial output and achieving economic growth will automatically lead to a significant decrease in unemployment – a misplaced belief in my view.

The report fails to address crucial questions, such as how Ireland can protect itself from the whims of mobile multinational firms. While it does say that indigenous firms should be encouraged, the kind of firms it talks about are simply Irish rather than foreign based multinationals.

No greens were asked to contribute to this report; neither were any unemployed people. Instead, the authors are six heads of firms, a trade union leader and an economist; only one of these was female.

A radical change in work, as well as work practices, is needed in what is now often called, the post-industrialist society. A shorter working week as well as work sharing, workers' co-operatives, early retirement options, and an unconditional guaranteed basic income for everyone, paid by the State, need to take their place to ensure that dignity is restored to all and that the mountains of work which needs to be done, such as food growing, house building, tree planting, road sweeping and child rearing can be done by people who are willing to work. A guaranteed basic income would end the concept of unemployment, it would end the effective prohibition on work for those who are in receipt of benefits and, above all, it would give citizens real choices so that they can work or not work, study, rear their children, do voluntary work, without the farce of pretending that they are looking for formally paid work.

Mr Brendan Dowling, the economist, costed a guaranteed basic income scheme for Ireland in both 1977 and 1982 and found it practical. He did not take into account the savings on civil servant's pay and pensions, the cost of office space or the reduction in the black economy if the effective prohibition on work were ended.

Meanwhile, we live in a very unequal society and immediate problems of great need must be alleviated. The Taoiseach sings the praises of the European Community for Structural and Cohesion Funds but for all the money mentioned, there is little evidence of it having been used where I come from in Dublin North. The Taoiseach mentions that Ireland will receive £3 million per day. A little over £1 million – or eight hours money – would finish a relief road in my town of Balbriggan, helping business and allowing the town centre to develop to suit pedestrians and passing visitors. Yet, this has been refused consistently by the Department of the Environment.

Also neglected are the harbours of north Dublin, factories lie empty, and there are well educated workers with no paid employment, that is, those who have not emigrated, and often no housing as the council has less money year by year. As we know, homelessness is causing deaths.

The railway and bus services are being run down and the most vital aspect of public transport in Dublin north, Aer Lingus, is seriously in need of equity from the government. Horticulture in north County Dublin is going to the wall as a result of foreign subsidised early crops flooding the Irish market.

Internationally, on some issues our government is seen to be seriously wanting. How is it that the barbarous activity of hare coursing is still allowed? This amazes 80 per cent of the Irish people, according to many surveys, and many outside Ireland too. Recently in Berlin, President Robinson was presented with a petition from German people against coursing in Ireland. Last week, according to a report in the *Nationalist* newspaper, the judge in Clonmel District Court noted that coursing 'involves the killing of innocent animals' and not for food but for entertainment.

Much less contentious is the need to object to a licence being granted to allow a huge increase in radioactive pollution from Sellafield; this is immediate. I formally propose that that matter be dealt with this week because by the end of the year it will be too late.

I look forward to working in this Dáil on behalf of the people of Dublin north and the Green Party with a Government who is compassionate and caring, who gives equal status to women and men in positions of responsibility and uses ecological understanding as a rule of thumb in all its decision making. In this regard the greens are proposing that the post of EC Commissioner be filled by a woman who would cherish our unique position in world affairs as a neutral country with no colonial axe to grind.

Following exploratory talks with parties to date, it would seem that Labour are the party most willing to accommodate a significant amount of Green Party requirements in any agreed programme for Government. Therefore I can say on behalf of the Green Party, that in the interim, I will be voting for Deputy Spring as Taoiseach, but ultimate support will depend on the outcome of discussions with various parties in the near future.

Mar fhocal scoir, is mór an trua nach bhfuil níos mó ná ball amháin den Chomhaontas Glas tofa an uair seo. I particularly regret that outgoing Deputy Roger Garland is not with me here today. He was a tireless worker in this House. Le cúnamh Dé, gan mhoill beidh seans ag Teilifís na Gaeltachta cúrsaí an Tí seo a chraoladh agus is cinnte go mbeidh mé ag iarraidh an mhéid Gaeilge agus is féidir a úsáid le linn mo thréimhse i Dáil Éireann.

In the summer of 1992 an event occurred that gave hope to environmentalists all over the World. The United Nation's Conference on Environment and Development, otherwise known as the 'Earth Summit', was held in Rio De Janerio, Brazil. It was meant to build on the work of the Brundtland Report of 1987. This conference came to an agreement on promoting and achieving sustainability throughout the world, known as Agenda 21. There was no direct Irish Green Party involvement in the conference, although it was attended by Mary Jordan representing Irish non-governmental organisations. Mary was a local election candidate for the greens in 1991, and later contested the Cork South West constituency in the 1992 general election.

Environmentalists placed a great deal of hope in the honouring of the agreements reached at Rio. The failure to follow through on these commitments would be a source of disappointment to greens worldwide.

Stiofán Nutty, Dublin

The first general election that caught my imagination was the 1973 campaign. I was twelve years old, and achieving a united Ireland seemed particularly important to me. I wanted Fianna Fáil to win. However my faith in Fianna Fáil declined during the 1977 election. Even to a young teenager, their 'give-away' manifesto jarred.

About this time, I became involved with a group who were trying to get Sinn Féin recognised as a society at Trintity College Dublin. These people seemed really genuine to me. I joined their hunger strike marches and was invited to join the movement. Though tempted, the spectre of the horrific impact of violence in the north prevented me from actually joining. I still couldn't find a political 'home'.

I was intrigued by Roger Garland's election in 1989. Who were the greens? I attended a very small meeting in Howth to hear Roger Garland and Máire Mullarney explain green politics. Something resonated with me, but I left that meeting feeling a bit despondent and unconvinced. However, the Green Party's performance in the 1989 European election and Trevor Sargent's 35,000 plus votes in Dublin convinced me to look at the greens again. Their outlook and philosophy fit well with me. I decided it was time to join up and 'suck it and see'.

On contacting head office, I was told that I should be part of the Dublin North-East group but it wasn't known if they were 'really a group on their own yet'. Eventually I found out that Dublin North-Central greens met in a pub in Clontarf called the Sheds. Within a few months I had joined a small group which included David Healy, Nora Kelly, Chris Morris and myself. We held monthly meetings in an office located in Chris's front garden.

The 1991 local elections provided this small group with a dilemma: we had two wards to contest and a budget of only £99. David stood in the Howth ward. Eventually, after much persuasion, Sadhbh O'Neill agreed to stand in the Donaghmede ward. I remember remarking that there '…wasn't a chance in hell of getting elected there without a canvass!' Our group concentrated on the Howth ward and abandoned Donaghmede to its fate.

We got 6,000 leaflets printed. David tirelessly rode his bike around the ward to distribute them. The Dublin County Council count was in the RDS and the City Corporation count in Bolton Street. At count the local FG director of elections tapped me on the shoulder. 'Congratulations', he said; 'Healy looks like he'll get elected and O'Neill just might make it.' He could see from my reaction that I had no idea that Sadhbh was in the hunt for a seat. Her amazing victory without even a canvass will remain etched into Green Party history for evermore.

By the 1997 general election I was active with both Dublin North-East and Dublin North greens. In the summer of 2001, Trevor asked me to be his Director of Elections for the forthcoming general election. I was delighted to accept the challenge but fearful of the responsibility of getting the party leader re-elected. Trevor had done the work on the ground, and his vote had increased with every successive election. We had a great team and I had really enjoyed the campaign. We created active 'cells' in each region of the constituency. We canvassed long and hard. It all came together on the day when Trevor topped the poll. The first Green TD ever to do so, and by an e-vote too. Trevor's electronic result was declared early on, so that allowed us to spend the next day touring the other Dublin counts and sharing in the victory celebrations as four more greens were elected as Dublin TDs. Then in the early hours of the next morning we watched with pure joy as Dan was elected in Cork as the sixth green TD.

When the party advertised for its first General Secretary I applied and to my delight I was successful. The first thing that struck me as I met our staff, public representatives and office holders ,was their enthusiasm and their strong desire to build on the success of the general election.

The primary focus ahead were the 2004 European and Local elections. One of the first issues I had to deal with was the refusal by RTE to grant live coverage to our upcoming Árd Fheis in Ennis. It was now the end of January and the party had to decide whether or not to fight this decision. It chose to fight and I was put in charge of the case. We were dealing with a High Court case. It was a whirlwind experience for me who had never before been in any court. The case exposed the party to the considerable risk of a major financial loss. I will never forget the words of our Treasurer 'Are you telling me, with your legs hardly under that desk, that we are going to be exposed to a six figure liability?' When the judge found against us I really felt that responsibility, but fortunately two factors rescued the situation. Firstly, Judge Mella Carroll stated that although she found for RTE, she felt six TDs plus two MEPs were at least equal to seven TDs (the number required to get live coverage). RTE subsequently decided to grant live coverage for our 2004 Árd Fheis. Also, RTE decided not to pursue costs. Our legal team was on a 'no foal no fee' basis so the case didn't cost the party one red cent.

Following the court case the greens returned to the work of improving the structure and procedures of the party. Colm Dunne's strategic plan was implemented. The Co-ordinating Committee (now the NEC) and National Council were restructured. Time was spent working with our staff to help improve their efficiency. A new head office was secured. New membership cards were introduced. Two Regional Development Officers were appointed to help local groups, increase active membership, and cultivate potential candidates for the upcoming local elections. Improvements were made to meetings of the parliamentary party. A Publications Officer was appointed. Gradually all the strands were drawn together to focus all energies and resources on the upcoming election campaign. The Green Party won thirty-two local council seats. This forms a good foundation which could reap a rich harvest in 2009.

An event that convulsed the party in 2004 was the issue of whether or not to contest the Presidency of Ireland. This coincided with my last days as General Secretary. It was a heady period. The meeting of the National Council was held in a small national school near Clonakilty. Members travelled from many parts of the country to voice their opinion on the subject. Did we take the right decision that day? To have taken on the challenge would have been a high-risk strategy. As with all high-risk situations there were great potential benefits but equally there were great potential risks. A successful campaign could have greatly increased the potential support for the party in any future election. However, an under-resourced campaign could have exposed the party to ridicule and humiliation.

I am optimistic about the future prospects of the party. Our political agenda is more relevant than ever. Our continued success will benefit both the fortunes of the party and the country.

Stiofán Nutty was Trevor Sargent's Director of Elections in 2002. He served as Green Party General Secretary from 2002 to 2004.

1993

The holding of the general election in 1992 resulted in some of the political activity continuing into 1993. This included the elections to Seanad Éireann, which the party decided to contest. In 1989 John Gormley had contested the National University of Ireland (NUI) constituency and Paul O'Brien the Dublin University (Trinity College) constituency. John's total of 1,700 votes was respectable but was never enough to be in the running for a seat. Paul O'Brien polled more modestly with just over 300 votes, again not an unacceptable poll for a Seanad election, but it was nowhere near good enough to place him in the running for a seat in that very competitive constituency.

In 1993 I choose to try another route. In the 1989 election the party had one vote for the 'Vocational Panels' that elect forty-three of the sixty members of the Seanad. The electorate for these five Vocational Panels consists of all city and county councillors in the country, newly elected TDs and outgoing Senators. The Green Party's voting strength in this constituency had by now risen to twelve votes.

Twelve votes were not much, but they did represent a foothold that could be used to gain further leverage. With this in mind I engaged in a consultation process with representatives of other political parties. As a result. an unlikely coalition formed between Progressive Democrats, Democratic Left and Green Party councillors to share votes. It succeeded it getting two PD senators elected and one senator for Democratic Left. I failed to get elected but was under no illusions that my prospects were slight. I was contesting the Culture and Educational Panel, which had only five available seats and a quota of over 120 votes. Nevertheless, I managed to secure a total of forty-eight votes and valuable lessons were learnt as to how the Green Party might approach Seanad elections in the future.

When the new Dáil assembled, differences arose between Roger and Trevor over whether Trevor should retain Anne Halliday (Roger's secretary) as his Dáil secretary. At this time secretaries were thought to be in the employ of a TD rather than the Houses of the Oireachtas. Trevor wanted a secretary who could conduct business *as gaelige* and thus was unable to meet Roger's request.

When Trevor Sargent was elected to the Dáil in the November 1992 election there was an expectation that he would resign his local authority seat in line with the party's policy not to hold a dual mandate. Opposition to the dual mandate was practiced only by the Green Party. Those greens who agreed to put this policy into practice placed themselves at a considerable political disadvantage. Opponents in the same constituency continued to be county councillors as well as members of the Oireachtas. Reluctantly ,Trevor complied with this responsibility. Members of his local Fingal branch chose Thea Allen to be his replacement as a member of Dublin County Council.

There was another reason why Trevor wished to remain a member of Dublin County Council. The 1991 local elections had seen a large amount of support in the Dublin area come to the Green Party because of the party's stance on the rezoning of land. A new county development plan was being debated and decided on for Dublin. Rather than learn the lessons from the electorate, Fianna Fáil, Fine Gael and Progressive Democrat councillors continued to rezone with abandon.

Their zeal for this activity became more understandable when Trevor received a letter from a developer. The letter asked for Trevor's assistance on furthering a rezoning application. Included with the letter was a cheque for £100 made out to the Green Party. At the next meeting of Dublin County Council Trevor brandished the letter and the cheque, and asked whether any of the other members of council had received the same. Uproar ensued. A number of councillors approached Trevor seeking to remove the cheque from his hand. Prominent in this group was Fianna Fáil councillor and Senator Don Lydon. Lydon engaged Trevor in a headlock as he sought to discover who the cheque was from and how much it was for. The meeting was adjourned in chaos as council officials escorted Trevor Sargent from the council chamber. These events were later to be investigated as part of the Flood/Mahon tribunals.

In the Dáil, Trevor was also to make clever use of theatrics. The Technical Group arrangement had given independent TD Tony Gregory an opportunity to move a private members bill that sought to bring an end to the practice of hare coursing in the country. Trevor was to be a key contributor to this debate. When he rose to speak he produced a hand held tape recorder to play in the Dáil chamber the sound of a hare being killed at a coursing meeting. This was in contravention of Dáil rules but did have the desired emotional and media effect.

On the second evening of this debate, when Tony Gregory was making his closing contribution, the Leas Ceann Comhairle Joe Jacob stopped the debate and asked that Leinster House ushers examine the contents of a shoebox that

Trevor Sargent had placed in front of himself in the Dáil chamber. There had been a fear that the box might contain a live animal. In fact the contents were nothing more dangerous than a petition that had been handed to Trevor by representatives of the Irish Council Against Blood Sports!

Bronwen Maher, Dublin

My introduction to the greens began when I agreed to distribute leaflets for Trevor Sargent in 1989, when he ran in the European Parliament elections. I had never canvassed before, but had a lot of experience as a market researcher, and these skills were very useful to me on the doorsteps. I was immediately impressed with Trevor's leaflet as it reflected many of the concerns I had as a young woman.

It was the Green Party's commitment to stronger local government, their call for active neutrality in foreign policy, and their commitment to equal opportunities for women that really inspired me to join in 1990.

A year later, we had our first major electoral breakthrough when Roger Garland succeeded in being the first green to be elected as a TD to Dáil Eireann. Along the way, I got the canvassing bug, knocking on doors and talking to people about issues that are important to us all. I still have a copy of that old '89 leaflet and must confess that I have a collection of Green Party canvassing literature right up to the last local and European elections.

I also joined the newly-formed Green Party Women's Group, a policy formation committee that tried to ascertain where the greens stood on some of the contentious moral and social issues of the time and to formulate policies that reflected these views.

Although the party had consensus on energy, transport and education policies, we had yet to confront issues such as divorce, that affected people's personal lives. The committee included a group of dedicated and talented women: Mary Bowers, Maggie Gibbons and Liz Kennedy to name but a few. We put long hours into drafting the policy and negotiating it through the party. The document proved challenging and controversial to many members, but was eventually passed by National Council in May 1991. The policy was ahead of its time. Many of the issues are still relevant today – the right to home-birth, valuing unpaid caring work and the call for rape victims to be allowed to appear as prosecutors in court, not just as material witnesses.

In 1991, I stood for the first time as a candidate in the local elections for the Artane Ward. It was, however, the European Election Campaign of 1994 that really gripped my imagination. The party had decided to run candidates in four of the European Parliament constituencies. The real emphasis was on the Dublin and Leinster campaigns where Patricia McKenna and Nuala Ahern were standing. To the surprise of the established parties and the media, the greens won two European Parliament seats. It was the third major breakthrough for us. Roger Garland's election to the Dáil in '89 and the local election victories of '91 being the first two. Along with Sadhbh O'Neill, David Landy and Colm Murray, I was delighted to have played a central role on Patricia's election team and spent the next five years as her assistant at her Dublin constituency office.

I ran in the 1999 local elections in Clontarf. While not successful, I knew from the response that a seat was there for the taking. Five years later, with the support of a dedicated North Central group, I took the fourth seat in a five-seat constituency. The following year the members of Dublin City Council elected me Deputy Lord Mayor.

I have held many positions in the party over the past seventeen years. I was Patricia McKenna's Election Campaign Manager in 1999 and a member of the Election Task Force, which organised our successful 2002 general election and 2004 local election campaigns.

On a personal level, I have an ongoing commitment to working on issues that directly affect women and children, and it is the everyday life of people that most inspires me. I see the greens' commitment to a sustainable environment as a key component to achieving a just and safe society.

Bronwen Maher was Green Party National Coordinator from 1993-94. She was Director of Elections for Patricia McKenna's European Parliament election campaign in 1999. She was elected to Dublin City Council in 2004 and became Deputy Lord Mayor of Dublin in 2005.

1994

At the beginning of 1994 there was little realisation within the Green Party that it was about to enter one of the most crucial stages of its history. The disappointing general election result of November 1992 had subdued the party and the time since had been largely a period of consolidation.

The five year cycle for elections to the European Parliament was nearing its completion and a new set of elections was to be held in June 1994. In addition the government decided that the local elections to Town Commissions and Urban District Councils would be held in 1994, after a gap of nine years.

These were the elections at which the Green Party had won its first elected office when Marcus Counihan was elected as a member of Killarney District Council in 1985. In 1989 Marcus had given all that he felt he could give to that position and wanted to quit. He was replaced by Michael Lucey, but having served for five years, Michael was not willing to stand again.

These were local elections that took place in small towns with rural hinterlands, areas in which potential Green Party candidates were scarce. The Green Party put forward twenty-two candidates and was successful in having six Urban District and Town commissioners elected.

In Dublin the only local authority to be contested was Balbriggan Town commissioners, where Colm Timmins was elected for the Green Party. In Greystones Patricia Feldwick was elected for the Green Party. Sean English added membership of Naas Urban District Council to his membership of Kildare County Council. In Kerry the party was unable to hold on to the Killarney Urban District Council seat but Conor Fitzgerald (a technician working with Radio Na Gaelteachta) managed to win a seat on Tralee Urban District Council. The party's other successes were both in County Cork. Liam Burke was elected on the first count to Youghal Urban District Council and Joe Snow was elected to Passage West Town commissioners.

Six seats from a base of zero at least gave the party something to build on in future. These were bases in areas that had not been well disposed to the Green Party in the past.

Of the six, perhaps the election of Joe Snow was the most significant. Joe Snow was not a natural Green. A strong community activist certainly, and active in a local environmental group, but by inclination and manner his representing of local community interests would not have been of a type that the Green Party would then have been familiar with. Joe had narrowly failed to be elected to the Passage West Town commissioners in 1985 as an independent, and had religiously attended any meeting that the council had held subsequently. There is no doubt that had he chosen to stand as an independent once again he would not have been easily elected.

I approached him a number of weeks before the declaration of the election and put to him the idea of people being elected on a Green Party ticket. He accepted and his election in the Cork Harbour part of Cork South Central was a significant help in my own success later.

While the town council elections were a trial exercise, it was the European elections that held out real prospects of success for the Green Party. However, there was no guarantee that the expectations raised by the 1989 European Elections would be built upon, leading to a breakthrough in 1994.

The party entered these elections more in hope than in confidence and selected candidates in each of the four Euro-constituencies, thus allowing every voter in the country the opportunity to vote for a Green Party candidate for the first time ever.

I was the candidate in the Munster constituency. Richard Douthwaite, the economist and author of *The Growth Illusion,* contested the Connaught/Ulster Euro-constituency. Nuala Ahern, a sitting county councillor in Wicklow, was the candidate for Leinster, and Patricia McKenna was the candidate in the Dublin constituency.

Both Munster and Connaght/Ulster (not having been contested before) were exercises in ascertaining what level of support existed for the Green Party. The Dublin and Leinster constituencies were different. A significant number of votes had been achieved in these constituencies by Trevor Sargent and Sean English in 1989. The party decided to divert whatever resources it had to these two constituencies to try and make a breakthrough at this level for the Green Party.

These decisions were taken by the four candidates and their election agents at a meeting in Crannagh Castle. It was still difficult to see what breakthrough could be made. The resources such as they were, were paltry. Access to the media remained miniscule.

With only ten days left in the campaign a further decision was made to pour any remaining resources into oversize posters for Patricia McKenna in Dublin. The placing of these posters in strategic locations in the Dublin area was organised by Steve Rawson, an inveterate campaigner for the party. It seemed to be the factor that worked. Patricia McKenna topped the poll in Dublin and won a seat in the European Parliament for the Irish Green Party.

While Patricia's election was greeted with huge excitement by the party membership, what occurred in Leinster was close to miraculous. Nuala Ahern, together with her election agent Mary Bowers, achieved a phenomenal breakthrough for the party by winning a European seat in Leinster.

Nuala had a number of personal characteristics that helped her campaign. She represented Wicklow and had lived there for a number of years, but she also had a family background in the northern part of the constituency in County Louth. These factors, allied with the existing green vote on the east coast and her willingness to campaign on the local radio stations dotted throughout the constituency, made Nuala the real surprise package of these elections.

Nuala's election had been frustrated by the decision of Peter Sweetnam, (son of a former Fine Gael Minister for Finance Gerard Sweetnam), to stand as an 'independent green' in the Leinster constituency. His intervention had no material effect as he received a derisory vote. He was asked to resign his membership of the Green Party which he duly did. Peter had been supported in his candidacy by Roger Garland. Efforts were made to expel Roger from the party as well. These efforts became bogged down in legal argument. Roger remained a member, which in retrospect was probably correct, given his role in helping to establish the party and in becoming its first TD.

In these elections the Green Party has won two of the fifteen Irish seats in the European Parliament. It was a magnificent achievement.

Nuala and Patricia both made their maiden speeches on the subject of the Northern Ireland peace process. (Nuala had been born in County Louth, while Patricia came from County Monaghan, so this was a subject in which each had a personal interest)

Inaugural Speech of Nuala Ahern to the European Parliament

I would like to thank President Hansch for his speech two weeks ago, acknowledging the importance of the peace process in Ireland to the European Union generally and to this Parliament in particular. As an Irishwoman born in the north who has seen and experienced the grief and misery caused by this conflict in Belfast and elsewhere, I request Parliament to congratulate the peace makers, and in particular a distinguished member of this Assembly, John Hume, for his courage in advancing the Hume/Adams dialogue, leading to the acceptance by the UK government that the people of Ireland must decide themselves their own political future, the Irish republican movement's rejection of violence and terror as a means of uniting Ireland, and its acceptance of a peaceful and demo-cratic progress towards an agreed solution.

I ask Parliament to grasp the opportunity to support the peace process in Ireland in a manner that respects all cultures and traditions; and I would request particularly that Parliament support educational, youth and commu-nity projects aimed at building a mutually tolerant society in Ireland. With regard to the Commission's reference to inter-regional and trans-frontier projects, I ask in particular that Parliament support inter-regional projects and cross-border projects that will build peace within Ireland, and I refer particu-larly to measures in support of European routes throughout Ireland. In parts of Northern Ireland the route between Belfast and Dublin is classified as a local road. It is not acceptable within our great European Union that a road link-ing two major cities on the island should be classified as a local road. I ask Parliament to support trans-frontier and inter-regional projects to upgrade inter-border connections. I ask Parliament to specify that the role of any assist-ance is not to impose any constitutional solution, but to use its impartial and benign influence, as a Union to which both the UK and Ireland owe allegiance, to facilitate debate and assist the progress towards peace.

I wish to welcome the acceptance of the resolution of the joint groups and to associate myself with such a resolution, which promotes non-violence, political dialogue and consensus as a method for conflict resolution. I would particu-larly make the point that political dialogue also includes community dialogue at grassroots level. As greens we are particularly keen that this avenue also be explored and that Parliament take note of the Opsahl Commission, chaired by the late Professor Opsahl, as a precedent for such community dialogue to take place. At a level of conflict resolution, a lot of work has been done by non-political community organisations on all sides, and I hope that Parliament can recognise that as part of this resolution.

Inaugural Speech of Patricia McKenna to the European Parliament

I wish to begin by congratulating all those who have contributed to the peace process. I welcome the belated recognition that Northern Ireland is an area of conflict within the European Union, and that the peace process is a mat-ter of European concern. It is definitely not an internal matter of the United Kingdom, which was the excuse used by Britain for too long.

It is necessary to support the developing peace process in a manner that respects all cultures and traditions as a condition for the long-term security of all citizens. It is also necessary to encourage the dialogue with and between all sections of society, and all involved in the conflict must have the opportunity of being involved in the process for a solution.

However, the role of any assistance should not be to impose any constitutional solution but rather to use Parliament's independence to facilitate debate and assist the progress towards peace and a true consensus.

I also suggest that the Committee on Civil Liberties and Internal Affairs organize a hearing with representatives of all the parties involved.

As someone coming from the border area, born and brought up there, I welcome the opening of some of the border roads which have been closed for the past twenty years. I also urge an end to the continued blocking of the border roads which are a vital link for people living in border areas between their extended families, their communities, their markets, and even with their own land. These links have been severed; communities depending on cross border trade, etc. have been devastated; the closure of roads has contributed to high unemployment, mass emigration and in some areas, total depopulation. These blockades and closures are unacceptable in a so-called 'Europe without frontiers'.

We would welcome and insist that funds being used to restore these small communities should be used in an ecological way that actually involves all of the people of the area. I would not like to see funds being misused as in the past.

Finally, I would urge all those still involved in paramilitary activity to cease now, and for the demilitarisation of all paramilitaries and all security forces. Peace cannot be achieved at the point of a gun either by paramilitaries or by the state.

In Mayo West, a by-election was held to replace Padraig Flynn who became European Commissioner. The greens did not contest the election which was won by Fine Gael candidate Michael Ring. Another election was held in Dublin South Central. John Goodwillie was selected as the party's candidate. His result indicated a possible support base that could be turned into a future Dáil seat. The victor on this occasion was Eric Byrne of Democratic Left.

The year 1994 was the year that the Civic Alliance on Dublin Corporation selected a green City Councillor as Lord Mayor of Dublin. There were four Dublin City Councillors, who were members of the Green Party, John Gormley, Ciarán Cuffe, Sabhdh O'Neill and Claire Wheeler. Those most interested in the position were John Gormley, Ciarán Cuffe and Sadhbh O'Neill. There followed an internal party selection that selected John and then selected Sabhdh as Deputy Mayor for the year.

The election of John Gormley as Lord Mayor of Dublin was an auspicious occasion for the party. Some thought was given to how a green Lord Mayor should operate. John Gormley lost no time putting many of these ideas into practice. One of his first actions was to refuse to use the official Lord Mayor's car. Instead he sought a replacement, a bio-diesel vehicle, in which he was successful.

John established a Lord Mayor's Commission into cycling in Dublin. The report was to become the template for cycle friendly initiatives that were subsequently followed by Dublin Corporation and later Dublin City Council.

The position of Lord Mayor of Dublin is one of the most media friendly public offices in the country. When John Gormley married his partner Penny Stewart, the ceremony was held at St Anne's Church, Dawson Street, and the wedding reception in the Mansion House, John's residence during his year as Lord Mayor.

During John's term of office the American Rock group REM came to visit Ireland. They stayed at Luttrelstown Castle. John, with some other friends and Green Party members, attended a party in the castle hosted by the group. This contact led to the group donating $1500 to the party. This was the largest corporate donation ever received by the Green Party before or since.

It was also during John Gormley's office as Lord Mayor that Prince Charles made his historic visit to Ireland.

John Gormley's term of office was very successful as regards local government achievements and the raising of his profile. It put John in an advantageous position to contest the next general election.

During 1994 a division arose within the higher echelons of the Progressive Democrats. Pat Cox had won a seat in the European Parliament for the Progressive Democrats in 1989. He subsequently contested the general election in the Cork South Central constituency in 1992, and won a seat there. He had been thwarted in his attempt to become leader of the Progressive Democrats. He was told by the party to step aside and to support Des O'Malley as the PD candidate for the European Elections instead.

Pat Cox reacted angrily to this suggestion. He resigned from the Progressive Democrats and announced his intention to stand as an independent candidate. He made a further commitment that, should he be elected as an independent MEP, he would resign his Dáil seat.

Pat Cox succeeded in being re-elected to the European Parliament. Within a number of months he resigned his seat in Dáil Éireann, thus necessitating a by-election in the Cork South Central constituency.

Around this time also, Gerry O'Sullivan, a popular Labour Party Minister for State who had been suffering a long term illness, passed away. This necessitated a further by-election for the Cork North Central constituency. It was decided to hold these elections in November.

A friend of mine, Eddie White, a neighbour from the Turners Cross area, was my election agent. He put his heart and soul into the by-election campaign. The Green Party establishment in Dublin did not realise what was possible in the Cork South Central by-election. The early stages of the campaign were largely done through my own local resources. It took the publication of a straw poll in the *Cork Examiner* to make the greens aware that there were three candidates in with a chance of winning the seat. Fianna Fáil's John Dennehy at 32 per cent, Fine Gael's Hugh Coveney at 24 per cent and myself at 18 per cent, with no other candidate coming close. With news of this poll Green Party members started to arrive in Cork by the dozen and widespread canvassing began to be achievable on the ground.

By the end of the campaign Hugh Coveney had recovered sufficiently to extend the gap between himself and myself, but the green vote at 16 per cent was still the highest that any Green Party candidate had won in any Irish electoral contest to date.

The Cork North Central by-election was won by Kathleen Lynch standing for Democratic Left. The vote won by Jane Power for the Green Party was a significant improvement to the party's performance in previous elections and indicated that if the party was doing well in constituencies like Cork North Central then the scope for improvement in Green Party votes and Green Party seats could exist anywhere.

The Labour Party took the loss of their seat in Cork North Central and their poor performance in Cork South Central particularly badly. It was a period of poor relations between the partners within the coalition government of Fianna Fáil and Labour. Relations were strained by Albert Reynold's attempt as Taoiseach to appoint his friend Harry Whelehan to be President of the High Court. When it emerged that the Attorney General's Office, for which Harry Whelehan was responsible, mishandled an extradition case involving a paedophile priest, Fr Brendan Smyth, the Fianna Fáil/Labour Government was torn asunder.

In its place a coalition was formed between Fine Gael, Labour and the Democratic Left under John Bruton as Taoiseach. The formation of this government was odd on a number of levels. Firstly, John Bruton and Fine Gael had agreed to a government that included the Democratic Left. Secondly, the recent by-election results enabled the formation of a Rainbow Coalition (which had not been possible in 1992).

Nuala Ahern, Wicklow

Seeing the pictures of planet earth taken from space was a defining moment for me on my green journey. When I saw our beautiful and fragile planet, vibrantly alive in the vast lifeless ocean of space, I came to a real awareness that planet earth is our only home.

I felt an awesome sense of responsibility as I tried to come to terms with the ability of humanity in the twentieth century not only to degrade the planet, but also to destroy it utterly through a nuclear catastrophe.

Coinciding with this vision, I was roused to political action by the example of two women. One was Petra Kelly, the founder of the Green movement in Germany. Petra was moved to oppose the nuclear industry by the death of her young sister from leukaemia. She believed that her sister's death had been caused by exposure to nuclear radiation.

The second woman who inspired me was Rachel Carson. She was a scientist working in the United States during the 1950s. She was the first person to alert humanity to the environmental damage that resulted from the use of chemical pesticides in agriculture. Her book *Silent Spring* gave a detailed explanation of the link between the use of pesticides to kill insects (that prey on crops) and the death of all bird life in areas where these pesticides were being used. She also described the adverse effects that pesticides in the food chain can have on human health. She advocated the study of ecology in order to examine the complexity of these links and to find a sustainable way for human beings to coexist with all life on earth.

Both Rachel Carson and Petra Kelly thought on a global scale about serious environmental issues. At the same time, they took action directly at a local level. This process of reflection on a planetary scale, followed by action at a local level, has become a slogan of the green movement: 'Think globally, act locally'. Green politics is about the linking of spontaneous action with global thinking; about explaining how an issue is connected to wider questions, such as climate change, or with famine and drought in the developing world.

Acting locally is where I started my environmental work. Two things motivated me. One was my work in the area of natural medicine, through which I became aware of the adverse effects of pollution on human health. The other was the waste crisis. I was convinced that the proper management of household waste could contribute to the resolution of this problem.

At a very basic level, it matters what comes into your kitchen, and how it goes out. It matters that you don't accept the 'plastic onslaught' from the marketing machine. It matters that you re-cycle it or refuse it. It matters that you compost organic waste where possible, and that you divide plastic, glass, metals and batteries into their respective recyclable components. It matters what kind of chemicals you pour down your sink, and what happens to your sewage. I campaigned against the disposal of the raw sewage, which could be seen every summer off the beach in Greystones.

It is important that we expand our view of our local territory to be not just our own homes and gardens, but also include the litter on our local estates. This might involve taking action to prevent the pollution in our air and water and to ensure that our sewage is disposed of properly and is not fouling our children's bathing places.

These all seem to me to be simple and straight-forward necessities. However when you see how things are done, and how vested interests prevent change taking place, then it becomes clear that simple demands for change (that would benefit all), becomes a political and social battleground.

A formative influence on my environmental activism is the fact that I grew up as a child on the Cooley peninsula in north Louth. This is the closest point to Sellafield on this island. I feel very deeply concerned about what effect a major accident at Sellafield, similar to the one that happened at Chernobyl, could have on the east coast of Ireland.

I was elected as the first Green Party member to Wicklow County Council in the summer of 1991. I was involved in a number of issues. These included the preservation of the last remaining part of the Coolattin estate: a beautiful oak wood called 'Tom na Finnogue' wood. The N11 motorway through 'the Glen of the Downs' was another issue. A complaint was made by a local green named Alex Perkins, to the European Commission. Alex made such a detailed submission to Brussels that Wicklow County Council had to make considerable alterations to their plans.

In 1994, I was chosen as the Green Party candidate to contest the Leinster constituency in the forthcoming European elections. After six months of hard campaigning I was elected an MEP in June 1994.

Representing Ireland in the European parliament was an exciting and challenging experience. I had campaigned against the reprocessing of nuclear fuel at Sellafield and, on election, made this campaign a priority. I promoted renewable energy and highlighted the need for energy saving. I was involved in the directive on electrical and electronic recycling, which a number of years later came into force in Ireland.

I was re-elected to the European Parliament in 1999 with an increased vote. In 2004 I stood down as the party candidate in the European elections and did not contest the seat.

During my period with the Green Party it has changed from being a group of idealists who had firm guiding principles but a weak grasp of practical politics, into an organization rooted in grassroots action with its sights on political power: the power to make change. This transformation was not achieved without much struggle and debate. This was always exhilarating, if a little intense at times!

Nuala Ahern was elected to Wicklow County Council in 1991. She was Green Party MEP for Leinster from 1994-2004. She is a member of the party's National Executive Committee.

1995

The formation of the new government caused some difficulties for Trevor Sargent. The technical group that had existed with the Democratic Left could no longer be formed. This meant that access to certain facilities and Dáil time was reduced.

Patricia McKenna and Nuala Ahern embedded themselves in the European Parliament and were appointed to a number of committees; fisheries in the case of Patricia and energy in the case of Nuala, who also had membership of the influential Petitions Committee. They both sought to maximise their influence as Irish green MEPs and brought strength to the green group in the European Parliament.

A consequence of Nuala Ahern's election to the European Parliament was the immediate surrendering of her Wicklow County Council seat. The Wicklow greens selected Emer Singleton as her replacement.

Patricia McKenna was not only finding her way around the European Parliament, she was also becoming familiar with the Four Courts in Dublin and the Irish judicial system. In the aftermath of the Maastricht Treaty referendum in 1992, Patricia challenged the constitutionality of the Irish government using taxpayers' money to persuade the electorate to vote according to its wishes. This applied to constitutional referenda and votes relating to treaties on the European Union, where public monies had been spent in embellishing the government's case.

In 1995 Patricia lost her High Court action. She appealed to the Supreme Court, where to the shock of the political establishment she won. This became known as the McKenna judgement. It found that the State was abusing its position in relation to the entitlements of voters to be properly informed and not have taxpayers' money used to promote only one side. It was an important judicial decision with significant political ramifications. The McKenna judgement established an important democratic principle in Irish political life.

The main environmental initiative of the Rainbow government during 1995 was the presentation by the Minister for the Environment, Brendan Howlin, of the Waste Management Bill. This bill was not totally to the satisfaction of the Green Party, as it for instance enshrined the principle of incineration into Irish legislation.

Patricia McKenna, Dublin

My first contact with the Green Party (or the Green Alliance as it was then known) was around the end of 1986 – just after the Coalition Government ratified the Single European Act (SEA) without a referendum. The late Raymond Clotty challenged this ratification in the Supreme Court. The Court ruled that the government were indeed acting unconstitutionally by ratifying the SEA and would first have to seek the approval of the people in a referendum. Out of this legal challenge grew the Constitutional Rights Campaign (CRC). A member of the Green Party, Grattan Healy, played a key role in that organization and it was Grattan who introduced me to the greens. It was during that SEA campaign of 1987 that I first met Petra Kelly, the charismatic and passionate campaigner and founder of the German Greens. Her conviction and vitality had a profound effect on me, inspiring me to get out there and fight for what I believed in. I remained friends with Petra and depended on her support on many occasions. We kept in touch with her right up to her sad and untimely death in 1992.

After the SEA campaign was over, I became very involved in the Green Alliance and never looked back. The Waterboys concert and the Environmental Emergency Conference were the first major events I was involved in as a member of the greens. Grattan Healy and John Gormley were the main organizers of these events. I remember working in my studio in Temple Bar, designing a poster and programme cover for the environmental conference and making small presentation sculptures for each member of the Waterboys, their manager and the legendary BP Fallon.

The Environmental Emergency Conference, although ignored by the mainstream media, was a great success. Participants included the world-famous David Bellamy as well as key players in the British nuclear industry. Held in the Synod Hall, Christchurch, the conference was opened by the Nobel Peace prize winner, the late Sean McBride. I believe it was one of the most significant environmental events of the decade, covering most of today's environmental problems.

Contributions to the event are even more relevant today than they were then. Had that event got the attention it deserved and the action it recommended at the time, we would be faced with fewer environmental problems today. Funding for the event came from the proceeds of two gigs very generously donated by the Waterboys.

In 1988 the greens got their first opportunity to appear on TV on Gay Byrne's *Late Late Show*. The researchers had contacted us to see if we could send two people along to the audience as they were discussing tourism and the environment with Gillian Bowler and others. John Gormley and I went along and we both made sure to get our few words in regarding the state of our environment. There was a prize that night for a weekend for two at the Chelsea Flower Show and it involved identifying a picture from bits of a jigsaw. When the first bit appeared on screen I knew immediately that it was the Botanic Gardens, as I had just finished an art project there. I told John to put his hand up and say so but it was almost the end of the show before Gay came back to say we were correct.

In June 1989 Irish voters elected the first ever Green TD, Roger Garland. During Roger's time in the Dáil, I helped out on a voluntary basis and one significant piece of legislation passed during his term in office was the EPA Bill. Our two key demands for that agency were that it should be truly independent and have the teeth and resources to deal with protecting our environment effectively. Unfortunately, our demands were not met and the EPA in its current form leaves a lot to be desired, with many environmentalists having no faith whatsoever in its ability to do what it was envisaged it would do.

The Maastricht Treaty referendum in 1992 was a real turning point for me. Having experienced the undemocratic behaviour of the government during the Single European Act, I was not prepared to sit back and let them get away with this a second time. As the referendum campaign progressed it was clear to me that it was going to be even more undemocratic than the previous one. Having gotten away with abusing their position in the SEA campaign to get the result they wanted, the government were clearly becoming more blatantly daring. They had put in place, at taxpayers' expense, a massive propaganda campaign involving billboards and newspaper advertisements, with crude simplistic propaganda slogans such as 'A vote against Maastricht will disempower women' or 'Vote Yes for £8 billion of EU structural funds'. I was convinced that such use of public monies, taken from both sides to push one side in order to get us to change our constitution, had to be in breach of the constitution itself. The constitution belonged to the people and it was up to the people to decide whether they wanted to change it or not. With help from a number of courageous Irish citizens, a case against this abuse of public money was put together. I went to the High Court to try to get an interlocutory injunction to stop the Government's propaganda campaign. Unfortunately, my case only got as far as the high court, and was thrown out by Judge Costello. I believed that, had the case gone to a full hearing, I would have won but time was against me. It was only a matter of days until the actual vote and the chances of getting the in-depth hearing the case deserved was slim, so I decided not go to the Supreme Court at that time.

However, the issue did re-emerge during the divorce referendum. I had been given assurances by John Bruton, the leader of Fine Gael, that he agreed with my argument that using taxpayers' money for propaganda purposes in referenda was wrong. I did not expect that the coalition government would adopt such an approach during the divorce referendum. But once again, my faith in politicians was misplaced, as the government did indeed start to spend public monies to get the result they wanted. While I was very much in favour of the constitutional amendment, and believed divorce should be available in Ireland, I could not stand idly by and allow a practice I firmly believed to be wrong to go unchallenged just because it suited me and the result I wanted in the referendum. So I was forced to go back to court and have the issue settled, once and for all. Many of my friends and party colleagues were outraged with me and tried to persuade me not to go ahead with the case. But I felt I had a duty to protect the interests of all Irish citizens, even those I may not necessarily have agreed with. It was a difficult time and probably one of the most stressful in my political carer. Aside from the pressure being put on me by friends and colleagues, I also had to contend with the possibility that I might lose the case and be faced with an enormous legal bill, putting my home and any money I had at risk. The McKenna case was so unpopular within the political establishment that I had no doubt the establishment would have thrown the book at me in relation to cost if I had lost. But fortunately for me, and indeed for all Irish citizens, the Courts were on the side of equality and fairness and ruled that such spending was unfair, unconstitutional and undemocratic.

The results of the European elections of June 1994 really demonstrated that the greens' time had indeed come. As the Green Party candidate for Dublin, I along with many other colleagues believed we had a slim chance of perhaps taking the last seat in Dublin. My campaign was a modest one involving a budget of about £6,000. Opinion polls and the media didn't give me much of a chance of success.

Most of my campaigning was done on a bike, with voluntary help from a number of key people within the party, including David Landy, Bronwen Maher, Sabhdh O'Neill and Steve Rawson as well as a few outside. On the morning of the count I phoned one of our members who was out at the RDS to see how things were going. She said 'Don't worry Patricia you seem to be doing quite well, in fact it looks like you are topping the poll'. When I heard this I was convinced that she didn't know what she was talking about and decide to go out the RDS myself. How could I be topping the poll? The Green Party had never topped any poll before! It just didn't seem possible. On such a low budget and a campaign that got so little media attention. On the way to the RDS, the radio commentator was saying that the Green Party's Patricia McKenna was topping the poll in Dublin so I knew it was true. From that moment on it was a roller coaster. I remember being really scared that so many voters had put their faith in me. In fact, I was so afraid I would let them down that for a few days I was almost afraid to do or say anything in case I would upset someone who voted for me. But then I realised I was elected to do a job, and I recalled the words of an old song 'you can't please everyone so you gotta please yourself'. In other words, stick to what you believe in and what you think is right, and that's what I have been doing since.

Patricia McKenna was Green Party MEP from 1994-2004.

1996

1996 was a year of marking time in Irish politics and for the Green Party. Some efforts were made in preparation for a general election expected in 1997. Two by-elections dominated the early part of the year. In Donegal North East the Independent Fianna Fáil TD Neil Blaney died. The subsequent by-election was won by the official Fianna Fáil candidate Cecilia Keaveney. Fianna Fáil were also successful in the second by-election in Dublin West. Brian Lenihan Junior won the seat that had been vacated by his father. He was pushed extremely hard by Joe Higgins running on an 'end-the-water-charges' ticket. The Green Party did not contest the Donegal/North East by election but did stand in Dublin West. Its candidate was Paul Gogarty who performed solidly but not spectacularly. However, the experience for Paul was to prove valuable to his eventual electoral success.

Later in 1996 the government decided to hold yet another constitutional referendum. This time it was in relation to removing any possible constitutional impediment to changing the Bail Laws. The Green Party campaigned against the passage of this amendment. It found itself very isolated in doing so. The amendment was overwhelmingly accepted.

From 1994 to 1996 the Dáil had established a forum for Peace and Reconciliation as a mechanism to advance the Northern Ireland Peace Process. Unlike with its predecessor, the New Ireland Forum in 1983-84, an invitation to participate was this time extended to the Green Party. The party was allowed one participating and one substitute member on the Forum, as well as a member on the Steering Committee. Trevor Sargent became the party's official representative at the Forum and attended many of its sessions. His substitute was Vincent MacDowell, a man who had had a strong personal history with Northern Ireland. Eugene O'Shea was the party's member on the Steering Committee that determined the work schedule of the Forum.

Eugene had been spokesperson on Northern Ireland within the Green Party for many years. He used his appointment to articulate a different approach to the problem. Greens in Northern Ireland, especially Peter Emerson, helped inform this process. The party acquired a reputation of being an honest broker when it came to issues that related to Northern Ireland. When George Mitchell was appointed as President Bill Clinton's representative on Northern Ireland, one of his first meetings in the Republic was with Trevor Sargent and the Green Party.

Part of the preparation for the upcoming general election was an upgrading of the party's corporate image. Changes were made largely at the behest of John Gormley. The party's logo was redesigned by a company that also supplied logos to Fianna Fáil and the SDLP. The tree above the waved lines was replaced by a stylised sunflower or maybe a sunburst, depending on who was looking at the logo. Realising the importance of this type of visual imagery, even using the term 'corporate logo', were further signs that the Green Party was moving in a different direction.

Mary Bowers, Dublin

I joined the greens many years ago, after reading a newspaper article on the policies and principles of the GP/CG. This was a time when the party was just a Dublin group and a Cork group. Shortly afterwards a convention was held in a restaurant I was managing at the time. A decision was taken to break into constituency groups. You know, after a few months I knew I had found my political 'home'.

For all the time I have spent on active roles in the party, I have got back great energy and experiences I would not have got elsewhere. The things I learned from the people around me will always stay with me. I have to say, I was very lucky to have met so many talented people over the early years in the party.

People like Richard and Marg Bach, who believed so strongly in the green message that they gave their time and energy on a voluntary basis, to keeping the office going and to developing and writing great policy. Policy that even when you read it today, you realise was written with great foresight and some really radical aims.

There have been many important moments in the growth and development of the GP/CG. Roger Garland's election to the Dáil and his willingness to donate his salary to the party helped to move us up a rung on the ladder. Next came the very successful local elections of 1991, John's year as Dublin's Lord Mayor and Trevor's election as a TD. Suddenly we were well on our way. We were fortunate in having John as Lord Mayor and Trevor as TD. They are two extremely competent and popular politicians.

For me, as National Co-ordinator going into a general election, the hiring of Edel Hackett as press officer was a great boost. We now had a manifesto we could be proud of and in Edel we had someone who could advise our candidates and deal with the press in a very professional manner.

After that was the hiring of Alison. She started to run the office the way it needed to be done, and gave the impression to the outside world that we had more than we actually did. Thank you both for making my time as co-ordinator so much easier.

I think I share a belief with many others I have met in the party over the years, that things could and should be better for everyone; that the world needs to be respected if we are to continue; and that the GP/CG is helping to change things. The journey is just beginning. Next year, next stage.

Mary Bowers is a long-standing member of the Green Party/Comhaontas Glas. She served as National Co-ordinator of the party in the late 1990s.

1997

1997 was a general election year. John Bruton as Taoiseach announced the election for June. If he had waited until the autumn then the government might have been in a stronger position to get re-elected.

The coalition government of Fine Gael, Labour and Democratic Left contested the general election on a common platform. Fianna Fáil under Bertie Ahern seemed energised. The PDs were less certain entering this election. The Labour Party was anticipating making losses because they had supported Fianna Fáil back into government in 1992.

Thirty-two candidates stood for the Green Party in this election. Knowing that the Labour upsurge of 1992 was not going to be repeated and that there could be space 'on the left' for the party to fill, there was some confidence that the greens could advance. In the end the election brought some progress for the greens. Trevor Sargent's seat in Dublin North became more secure but doubt remained for several days after the election if any other green would join him in the Dáil. The 1997 Manifesto offered the electorate a real political choice:

> The General Election of 1997 will involve the deepest inspection of the Green Party/Comhaontas Glas ever. We are looking forward to the challenge because we feel that we are the only political party which can offer Irish voters a true political alternative for a sustainable future.
>
> Since 1989 five of the six political parties represented in Dáil Éireann have participated in government. In that time they have shown themselves to differ little from each other, in their policies, in their philosophies, or in their practice of government. They have been shown to be pale imitations of themselves, and have deprived the Irish electorate of a real political choice.
>
> A vibrant democracy depends on the discussion and examination of competing ideas and differing visions of society. Through this manifesto the Green Party / Comhaontas Glas offers Irish voters that choice.
>
> Contained here are policies we will aim to implement when in government. We will look for economic change and ways to bring about a new politics, leading to a major improvement in the quality of life for all Irish people. Our

policies also take into account Ireland's role in the wider world.

The Green Party/Comhaontas Glas is more than a one issue party. *Is gné glas gach gné.* We are an every issue party which offers Irish people an exciting and sustainable programme for government. The Green Party plans for the future, other political parties plan for the next election. We want you to be part of our vision for the future in Ireland.

For myself in Cork any expectation that had arisen through my by-election performance of 1994 was not met in 1997. My vote tally, while significant, never put me in the running for any of the five seats in Cork South Central. There was a strong first-time performance by Mary White in Carlow/Kilkenny, but again no seat was realised. Gerry Boland, a long time party member, animal rights and vegan activist, polled well and raised the party's vote in Dublin South, indicating that the party could regain a seat in the future.

The only opportunity that remained for the greens to advance was in Dublin South East. There a recount was called for the final seat between the sitting TD Michael McDowell of the PDs and John Gormley of the greens. At the final count a mere margin of twenty-seven votes separated the two. The PDs called for a recount and for several days votes were looked at inside out and upside down to see if that margin could be overturned. The reality, however, was that whatever votes were found to be deficient were in John Gormley's favour. The transfer patterns from Fine Gael and Labour favoured John Gormley. The original count verdict was upheld.

During 1997 a factor that made life difficult for the party was that sometimes mixed messages were sent to the electorate. In Wicklow for example, a major environmental issue was the road-widening proposal at the Glen of the Downs. Green Party representative and general election candidate Alex Perkins negotiated with Wicklow County Council and the National Roads Authority for a slight variation to the their proposals. Those taking part at an eco camp at Glen of the Downs were adamantly opposed to such a compromise, as were many Green Party members and supporters. This double think did not go down well with Wicklow voters.

While the 1997 general election was disappointing for the greens, at least the party now had two TDs in the Dáil. It was an odd situation for the party to have only 2 out of 166 seats in the Dáil while holding 2 out of the 15 Irish seats at the European Parliament.

Eamon Ryan contested the National University Panel in the Seanad election. It was his first election as a Green Party candidate and he polled 970 votes (2.8 per cent of the poll).

I also stood in these elections, this time contesting the Industrial and Commercial panel. A further difference between my campaign in '93 and that of '97 was that I chose to go on this occasion on to an 'inner panel' where candidates are selected by members of the Oireachtas. Four signatures were required to sign my nomination papers. I was assured of two, finding two others would prove difficult. I was fortunate to secure nominations from Professor Joe Lee and Senator Mary Henry, a Cork woman who represented Dublin University. Being on the inner panel gave me some advantages that I would not have had if I was seeking a nomination from an outside body. Of the nine seats available on the Industrial and Commercial panel, three are for people on the outside panel, three for those on the inside panel, and three can come from either panel.

As in 1993, I had to find a coalition of votes, which was to prove difficult. I managed to secure the support of forty-three Seanad voters. This was five less than the forty-eight I had won in 1993. Had I managed to repeat the forty-eight votes I had won in '93, I believe I would have been elected to the Seanad. As the Industrial and Commercial panel count progressed, I found myself in fourth position where three seats were available. I ended up just two votes behind the person who won the third place.

The formation of a new government would prove problematic. The outgoing Rainbow government of Fine Gael, Labour and the Democratic Left did not have the number of required seats to be returned. The alternative of Fianna Fáil and the Progressive Democrats also fell short of the eighty-three seats required. Fianna Fáil had won seventy-seven seats and the PDs had four seats. Both parties had contested the election on a common platform and had a vote-sharing arrangement, but they would need support from elsewhere to bring them into the position they needed to become the next government.

While the Green Party was never seriously considered as an option, an impromptu meeting was held between Trevor Sargent, John Gormley, Bertie Ahern and Noel Dempsey, the Fianna Fáil spokesperson on the environment. This meeting was a disappointment on a number of levels. It was held without any degree of seriousness, indeed it seemed to be treated by Fianna Fáil as an exercise in 'going through the motions'. The brief meeting centred on what the incoming government would do in relation to environmental issues. It was really about seeking Green Party support for the election of Bertie Ahern as Taoiseach. One formal offer was made to the Green TDs, that if their support for Bertie Ahern was forthcoming, then the new government would offer the greens the chairmanship of a number of committees.

Trevor and John later had a meeting with John Bruton in the Dáil restaurant. Bruton knew that he could not form a government on this occasion. However

,given the fragile nature of the government that was being formed, he had an expectation that he might do so in the near future. With this expectation in mind, John Bruton informed the Green TDs that if their support was forthcoming in the formation of a government involving Fine Gael, then an offer of Minister for State for Environmental Protection would be made to them.

As it happened, in the end the government was formed quite comfortably. Seamus Pattison accepted the position of Ceann Comhairle. This move took one vote away from the opposition. Three independent members were found to support the government's programme. These were Harry Blaney of Donegal North East, Mildred Fox, and Jackie Healy Rae, who represented Kerry South.

Having two members in the twenty-eight Dáil gave the Green Party some advantages that they had not enjoyed before. With two TDs, the party could ask about the order of business at each Dáil sitting. Democratic Left was again in opposition so it was possible once more to form a technical group that would give the greens some access to speaking time and the ability to contribute to set piece occasions such as the Budget. A second member in the Dáil also meant some extra state funding for the party. Some of this was used to hire additional staff. Jan O'Connell, who came from radio journalism, was employed as press officer for the party. She replaced Edel Hackett, who had worked as press officer in the run-up to and during the general election.

Paid administrative staff was hired for the party's national office. Alison Martin was appointed as the party's first paid administrator. I was employed on a part-time basis as a researcher based in Trevor's office. I had the responsibility of coordinating Dáil business on behalf of the party, with particular responsibility for drafting parliamentary questions. This was a valuable learning experience as I wanted to learn as much as I could about the technical workings of the Dáil.

The introduction of state funding for political parties had come as a welcome relief to the Green Party. Up until then the only sources of funding available were membership subscriptions (from a small membership base) and the donation by the TDs of up to 10 per cent of their salaries. The party's treasurer was then and still is Martin Nolan, who worked on a purely voluntary basis.

During 1997 there were also significant developments internationally for green and environmental politics. In May the German Greens, led by Joschka Fischer, became part of the German government. This meant that there were now greens in government in Germany, Belgium, Finland, Italy and France.

In December an important international agreement was signed in Kyoto, Japan. This treaty sought to limit the creation of greenhouse gas emissions. It put in place targets for countries to attain, with penalties for failures to reach these targets.

Bertie Ahern appointed Ray Burke as Minister for Foreign Affairs in the new government, despite the fact that serious questions of corruption had surrounded Ray Burke throughout his career. The establishment of inquiries relating to the affairs of Charles Haughey and Michael Lowry brought these doubts about Burke's suitability back into the picture. Because of the questions now being asked – within three months of the new government being appointed – Ray Burke resigned his position as Minister for Foreign Affairs and also his seat as a TD for Dublin North. Subsequent events were to vindicate the pressure that was imposed and to justify his resignation. It was beginning to seem that this government would not serve a full term in office. Many were waiting for the next crisis that would topple the government and precipitate another general election. That general election, however, never came.

The election that *did* come before the end of 1997 however was an interesting one. Mary Robinson was nearing the end of her seven-year term in office as President. She made it clear that she would not be seeking re-election. She resigned from the office before the completion of her full seven-year term. This was to accept the position of United Nations High Commissioner for Refugees.

The Labour Party insisted that there be an election for the position of President. With great fanfare the Labour Party announced it would be supporting the candidacy of Adi Roche, the Anti-Nuclear and Chernobyl campaigner. While this was a Labour Party initiative, a day or so before the official announcement came, approaches were made to the Democratic Left and the Green Party in an effort to have a joint platform to support this candidacy. As with Mary Robinson before her, Adi was to be an independent candidate. The Green Party had little difficulty in supporting her candidacy, Adi after all had been a Green Party member at one time and her husband Sean Dunne had been a candidate for the party in the local elections in Cork in 1985. It would have been churlish of the Green Party not to support the candidacy, despite any unpleasantness in the past.

The official launch of the Roche campaign was held at the Royal Hibernian Academy in Ely Place near the Labour Party headquarters. Everyone there was full of smiles, but behind the scene there existed a great deal of uncertainty as to how the campaign was going to be organised and how each of the parties was to take responsibility for the campaign. The Labour Party largely financed the Adi Roche campaign, but there was an expectation that each of the other political parties would fund their part of the campaign. This assumption was made without any discussion with the Green Party, whose scarce resources were already depleted by the general election in 1997. It was a cause of dissension throughout that campaign and for sometime afterwards. Large personal donations were made by Trevor Sargent and Patricia McKenna. A large number of Green Party activists involved themselves in the campaign. Fine Gael chose their MEP for Dublin, Mary Banotti, as their candidate. Fianna Fáil had an internal candidate selection process amongst its TDs, Senators and MEPs. It seems that those at the top in Fianna Fáil had decided that the candidate should be a woman and chose Dr Mary McAleese as their candidate.

Two other independent candidates, Dana (Rosemary Scanlon) and Derek Nally, also contested the presidency. They were nominated by receiving the support of four city and county councils.

The first opinion poll of the campaign showed Adi Roche to have 26 per cent support and to be one of the prime contenders. However, she succumbed to a series of highly personalised campaigns against her in the media.

These media stories had two effects. First of all, support for Adi started to slide and, more importantly, on the ground support for Adi (in terms of people willing to campaign on her behalf) started to diminish. This was particularly true of Labour Party activists. In Cork, for example, there was little Labour Party involvement in Adi's election campaign. As a result there was the strange situation where a campaign, which was largely funded by Labour, had activists who were choosing not to get involved.

Mary McAleese was ultimately successful in becoming President. Mary Banotti finished a very credible second. Finishing third and a surprise to many was Dana (Rosemary Scanlon). The Adi Roche campaign had petered out to a disappointing six and a quarter percent of the national poll, a little above that of fifth-placed candidate Derek Nally.

Meanwhile in the Dáil the new government was irritated by the use that journalists were making of the Freedom of Information Act to examine documentation sent between government Ministers. The new government was not comfortable with this degree of scrutiny. They proposed a constitutional amendment on the question of cabinet confidentiality.

The referendum for this amendment was held on the same day as the Presidential election. The Green Party opposed the government's attempt to limit the effect of freedom of information on the accountability of the political system to the wider public.

The government succeeded in winning the referendum by a narrow margin. This victory gave it further confidence to later emasculate other aspects of the Freedom of Information Act.

Towards the end of the year Ray Burke resigned as TD and Jim Kemmy died after a long period of hospitalisation.

Colm Ó Caomhánaigh, Dublin

Like most people who join the Green Party, I had never been involved in any political party before. While my parents were active in community groups, there was nobody in my immediate family who had involvement with any party.

I joined in late 1983, what was then The Green Alliance. It was the presence of Ecology Party candidates in the previous general election that had first brought the party to my attention.

I entered college with quite conservative views, and despite all the left-wing activism in Kevin Street at the time, left with them largely intact. I also shared a flat with friends who were active on the left of the Labour Party. I never really took to left-wing politics, largely because I found it all very aggressive, I don't have any ideological opposition to state control of certain enterprises – there are many fine examples across Europe where it works well, but it is difficult to sell in Ireland with so many inefficient state enterprises.

At first I thought that the greens were only concerned with environmental issues. I was pleasantly surprised to discover that the party had policies on a broad range of topics – and in most cases its principles coincided with my own.

There was one local group for all of Dublin at that time. In a seemingly determined attempt to confuse the public, it was called the Dublin Green Movement. There wasn't a peep out of me for the first few months but I ended up being Treasurer for the Christopher Fettes European election campaign in June 1984.

Christopher, Roger Garland, Máire Mullarney and Tommy Simpson would have been the main movers at the time. The 1985 local elections came around and, since no other member living in my home town of Malahide was prepared to put their name up, I was nominated.

Standard A5 leaflets were printed up with a blank space for the candidate to manually stamp on their name. I delivered a few thousand around Malahide with help from a couple of local members and a good number of friends.

On election day, I had no leaflets to give out at the polling station, so I made up a collage poster with photos of environmental black-spots. I propped this up by the gate. It was different anyway and got people's attention. I only mustered 161 votes and narrowly managed to avoid coming last.

In the same election, Trevor Sargent was the candidate for Balbriggan. Together we used the opportunity to kick-start the Fingal Greens. I continued to be more involved in the local politics of that area rather than in the city where I lived.

During the mid-1980s a significant minority of members were indifferent to contesting elections at all. They were more interested in 'direct action'. They hived themselves off into the GANG (Green Action Now Group) as a separate group alongside the main Dublin group. It wasn't long before there was a bust-up. GANG's obsession with absolute consensus went as far as overprinting party leaflets with the caveat 'The policies in this leaflet are not necessarily shared by all groups in the Green Alliance'. This rendered the leaflets utterly useless and the GANG was expelled. The upside of the split was that it resolved the question of whether or not we should focus primarily on contesting elections.

Success often came from the most unexpected sources. For example on the night after the 1985 local elections, we had gathered for a post-election party, to celebrate the few per cent of votes we had got, when news came through on the phone, that Marcus Counihan had been elected to Killarney UDC. The Kerry Greens were a strong force in the party at the time but up in Dublin we had no idea that a seat was a real possibility.

In 1989 Roger Garland's election to the Dáil in Dublin South took everyone by surprise. It was highly unusual for a party to win a Dáil seat before it even had a single county council seat anywhere in the country.

At that stage, I had switched my efforts to the Dublin South East constituency, where I lived. At the count in the RDS we surprised everyone, not only with the 10 per cent vote that John Gormley had received, but also by being the first party to have a computer that worked out the tallies. The FG and FF election agents poring over their paper charts spread on a table glanced disapprovingly at the crowd gathered around our computer that could give an updated total after every box was entered.

When our tally was done, we scooted over to the Dublin South count from where rumours of Roger's likely election were emanating. We discovered that Roger had left the count, refusing all requests for interviews from the media. His attitude was that the media had ignored us during the election so they could now get lost. I was despatched to Roger's home in Rathfarnham to try to talk him out of that. He eventually came in to the RTE studio that evening.

In 1989 I had been appointed Director of Elections for the European Parliament election of that year. However when a general election was called to coincide with the European one, I found myself with a much bigger job on my hands. In the end I was Director only in name. I had a regular job with the ever-patient ENCAD Computer Systems, so I was limited in what I could do. Others jumped in to do most of the real work.

On the night of the election, I found myself giving interviews with the BBC and the Sunday newspapers, because Roger was still reluctant to talk to them. You rarely get to celebrate properly on an election night. The media are still buzzing around looking for comments from the candidates and talk has usually started about potential coalitions and all that. On those occasions you are on the winning side, it's such a buzz!

Roger's period in the Dáil proved to be difficult both for him and for the party. Roger was not your typical green. He was definitely on the conservative side of the party, which led to tensions within the party. Our insistence on voting against all of the other party's nominees for Taoiseach did not go down well in the media. But we were determined to mark out our independence from the start. Roger's demise was brought about by a single sentence from Mary Harney, I will never forgive her preposterous accusation that Roger, (because he opposed the extradition of Dessie Ellis) was 'a fellow traveller' of the IRA. The charge stuck, and Roger's family were subjected to constant abusive phone calls.

In 1991 we won our first city and county council seats at the local elections. Thirteen in all. In Dublin South East we were particularly pleased to be taking a seat in each of our local constituencies.

Winning four seats on Dublin City Council brought the party its first taste of power. We were part of a coalition involving Fine Gael, Labour, the Workers' Party and Independents. We were determined that the arrangement should be based on policy agreement, rather than simply making up the numbers, so the coalition agreed a 'Civic Charter' for the city.

The coalition was shaky enough and in its fourth year we could not be certain that John Gormley was going to be elected mayor until he emerged with the chain over his shoulders. It was a particularly proud moment for me to see Dublin becoming the first capital city in Europe to have a Green mayor. John made quite an impact with the public that year. His initiative in getting a bio-fuelled mayoral car was far ahead of its time, especially when one considers that more than ten years later, government ministers are still driving around in fossil-fuelled cars.

Hopes were high going into the 1992 general election. Unfortunately, our vote dropped amid the surge in support for Labour. Roger did not recover from the damage inflicted by Harney and lost his seat. Fortunately, Trevor Sargent benefited from a huge Labour surplus in Dublin North and took a seat there.

The rate of progress was frustratingly slow and expectations going into the 1997 general election were limited. I had made my mind up that if John Gormley did not get elected this time, I would probably throw my hat at the whole thing.

In the event, John scraped in by twenty-seven votes. The week-long recount had John pitched against Michael McDowell. It was a surreal experience. Once the first re-check of ballot papers had been completed on the Sunday night, everyone knew the result was not going to be overturned. The process was deliberately drawn out because Fianna Fáil and the PDs were in negotiations with independent TDs about forming a government and wanted them to think that another seat might be gained in the re-count. Most of the time in the RDS was spent leaning over the barriers nibbling at stale sandwiches while barristers engaged in intricate arguments or election agents examined ballots with magnifying glasses. It was all a sham and a monumental waste of everyone's time.

Despite John's success I was still disappointed with the overall performance of the party. The 1999 local elections proved to be a further setback. We dropped back to just eight councillors nationally. I felt like giving up but having witnessed the immense personal commitment made by John, Trevor and others, I just couldn't walk away. I remained involved, but mostly at a local level.

The membership of the party had great faith in our two TDs and supported them to push through reforms that have made significant improvements to the organisation. Leading up to the 2002 General Election a party leader was elected and a policy of targeting our strongest constituencies was put in place. Seven were identified as possible gains and in the end four of those got elected. When it was decided that our new parliamentary group of six would need a Parliamentary Group Secretary, I just had to apply for the position. This involved me leaving my job of the past twenty years with a small company. It was not easy. I can think of no other job that could have tempted me away, but the opportunity was too good to refuse. I am very fortunate to be in a position where I am now paid to do the kind of work that I had been doing in my spare time for years.

The Green Party under-performed again at the 2004 local elections. While we more than doubled our number of city and council seats, we should have many more than eighteen at this stage. The loss of the European seats, at the same time, was a major cause of gloom in the aftermath of the 2004 elections.

Holding the local and European elections on the same day is a major problem for a small party. We had five times as many candidates in the local elections as we had in the general election. Servicing that alone is a huge job, without having the European elections thrown in on top.

Research by Michael Marsh of Trinity has shown that only one quarter of the voters who voted Green in the 2002 General Election voted Green again in the 2004 local elections. In fact, only one third of the voters who voted Green in the local election also voted Green in the European election on the same day! This research shows how new parties do not command the same loyalty from election to election as the more established parties. We have to work much harder for our votes.

As regards the next General Election, there is no doubt that the party is better prepared than ever. The candidates in our strongest constituencies were all selected by the spring of 2005. Much of our policy development work for the election has been done a full year in advance.

That said, the bar is being raised all the time and the fact that this government has raised the limits on expenditure is a fair indication of their intentions. Experience has shown that we do not need to match their spending but we still need to spend more than ever before, just to make sure that we are not swamped.

The Green Party has on occasion in the past reached seven or eight per cent in the polls. However we have never been able to maintain that level of support over a long period. The run-up to the 2006 Annual Convention saw the party under sustained attack from the government parties. I always love to see this. It means that they are worried about us. The challenge now is to maintain that level of performance until the next election.

A major concern I have is how the Green Party would handle being in government. It seemed to me that we would only be in government for a month or two before some issue would come up that would result in calls for us to pull out. If we are to go into government, we would have to be prepared to fight at the cabinet table for the best deal and then live with it. The membership is now hungry enough to get into power and mature enough to face up to the difficult choices ahead.

Colm Ó Caomhánaigh joined the Green Party/Comhaontas in 1983. He was local election candidate for the Malahide constituency in 1985. He was Director of Elections for the General and European Elections in 1989. He has been a full-time employee of the party (Parliamentary Group Secretary) since 2002.

1998

Early in 1998 two by-elections were held. In Limerick East, the Labour candidate Jan O'Sullivan replaced her friend Jim Kemmy. In Dublin North Sean Ryan won the seat that had been made vacant by the resignation of Ray Burke.

The Green Party contested both by-elections. In Limerick East, Eric Sheppard, a community activist, polled 800 votes. In the Dublin North by-election Paul Martin from the Swords area was selected to represent the Green Party and won just over 1000 votes. The party shrugged its collective shoulders and rationalised that by-elections run under different sets of rules.

In 1998 two further constitutional referenda were held. The IRA ceasefire of 1997 was holding and this assisted an agreement being reached between the political parties in Northern Ireland with the British and Irish governments. The signing of the Good Friday Agreement had to be ratified by all the people on the island of Ireland.

The Government thought that this presented an opportunity for the people to decide on the Treaty of Amsterdam, part of the process in the deepening of the European Union. All political parties supported the Good Friday Agreement. Most parties supported the Treaty of Amsterdam. The Green Party was forced to campaign yes to one referendum and no to another.

In the end the Treaty of Amsterdam passed easily enough, and the Good Friday Agreement was accepted overwhelmingly in the Republic of Ireland.

During the summer of 1998 Patricia McKenna and Trevor Sargent involved themselves in an unusual piece of political activism. For a number of years events at Drumcree near Portadown in County Armagh had been a source of sectarian tension and strife. After allowing an Orange Order march to pass through on two previous occasions the British authorities that year refused to allow the march to pass through the nationalist Garvahy Road area.

Patricia and Trevor went to Portadown as witnesses. As a member of the Church of Ireland, Trevor Sargent attended the church service at Drumcree. He wanted to discover the extent to which a religious event was linked to a sectarian march. Later he joined residents on the Garvahy Road, where Patricia McKenna had been, and spoke with community activists. Among the representatives who spoke to Trevor and Patricia was local solicitor Rosemary Nelson, who spoke of her fear on receiving death threats. She was later brutally murdered.

Later in the year Hugh Coveney, Fine Gael TD for Cork South Central ,died in a tragic accident. The by-election was called for October 1998. Fine Gael chose Hugh Coveney's twenty-six year old son, Simon, as their candidate.

This was always going to be a by-election that the Green Party was not likely to win. What was important for me as the Green Party candidate was to be able to hold my vote, possibly increase my vote share and to remain in a strong position for the following general election.

Simon Coveney easily won the election. I held the vote I had won in the general election of 1997 and gained a marginal increase for the Green Party share of the vote. In this I was strongly helped by Steve Rawson, who served as Director of Elections.

Edel Hackett, Mayo

I was appointed press officer to the Green Party in 1997 and was the party's first full-time employee.

Things were quite different then. In the Leinster House office there was just a fax machine, Trevor, his wormery, and myself. Over in Fownes Street, Mary Bowers seemed to be stationed permanently in the party's office, despite the fact that she had her own business to run as well. Colm Murray was the campaign co-ordinator, patient and tireless in dealing with the needs of all of the candidates, day and night.

My most vivid memory from that year was the launch of the election campaign. We didn't have a budget for venues so decided on an outdoor launch, at the gates of Leinster House. Thankfully, the weather was kind. We had no budget for fancy backdrops, so Colm Murray was drafted to hold up the sign. The launch was covered in all the papers – primarily because it was outside. Colm's right hand made it into every picture!

This election will be remembered for the re-count between John Gormley and Michael McDowell. For the greens, it was essential to see John elected to join Trevor. From my point of view, it presented a golden opportunity to ensure that the Green Party made it into the papers every day. There was nothing much to report. Green and PD heads hanging over the shoulders of the counters: analysing the validity of each ballot. The media, to pass the time, turned to things like the choice of sandwiches, or the contrast in footwear between Greens and PD supporters. In the end, John won by twenty-seven votes and became TD for Dublin Southeast.

A year later, with a general election, a presidential election and countless late nights in Kildare House behind me, I decided to become a member. By then I had spent so much time with people who passionately believed in the green vision and who gave their time tirelessly to support the few who actually stood for election, it was impossible to just walk away. Besides, it all made so much sense; even if issues such as renewable energy or global warming were treated as a political sideshow at the time.

The 2002 election is, to my mind, the party's most significant achievement to date. When Dan Boyle was elected as the sixth Green Party TD to the Dáil, the promisedbreakthroughhadhappened.GreenswereagrowingpartofIrishpolitics.

The past four years since that election have seen a rise in support for the greens. What was in the past portrayed by the media as an issue of concern to only a few has become the reality for many. Diminishing supplies of fossil fuels, poor public services, defective spacial planning, the exodus of jobs to cheaper markets and no support for indigenous industries, are factors that now affect everyone. Green issues are no longer political sideshows.

Edel Hackett was employed by the Green Party/Comhaontas Glas as Press Officer from 1997 to 1998 and during the 2002 general election campaign. She is currently secretary of the Mayo Green Party group.

1999

The government finally decided that the local elections could no longer be postponed. These elections now coincided with elections to Urban District Councils and Town commissioners.

The Green Party decided to adopt a slightly more professional approach to these elections. For the six-month period prior to the elections, I was appointed fulltime election organiser.

This involved trying to get as many people as possible to contest on behalf of the Green Party, by offering assistance and organisation for their campaign. Finding new candidates was becoming easier for the party. On this occasion there were eighty-two Green Party candidates for city and county councils elections. There were twenty-seven for the Urban District Councils and Town commissioners elections. In these elections the Green Party would have 109 people in total on ballot papers throughout the country.

A number of factors militated against the Green Party running an effective campaign for these elections. There were insufficient resources available to run the campaigns. The resources that did exist were spread far too thinly with not enough effort being made to prioritise resources to maintain existing seats or to target specific seats that could be won.

Also the lack of candidate consistency was a problem. Success in local elections is highly dependent on voters having an intimate knowledge of the candidates contesting. Because of a combination of factors – retirement, ill health and the party policy on duel mandates – the greens were facing these elections with an erratic array of candidates. For example when Trevor Sargent resigned his local authority seat he was replaced by Thea Allen, who was subsequently replaced by Therese Fingleton. Nuala Ahern's replacement on Wicklow County Council, Emer Singleton, was replaced in turn by Alex Perkins. After long service to the party, Máire Mullarney resigned her seat on South Dublin County Council in favour of Andrew Shorten. Betty Reeves, who had contested the 1985 local elections, stood aside from her place on Dún Laoghaire/Rathdown County Council, on health grounds and was replaced by Bernadette Connolly, who subsequently decided that she was not to be a candidate in the 1999 election. Sabdbh O'Neill, who had been very successful as a councillor, felt the extended term of office interfered with her need to get on with her life, and so resigned from Dublin City Council and was replaced by Donna Cooney. In 1998 John Gormley stood aside from his Dublin City Council position. He was replaced by Eamon Ryan.

This meant that of the thirteen councillors elected for the Green Party in 1991, only five would be seeking re-election. Even among those five councillors Ciarán Cuffe and myself were (due to boundary changes) contesting new wards.

The upshot was that the party failed to progress in the 1999 local elections. Only eight seats were won, compared to thirteen in 1991. In the event only two of the thirteen councillors that the party had elected in 1991 continued to be councillors after the 1999 elections, Ciarán Cuffe on Dublin Corporation and myself on Cork Corporation.

The only upside of these elections to the City and County Councils was that the eight people elected would help the party in future elections. Amongst these people were Mary White, topping the poll in a three-seat ward in County Carlow, and Deirdre De Burca, elected on her first attempt in Bray to Wicklow County Council, continuing the party's presence there. Vincent MacDowell, a long-time servant of the party, father of Nuala Ahern, finally succeeded winning a seat in Dún Laoghaire/Rathdown County Council. Eamon Ryan, having been co-opted on to Dublin City Council in place of John Gormley, performed spectacularly in topping the poll in the Rathmines Ward. Paul Gogarty performed excellently and was elected to represent Lucan on South Dublin County Council. Heidi Bedell won a seat on Fingal County Council in her own local area of Malahide.

A sad footnote to the 1999 local election campaign was the death before polling day of Limerick City Council candidate Eric Sheppard. Eric had been a candidate for the greens in the 1997 general election and had also contested the 1998 by-election in Limerick East.

The Urban District Council and Town commissioners elections told a similar story. The number of candidates was up, the vote totals increased, but winning seats still proved difficult. The party won five seats as opposed to the six seats won in 1994. Two Cork seats were retained by Joe Snow and Liam Burke. Therese Fingleton managed to be elected to Balbriggan Town commissioners. Sean English had retired from both Kildare County Council and Naas Urban District Council and the person who had replaced him, J.J Power, had come close but not close enough to retaining both seats.

Conor Fitzgerald failed to be re-elected to Tralee Urban District Council, mainly because of his support for traveller issues, something which also damaged the re-election campaigns of David Healy and Larry Gordon in Dublin.

The one bright spark for the greens at this level was the breakthrough in County Clare. Donal O'Bearra handsomely won a seat on Ennis Urban District Council and Paul Edson was elected on the party's behalf to Kilrush Urban District Council. It could have been a hat-trick as Brian Meaney, who contested the '97 general election on behalf of the party, saw himself tied for the final seat to Clare County Council for the Ennis Electoral area, but was denied that seat on the basis of having a lower first-preference vote total.

Local Election Day also saw the holding of a referendum to insert a reference on local government into the Irish Constitution for the first time. It was a non-contentious amendment fully supported by the Green Party. At least it gave the certainty that the next local elections would be held in 2004 and every five years after that.

That five-year cycle would also coincide with elections to the European Parliament. The contrast between the party's performance in the local elections of 1999 and the European elections of the same day was striking.

Political opinion coming into these elections was that the greens would struggle to hold these seats, and that the winning of them in 1994 was an aberration. Commentators felt that the party's opposition to the European Treaties would damage the party. They failed to realise that a growing number of voters seemed to be questioning the European Union project and wanted a more reasoned debate on a different type of Europe.

The party selected three candidates in 1999. The green candidate for Munster was Ben Nutty, who performed quite well, gaining a similar level of votes I had achieved in 1994. However, it was the performance of Nuala Ahern and Patricia McKenna that again astounded the pundits in these elections. Both significantly increased their vote. Both were elected comfortably. Once again the Irish Green Party had won two out of fifteen seats available in Ireland.

It seemed that the Irish voter was treating the Green Party candidates distinctly and differently, depending on which election was being contested. Voters were willing to give support to the greens in any European election, but were less willing to vote green in elections to Dáil Éireann and less willing still in elections to local councils.

For the party to make progress it had to figure out why these distinctions were being made by the voters and what could be done about it.

Later in the year, another by-election was held in Dublin South Central because of the death of Labour Party TD Pat Upton. The seat was won by Pat Upton's sister, Dr Mary Upton. There was a very low turn-out in this election but nevertheless the Green Party candidate Kristina McElroy performed well.

Carol Fox, Dublin

My formal involvement with the Green Party began during the 1997 general election when John Gormley asked me to be his Director of Elections. It proved to be a real 'baptism of fire' with a dramatic week-long re-count. We all know how it ended: with John's victory and the defeat of sitting TD Michael McDowell – by twenty-seven votes! The image of suited PD lawyers facing John on his bike as the recount began is one I shall long treasure.

My informal involvement with greens had begun a decade earlier during the 1980s, at the height of the Cold War, when the use of nuclear bombs seemed a real possibility. My work with the Irish Campaign for Nuclear Disarmament had enabled me to make contacts and friendships with a number of greens in Europe, including the late Petra Kelly, founder of Die Grünen in Germany. Petra supported Irish neutrality and the positive moral role Ireland could (and at times did) play internationally in promoting disarmament, peace and justice. Her active campaigning in Ireland against Carnsore Point, Sellafield, and the militarization of the EU helped to spread the green ethos and reinforced the identification of the Green Party with anti-nuclear and peace issues.

It has also been a pleasure to be involved with the Irish Green Party and to work closely with the TDs and colleagues like Alison Martin, Steve Rawson and Colm Ó Caomhánaigh.

One of my greatest Green Party memories must be the election of Nuala Ahern and Patricia McKenna as Green MEPs to the European Parliament. To succeed the first time was a remarkable achievement (of which the other parties were justly jealous). To do it twice was truly significant. I also remember that glorious day, following the 2002 general election, when our six Green Party TDs walked into Dáil Eireann.

The Green Party has contributed enormously to political debate in this country. Greens have also contributed to *how* that debate is conducted. The landmark McKenna Judgment of 1995 provided clear proof that green politicians had the courage of their convictions. Patricia McKenna MEP risked her all to ensure that future referenda in Ireland were conducted in a democratic fashion and that public monies were not used to fund one side only in a campaign.

As a result, the Referendum Commission was established and entrusted with providing factual and unbiased information to voters on referendum issues. Recent referenda, despite the government's best efforts to undermine them, have been conducted in a more equitable manner because of this judgment.

In terms of political debate, the Green Party has had an influence far beyond its size. This is partly because of its association with a large and influential political grouping in the European Parliament, and also because the greens are articulating a new and different message from the other political parties – a message voters are beginning to see as increasingly relevant.

Since 1997, I have worked in the Dáil, as a Green Party researcher and the following observations are based on that experience.

Green Party TDs in opposition have played important roles in amending legislation, holding ministers and An Taoiseach to account, and in contributing to Dáil debates.

Trevor Sargent amended the 1999 Electricity Act to prohibit nuclear power being developed in Ireland. In the early 1990s, it was Trevor who first proposed a plastic bag levy in the Dáil.

In 1998, during the debate on the Amsterdam Treaty referendum, John Gormley proposed an amendment which would have put Irish neutrality into the Constitution. Thus he managed to get a serious debate on neutrality on to the floor of the House, into the media, and on the Dáil record. The debate highlighted the ambivalence of the larger parties to the issue of Irish neutrality.

In the debates on the Amsterdam and Nice Treaties, and on the question of joining NATO's Partnership for Peace, the Green Party became the main opposition party in the Dáil to government policy.

The Greens have made a difference to debates on the war in Iraq and the use of Shannon airport by US army personnel, salmon fishing stocks, renewable energy, equality and children's rights – indeed a wide spectrum of issues ranging from agriculture to zero waste.

I am a strong believer in the Dáil record. It helps to hold the government of the day accountable but it also provides an all-important historical marker. The Green Party will be well-noted.

The Irish Green Party has reached an important point in its development. Our issues have become *the* issues. Climate change, the energy crisis, quality of life and the need for good health services, healthy lifestyles, the effects of globalization, war and peace – these are all issues at the core of green thinking and green solutions.

The other political parties know this. One of our tasks in the upcoming general election will be to remind the voters that it was the greens who offered the new ideas and the solutions in the first place. It's certainly not the other parties who are now lining up to try to steal our green credentials. Many of them have already served in government and shown their true colours. They are not to be believed. If the electorate wants action on issues that matter, it must vote for the real thing.

The year 2007 should see more electoral gains for the Green Party and who knows, maybe even our first ministers in an Irish government. Personally, that would be something to behold, just a decade after my first official involvement with the Green Party. For so many others who have campaigned on behalf of the greens for up to twenty-five years, who could think of a better birthday gift.

Carol Fox was John Gormley's Director of Elections for the 1997 and 2002 electoral campaigns. She has been a Parliamentary Researcher for the Green Party since 1997 and is currently Head of Research.

2000

This was a relatively uneventful year for the Green Party. As the country entered the new millennium, there seemed to be a period of consolidation in Irish politics. There was only one election in Tipperary South, when Labour Party TD Michael Ferris died. Labour was not successful in retaining this seat, which was won by the independent Seamus Healy. The greens did not contest this by-election as the party had no presence to speak of in Tipperary South.

During 2000 Trevor Sargent and John Gormley sought to push the environmental agenda as hard as they could. The party published a position paper on climate change entitled 'Ways out of the climate crisis', which maintained that the imposition of a 'carbon levy' on industrial processes would be required to reduce the level of carbon dioxide emissions.

John Gormley consistently pestered the Taoiseach as to if, and when, the government intended to introduce a plastic bag levy. This proposal had been raised initially in the Dáil by Trevor Sargent as far back as 1994.

Since 1997 the Green Party TDs had published a number of private members bills. These included the Public Office Bill (1997), which sought to end the dual mandate; the Road Traffic Reduction Bill (1998); and an Amendment of the Constitution Bill (1999), which sought to insert a clause enshrining a policy of neutrality into the constitution. None of these bills were given an opportunity of being debated in the Dáil.

There had always been an internal publication of one sort or another within the Green Party. *Eco News* was the first version of such a newsletter. When the party name was changed to the Green Alliance, the magazine reflected this and became the *Green News*. After the election of Roger Garland TD a more professional publication, *Nuacht Ghlas,* began to appear. A smaller typed *Green Newsletter* was also made available monthly through the heroic efforts of Sheila Hussey, a Dublin South member, now sadly deceased.

In the mid-1990s *An Caorthann* (The Rowan Tree), a substantial party periodical edited by Laurence Cox, was produced for a number of years. Since 2000 *The Green Voice* has been the publication distributed to party members and to those interested in joining the party, as the means of keeping in touch with party events.

Niall Ó Brolcháin, Galway

Like many Irish people of my generation, I worked abroad in the eighties and early nineties. While I enjoyed living in England, Scotland and Europe, Ireland has always given me that sense of place that makes me feel at home.

I returned home in the early nineties and immediately got involved in the anti-war movement. I remember marching down O'Connell Street in Dublin with pitifully small numbers of people. I got to know most of them personally and met my wife Niamh at a fund-raising table quiz for the Gulf peace campaign. At the same time I became interested in self-sufficiency and with a few people bought a small farm in a beautiful part of county Cavan and grew organic vegetables on a small scale. I also became a vegetarian.

While Niamh had been a member of the Trinity College greens many years beforehand, it was the election of Patricia McKenna and Nuala Ahern as MEPs that inspired me to join the Green Party.

I was living in Dundrum in the Dublin South constituency at the time. Máire Mullarney and Larry Gordon were the local Green Party councillors and Sheila M. Hussey was the secretary. The green group was full of great characters. Gerry Boland had been selected to stand for the next general election and Miriam Hennessy was his Director of Elections. I had no intention at that time of ever standing for election myself and was delighted to support Gerry in his bid to become a TD.

Around the time of the 1997 General Election, I was offered a job in Cork and decided to go but I managed to see the election through in Dublin first. Many greens were of the view that we would get up to ten seats. The grounds for this optimism were based on our success in the previous European and local elections. It was amazing to hear candidate after candidate utterly convinced that they would get elected to the Dáil at their convention in Malahide.

The overall result was disappointing but we managed to double our seats. John Gormley joined Trevor Sargent in the Dáil. Both were elected by narrow margins. The thin line between success and extinction was measured by just a handful of votes. Gerry Boland performed well, gaining around 3,500 first preference votes, but he failed to get elected. He subsequently decided not to continue in politics. His retirement was a great loss to the greens.

When I moved to Cork, it took me a while to get connected with the local greens. Cllr Dan Boyle and Sean O'Flynn were the most active figures at the time. Joe Snow and Liam Burke were local elected representatives. Dan's father Joe took me under his wing and it was only a matter of weeks before I was press-ganged into becoming the Secretary of the Cork South Central group. It was a fairly steady but small group, who met regularly in a community centre at Turners Cross. While I enjoyed my time in Cork I didn't stay too long as work took me elsewhere. I moved to Galway in 1998.

There was no Green Party group in Galway at the time. Just before the local elections of 1999, I got an email from Lucille O'Shea, the Connaught/Ulster convenor who lived in Mayo. It was also addressed to Janice Fuller, an old friend of my wife from her Trinity days. We got together and decided to start a green group in Galway. There was a considerable degree of interest. We had no intention of running any candidates in the 1999 local elections but Pat Fitzpatrick, who had run for the greens in the 1997 general election in Galway West, turned up to a meeting and said he'd give it a go. I offered to act as his director of elections. Fintan Convery, a friend of Pat's, also decided to run as a supporting candidate at the very last minute. Pat was sixth in a four-seat ward. Not a bad result considering our resources.

For some unknown reason I decided to put myself forward for the general election of 2002. I had been campaigning on a multitude of environmental and community issues since the local elections of 1999. I did quite well, finishing seventh in a five-seat constituency. Not quite good enough though. The greens did very well overall, trebling the number of Dáil seats from two to six.

The green group in Galway West is going from strength to strength. In 2004 I was elected to Galway City Council and thus became the first Green Party member to be elected to anything in Connaught. I am the Mayor of Galway City for 2006/2007.

What of the future? It is my belief that the greens are fundamentally necessary for the times we are facing. Irish society is based on an economy heavily dependent on diminishing finite resources imported from abroad: most notably oil. This will not continue. We need to get into Government to achieve a sustainable future. I'm not too sure if we can achieve this in time to prevent our society running into enormous problems. I know we will try.

Niall Ó Brolcháin is currently Mayor of Galway city, having been elected to the council in 2004. He was recently employed as event manager by the Green Party and was responsible for organising the Annual conventions in Galway, Cork and Kilkenny.

2001

An agreement called the Treaty of Nice was reached in early 2001. The Irish government, wishing to be seen as good Europeans, decided that Ireland would be one of the first countries to hold a referendum to ratify this treaty. The Irish political establishment was confident that the Nice Treaty would pass in Ireland with a healthy majority.

To make doubly sure, the government decided to hold a number of referenda on the same day. The first was on Ireland ratifying a treaty in relation to the International Criminal Court. The second concerned the abolition of the death penalty. The third question was on the ratification of the Nice Treaty. This was part of a political strategy to ensure that voters would be conditioned into voting yes, yes, and yes.

The Green Party faced the Nice Treaty referendum campaign with enthusiasm. While other political parties were also opposed to it, it was the Green Party who provided the intellectual weight in relation to campaigns on European Union treaties.

When the count for the Nice Treaty was completed, the political establishment was in shock. 54 per cent of the electorate had voted against ratifying the treaty. As no European Union Treaty can proceed without being ratified by all member states, the question arose now as to whether the Nice Treaty would ever come into being.

The Government responded by establishing a 'Forum on Europe' to which all political parties were invited. The Green Party accepted the two Forum places it was allocated. These were officially occupied by Trevor Sargent and John Gormley, but in reality most of the sessions were attended by Paul Gogarty and myself. As MEPs were considered full members of the Forum, Patricia McKenna and Nuala Ahern were regular attendees.

The government had now been in power for over four years, and consequently the next election had to be held within the following twelve months. In preparation for this, the selection of candidates to stand for the Green Party took place throughout 2001.

There was only one electoral contest in 2001. It was another by-election again in Tipperary South due to the death after a long illness of Fine Gael TD Theresa Ahern. Tom Hayes managed to hold the seat for Fine Gael.

This was the year the Green Party finally tackled the vexed question of the leadership of the party. A special convention was held in Kilkenny to determine who would be the first leader of the Irish Green Party. Three candidates put themselves forward: Trevor Sargent, Paul Gogarty (then a councillor on South Dublin County Council) and Niall Ó Brolcháin from Galway West. Trevor was elected, winning more than eighty percent of the vote.

The selection of a deputy leader was a more straightforward affair. Only one candidate, Councillor Mary White, came forward. Members were happy that this combination presented a balanced concept of leadership within the party. Male/female, Dublin and rural, a Dáil representative and a local government member. The party looked forward to seeing what difference this leadership structure would make as it prepared for the general election of 2002.

Mary White, Carlow

The potato crop of 1996 is probably the reason I am in the Green Party today! September 1996 was a glorious month and the potato crop was huge. I was harvesting them one day when a red car drove up to my hall door. I did not know it at the time, but this visitor was on a mission. His brief was to get me to stand for the Green Party at the next election, in the sprawling constituency of Carlow/Kilkenny. I stopped picking the potatoes, went in and had a cup of tea with my visitor, John Bolger. I did not agree to stand at once. It was not an easy decision and it took John several calls and visits before I did what I felt in my heart I would always do – commit to standing.

The decision changed my entire life. Up to that time, I had been a bookseller; a 'stay at home' mother and keen organic grower. All that was to change.

A few weeks later, I hit the canvass trail, in November 1996, turning the hearts and minds of the people of North Kilkenny, asking them to support me at the next election. Callan had never seen anything so bizarre before. An eager, novice Green Party candidate handing out leaflets in the freezing cold winter of 1996.

I knew I had little chance of winning a Dáil seat. I also knew I needed to do something different to catch the headlines. I decided to walk the entire length and breadth of the constituency, staying with friends, walking the lonely back roads of Thomastown and Inistioge.

I walked over 3,000 miles – the equivalent of walking to Berlin and back. I wasn't elected, but polled over 3,000 first preferences. That's what I wanted to achieve.

Hardly had the dust settled before the local elections came around in 1999. To make matters worse, my electoral area had been cut, from a four-seater to a three-seater. I kept canvassing. On that memorable June day in 1999, I topped the poll in a rural three-seater, dumping out Fine Gael in the process. It was heady!

In the Green Party I found like-minded people with a passion not only for things that I had campaigned for (clean water, proper planning, safe food, protecting wilderness areas), but also infused with a strong sense of social justice. For me it was like entering a room with a host of friends with similar interests, who wanted to change things for the better. I felt at home.
Life on Carlow County Council has been a roller coast ride of incredulity, rage, astonishment and anger. Being an elected representative of the Green Party gave me courage when I found myself in tight corners.

Two events, I believe, catapulted the party into the 'big time': the decision to elect a leader and the appointment of a general secretary. We needed a leader badly, not because we advocate hierarchical structures, but because we were missing out when the media came to assess the political strength of our party. The election in 2001 of Trevor Sargent as party leader was a pivotal point in the party's recent development. He has been a guiding influence in the party and had the joy of leading five new TDs into the Dáilchamber in 2002.

The appointment of our first General Secretary, Stiofán Nutty, is the second decision that, I believe, put the party on professional footing. His contribution has been incalculable. With the party's Strategic Plan in place, and with the benefit of increased staff and funding from the ETF the party moved into a different gear. It is now in a good position to increase its parliamentary strength at the next election. I am keeping my fingers crossed that some green women will be among the newly elected TDs!

On a personal note, I was astonished when I was elected as Deputy Leader. This has been a tremendous honour and I have tried hard to give the party a more rounded image, in terms of its gender balance and geographical spread. It has been a privilege to represent the party throughout the length and breadth of the country.

I will slide over the 2002 general election. I came so close – polling almost 5,000 first preference votes. I came within a whisker of getting a seat. But there is no point looking back – it is onwards towards the general election of 2007.

No contribution to a book on the Green Party would be complete without reference to the extraordinary dedication of all those quiet backroom members who turn up again and again to meetings. They fundraise for us and give us courage and inspiration. They never seek the limelight nor run for office, but they are committed greens: quiet lovers of the biosphere and passionate about their local environment.

One such man stands out for me. The late Tom Nolan, who encouraged me every step of the way. He lived a quiet life in County Carlow with his furniture business and his permaculture garden. A man of few words but with huge vision, Tom sadly died a few years ago. He remains, for many of us in Carlow/Kilkenny, an example of what a good green should be. We miss him.

Mary White is Deputy Leader of the Green Party/Comhaontas Glas. Elected to Carlow County Council in 1999, she was re-elected in 2004. She is a Member of the Management Committee, and of the National Executive Council. She is spokesperson on Agriculture, Food and Rural Development.

2002

The party's annual convention of 2002 was held in Cork. John Gormley was elected to the position of party chairperson at this convention.

The party established a youth wing, the 'Young Greens' during 2002. There had been reluctance over the years to form such a group within the party because the greens perceived themselves to be a party where young people were always welcome to become involved. However, after twenty-one years, the party membership was now ageing and it was felt that there was a need for a special group that would attract more young people into the party.

As 2002 advanced it was clear that another general election would be held soon. There was an expectation that the party might add to its presence in the Dáil by winning perhaps two additional seats. Mary White in Carlow/Kilkenny had her eye on one, and I hoped that I might finally succeed in Cork South Central. The optimists within the party spoke of winning seven seats, seven being the critical number to be recognised as a distinct group and having full access to Dáil facilities.

The outgoing government had a good election. Fianna Fáil won eighty-one seats and came close to winning an overall majority in its own right. The PDs won eight seats, thus giving the outgoing coalition government a healthy working majority to form the next administration.

The big surprise of the election was the collapse of the Fine Gael vote. They lost twenty-three seats in all and were shocked at the result.

Labour was returned unchanged. Sinn Féin won five seats. Fifteen independents were elected. The Green Party did well. Trevor Sargent topped the poll in Dublin North, John Gormley was elected in Dublin South East, Paul Gogarty was elected in the new three-seater Dublin Mid-West. Ciarán Cuffe was elected in Dún Laoghaire. Eamon Ryan was elected in Dublin South and finally at two o'clock in the morning and after a five-day recount, I was elected in Cork South Central. The major disappointment was the failure of Mary White to make a breakthrough in Carlow/Kilkenny.

Despite not having seven members in the Dáil, the party had at least a parliamentary party: the six TDs and two MEPs. This point was used when applying for full Dáil status. It was not, however, an argument that was accepted by the Dáil authorities. The greens felt aggrieved and on the opening day of the Dáil, before the start of the opening session, the six Green Party TDs occupied the Government front bench seats in protest at the inflexibility of the Dáil's rules and procedures. There was a mixed reaction to this protest. Some felt that the Green Party might add some colour to the rather staid Dáil proceedings. Others, however, felt that it merely showed that the greens were more dedicated to stunt politics than to being taken seriously.

One benefit of having a larger parliamentary group in the Dáil was that additional resources were available to the party. This enabled the party to appoint new people to work on its behalf, particularly at constituency level. Many of the new constituency secretaries were appointed over the course of the summer.

Internationally, eco-politics came to the fore again with the holding of a conference in Johannesburg on environment and development. This was a follow-on to the Rio conference of 1992. John Gormley managed to secure a place on the Irish parliamentary delegation. Despite the fact that the recommendations of the Rio conference had not been adhered to, there was hope that the emphasis of this conference on environmental protection linked with social justice might evoke a better response.

The Dáil met for a special session in September 2002, with the sole purpose of passing a referendum bill that allowed for a second referendum to be held on the Nice Treaty. The government was determined that the people of Ireland would vote Yes.

The Green Party once again campaigned for a No vote. Surprisingly, it appeared to be benefiting from articulating its opposition to this treaty. An *Irish Times* TNS/MRBI poll showed that the party's public support had increased, and had in fact doubled since the general election four months previously.

During the summer of 2002 the smaller opposition groups in the Dáil met to discuss how they could improve their situation. This resulted in an agreement between the Green Party, Sinn Féin, Joe Higgins the Socialist Party TD and ten other independents to form a Technical Group. This grouping excluded those independents who had supported Fianna Fáil and the PDs in the previous government.

This technical grouping, which gave the green TDs full access to Dáil facilities, guaranteed speaking time and the use of certain resources. This was purely a technical arrangement with no policy implications for the participants.

Membership of the Technical Group in the Dáil gave the Green Party an opportunity for the first time to publish private members bills and to have such bills debated and voted on in the Dáil chamber itself.

A Waste Management Amendment Bill presented in the names of Trevor Sargent and myself offered the greens an opportunity to show that we were prepared to introduce legislation and to honour their manifesto commitments. The bill was voted down by the government. The greens knew in advance that the bill would fail, but the mere holding of such a debate in the Dáil, and forcing the Minister for the Environment, Martin Cullen, to defend the government's record, confirmed that the Green Party was coming of age.

It was around this time that the Green Party became the first political party to express its reservations about a deal that the government had struck with the Shell oil company in relation to bringing gas ashore from the Corrib Field, off County Mayo.

Paul Gogarty, Dublin

On 1 August 2006, my dear friend and colleague, Green Party Councillor Fintan McCarthy, was tragically killed in a freak road accident in Beijing, China. His life, along with that of his girlfriend Sonya Rabbitte, and a Dutch tourist who were on the same minibus, was taken in such a random, unimaginable and arbitrary way that it will take many years, for those who loved him to come to terms with their loss, if they ever do.

My friend is gone and I miss him terribly. I knew Fintan since I was a child. We grew up together, played GAA together, went out clubbing together. We travelled together, laughed and joked together and argued continuously. Yet we never fell out.

We did not need politics and the Green Party to mark our friendship. Yet that is the context in which our relationship will mostly be remembered, because together we made an impact.

I joined the Green Party in 1989 and had stood without success in several elections before Fintan ever became a member. He eventually joined around

1995 because in his own words, 'I grew up in Lucan and have seen the way it has been destroyed by bad planning. I'd rather see someone elected who cares about the way the area is developed'.

At that stage, Fintan was involved in the local community council, planning council and several other community groups. While we both had always had a general interest in the political system, he came to his own opinion that the Green Party's policies need to be implemented urgently.

After joining the local Green Party group, Fintan assisted in my campaigns in the 1996 by-election in the old Dublin West, becoming Director of Elections for the 1997 general election. We made a huge effort with limited resources during the three weeks, but as with my 1991 local and 1992 national campaigns, the final result left me well short of taking a seat.

The 1997 campaign left both of us tired and frustrated and genuinely wondering if there was any point in going on. Yet history will show that we did go on. We learned our electoral lessons and two years later I topped the poll in my electoral area in the 1999 local elections. Three years after that I became the first ever Green Party candidate to be elected to the Dáil in a three-seater, the newly formed Dublin Mid-West constituency.

Fintan was the natural successor to take over my council seat and, having been co-opted on to South Dublin County Council in January 2003, he was comfortably elected in his own right in the June 2004 local elections. Working efficiently together as a 'green team', we can look back with pride on many local achievements.

We worked extremely well together, combining our efforts at local and national level to the benefit of our constituents. It was of course a huge bonus to be friends. We spoke on the phone every day. We understood how the other operated. I was the gung-ho impulsive and he was the diplomat, yet somehow we reached a happy medium in terms of how we worked as a unit. Going to meetings and functions together was never a chore because of our close friendship and shared wicked sense of humour.

But the most important attribute we shared in the Green Party was being politically grounded. Our political antennae were finely tuned and if one didn't pick up the signal the other most certainly would.

And both of us got the signal after the 1997 general election, which for us turned out to be a sharp kick up the arse. We eventually realised that there was no point in waiting around until the next election to appear on someone's doorstep, no matter how worthy the 'cause'. They needed to be consulted and kept informed regularly.

So I started knocking on doors, organising campaigns and dropping regular leaflets on issues of concern to voters locally. And, as mentioned earlier, I topped the poll in the 1999 local elections. With an actual 1999 local election budget of just £460, it is clear that it was the work I did before the election that got me in, rather than any miracle campaign during the election itself.

Our poll-topping success out of nowhere was a vindication for following what (in Fintan's honour) I will now call 'The McCarthy Doctrine' – a doctrine of public service, personal sacrifice and regular, direct communication.

My motto from my early career as a councillor and into the Dáil has been 'Not Just at Election Time'. When Fintan took office we added the second motto 'Putting Our Community First'. These are the two fundamentals of the McCarthy Doctrine. In essence, whether you are seeking election or re-election you must first and foremost remember who elects you and what you are elected for. Before the grandiose ideals of the green revolution must come the small steps that enable political evolution.

Fintan and I often discussed how the electoral success of the Green Party has taken place in fits and starts. The initial breakthroughs of the late 1980s and early 1990s were not followed up. Seats were not consolidated. Breakthroughs outside Dublin had more to do with individual flair than strategic nous.

By 1999 we may have had two TDs and two MEPs, but we had lost council seats when compared with 1991. Our 2002 breakthrough of six TDs was hailed as a new beginning, but our local election effort in 2004 was a comparative failure and our European effort was an absolute failure. To add insult to injury we ran two absolutely abysmal by-election campaigns in 2005, even though we had months and months to build up a profile on the ground.

These downturns frustrated Fintan immensely. All the more so because with a little bit of planning and dedicated preparation at local level we could have obtained at least double the current amount of council seats. We could have increased our vote in the by-elections to an extent where a Dáil seat next time around was a probability rather than a remote possibility. But it didn't happen and while the party nationally must shoulder some of the blame, nothing beats consistent hard graft at local level.

We don't have a God-given right to be elected. It is an honour bestowed on very few. But it is an honour that needs to be worked for from council level upwards if you are in a small party with meagre resources.

As I write this piece at the end of August 2006, we are performing well in the polls. There is a discernable swing to the Green Party and green issues are in vogue – especially as they relate to areas such as transport and energy. But the worst mistake that has been made and must not be made again is to expect that the electorate, busy and distracted as they are, will recognise the importance of these issues. So many have fallen, myself included, by assuming that if I am green, if I am principled, and if I turn up at election time, I will do well.

Yes, we will get a certain vote for being 'green' and will benefit from national swings from time to time. But nationwide, with only a few exceptions, we will get far more votes for being diligent, hard-working representatives on a variety of issues. Remember, along with energy and transport, issues such as healthcare, education, crime and housing/planning all relate to the community and are all fundamentally green issues. It is just that they are not always seen as green issues by the electorate.

But it is the votes garnered from work on these issues that will enable us to get elected and make a real difference in government. That is why we also ignore them nationally at our peril.

What do we truly want as greens? We want a just, sustainable world. We want to protect our global and local environment, secure our energy supply and safeguard our quality of life for future generations. That is our goal.

As a political party, we can only achieve our goal through attaining elected office. And to do that sometimes means putting the longer-term objectives on hold while dealing with the issues that are more immediate to the electorate. Once we get into government, we can look at the bigger picture.

As a party, we have much to gain by following the McCarthy doctrine of putting in the work on the ground and letting people know about it constantly. The process of knocking on doors, dropping leaflets and meeting people must be engaged in with religious zeal by both candidates and party members. The direct, personal form of communication works the best. But, while we feel it is our green mission to educate, we mustn't preach. Above all, we must listen and we must serve.

Paul Gogarty joined the Green Party/Comhaontas Glas in 1989. He was elected to South Dublin County Council in 1999. He became TD for Dublin Mid-West in 2002. He is party spokesperson on Education and Science, and Arts, Sport and Tourism.

2003

As the new year began, it became clear that the United States of America was planning to lead an attack on Iraq. In the Dáil, the Green Parliamentary Party demonstrated its opposition to the impending war by holding up large printed letters which spelt the slogan 'No to War' just as An Taoiseach Bertie Ahern rose to speak during leaders questions in the House. The protest was the subject of a humorous article by Frank McAnally in *The Irish Times*. In the article he pointed out that while each Green Party TD held up one letter, Ciarán Cuffe had to hold the final two, as our parliamentary party was still one seat short of a full slogan!

The party was in tune with public opinion. In February a national demonstration was organised for Dublin. More than a hundred thousand people marched in protest against US policy in Iraq and the Irish government's support for that position. There was a large Green Party presence at that demonstration, where Patricia McKenna was one of the platform speakers.

The protest did not have the slightest effect whatsoever on the government's policy. The day after the Taoiseach presented the annual St Patrick's Day offering of shamrock to George Bush in the White House, the US began its military action.

The use of Shannon airport by US military personnel became a focus for Irish opposition to the war. Green elected representatives participated in many demonstrations at the airport. Green Party member Tim Hourican (who had been a general election candidate for the party) and retired Irish army colonel Ed Hogan were actively involved in the surveillance of US troop movements at the airport.

The Green Party carried out some personnel changes in its organisation towards the end of 2002 and the beginning of 2003. A full-time general secretary, Stiofáin Nutty, was appointed. Colm Ó Caomhánaigh was appointed as the Dáil administrator to help oversee the party's business in the Dáil. The party's research team was increased, with the addition of two more researchers.

The party's spring convention was held in Ennis. It was preceded by a court action taken by the party against RTE, because of the broadcaster's refusal to grant live coverage to the conference. RTE uses an arbitrary rule that stipulates that a party must have at least seven TDs elected and over 5 per cent of the national vote to qualify for a live broadcast of its party conference. The Green Party fell below both these criteria, but only marginally so. RTE refused to take into account the two sitting MEPs who were officially part of the Green Parliamentary Party.

Around this time the Green Party produced its second Private Members Bill of the 29th Dáil. This was a bill to introduce a National Transport Authority. This would involve combining the National Roads Authority and the Rail Procurement Agency so that a single authority would have overall responsibility for all transport planning, with a particular emphasis on public transport. It was voted down by the government.

Then, during the summer of 2003 a controversy arose within the Green Party when the *Sunday Independent* examined the 'declaration of interest' given by TDs in relation to their shareholdings as is required by the Standards in Public Office Commission. Ciarán Cuffe TD had never bought any shares, but had been bequeathed a share portfolio by his mother on her death. When he detailed the contents of this portfolio, his declaration listed a number of companies with whom the Green Party would have ethical difficulties. There was nothing illegal about the shares per se, but Ciarán resigned his position as party spokesperson on the environment. The offending shares were sold and transferred to more ethical investments.

The controversy revealed that the party had no internal mechanism to deal with such situations or to bring similar matters to the attention of an appropriate party official for vetting, advice or approval. As a result the party drew up a set of guidelines for the vetting of all future party candidates.

The difficulties that surrounded this issue were exacerbated by the less than supportive approach adopted by some members of the party. Patricia McKenna MEP was particularly dismissive of Ciarán's difficulties. This led to a certain cooling in personal relations within the party.

Shortly afterwards the party presented its third private members bill in the name of Ciarán Cuffe. This bill sought to amend the Planning and Development Acts. The debate that followed the bill allowed the party an opportunity to criticise the government's lack of a housing policy, especially in relation to the excessive profits being made by property developers.

Meanwhile, Patricia McKenna had managed to secure journalistic accreditation to attend the EU Summit of Leaders held in Greece that July. This caused some media comment. Patricia pointed out that as an elected member of the European Parliament she did not have the same access as that given to journalists. As this was a major decision-making forum within the European Union, she was happy to expose that particular double standard.

Over the years the Green Party had questioned the effectiveness, and indeed the impartiality of the Environmental Protection Agency. Just after the general election of 2002 the government appointed Dr Mary Kelly as Director General of the EPA. The greens objected to this appointment, given Dr Kelly's previous position as a director of the business organisation IBEC.

In the summer of 2003, Dr Kelly made a public statement outlining the need to build waste incinerators in Ireland. This was a compromising statement, coming as it did from the Director General of the agency which would be adjudicating on whether or not there should be incinerators in the country. The Green Party called for both the resignation of Dr Kelly and for the restructuring and reform of the Environmental Protection Agency itself.

In September, there was sadness within the party when we learned of the death of Vincent McDowell, father of Nuala Ahern. Vincent had been an active member of the party over many years and had once served as co-ordinator. He was elected to Dún Laoghaire/Rathdown County Council as a representative for the Dún Laoghaire ward in June 1999. He had also been a general election candidate on behalf of the party. He resigned from the party following a dispute in which Ciarán Cuffe was selected as the candidate for the Dún Laoghaire constituency in the 2002 election. Vincent continued to serve on the county council as an independent member. He subsequently became a Labour Party councillor, having had a history with the Labour Party and with the Republican Labour Party in Northern Ireland throughout what had been a colourful life.

Because Vincent had won the seat originally as a Green Party representative in 1999, local government legislation meant that it was up to the Green Party to choose a replacement. The greens selected Kealin Ireland as their councillor to represent the party on Dún Laoghaire/Rathdown County Council.

This period saw the first of a number of postcard campaigns the party would organise over the following years. This particular campaign called for the linking of the two LUAS lines. It was sponsored by Ciarán Cuffe and Eamon Ryan. Thousands of postcards were distributed to put pressure on the government to bring about a more co-ordinated public transport policy.

This year also saw the beginning of the next step in the integration process of the European Union, with the holding of a 'Convention on the Future of Europe'. This was eventually to produce a constitutional treaty. It was a document with which the Green Party had considerably difficulties. The party postponed making any definitive decision on the document until it had conducted its own internal consultation process.

John Gormley was one of the Irish Parliament's alternate members in the Constitutional Convention. He contributed significantly to its deliberations and brought several proposals to the convention in relation to citizens' initiatives and the decision-making process that should be followed in deciding on the constitutional treaty itself. He suggested that this be done by securing the support of both the majority of citizens within the European Union and the majority of member States.

In October the party published a policy document called *Re-inventing Democracy*, which outlined a number of reforms the Green Party believed would help make the Irish political system more open, more accountable and consequently more democratic. Among the proposals put forward was the reduction of the voting age, different ways of proceeding with referenda, reducing the number of seats in the Dáil, changing the modus operandi within the Dáil, and reducing the size of the cabinet and redistributing many of the roles and functions of central government back to local authorities.

The greens were reminded that reality had not changed when the Houses of the Oireachtas Commission was formed. This commission took over responsibility for the affairs of Leinster House from the Department of Finance. The members of this commission specifically excluded representatives of the Technical Group and attempts to raise the issue were ruled out of order during the passage of the legislation that brought the commission into being.

During December 2003 the fourth private members bill to be introduced by the Green Party was debated in the Dáil. The Broadcasting (Amendment) Bill was moved in the name of Eamon Ryan. This bill attempted to put in place a code of practice that would limit and restrict certain types of advertising that overtly tried to influence young people in ways that could harm their health and well-being. The code was aimed in particular at advertisements for junk foods, sweets, and sugar-based soft drinks. The proposed code would also consider the type of advertisements that accompany the sale of toys, or any advertisements that make use of 'pester power'. Once again the bill was voted down by the government. This was the fourth private members bill introduced by the Green Party to the 29th Dáil. Support had been forthcoming on each occasion from the opposition parties and from many of the independent TDs.

Before the Dáil rose for the Christmas recess in December 2003, figures were released that showed almost 100 members of the Oireachtas had resigned their local authority seats, as was required of them under legislation that had been passed by the Houses of the Oireachtas. Each of these TDs and senators qualified for a €5,000 payment for surrendering their local authority seats.

The criteria for receipt of this payment was that they had resigned between 4 May and 30 September 2003. Unfortunately for them, the four Green Party TDs had already resigned their positions before May 2003. Consequently, none of the four received the €5,000 payment.

Brian Meaney, County Clare

I was born second in a Catholic family of seven. My mother had to stop nursing due to the marriage ban in the local psychiatric hospital where she had met my father. Our family life was nothing out of the ordinary in the late 1960s and early 1970s. Plenty of work, Mass, school, lessons and hurling.

The discussion around the feeding table of my childhood was never political or topical. I can mostly remember a lot of squabbling about tomato sauce!

Being a one-channel, one-telly, one-radio, one-*Irish-Press*-newspaper per day house, combined with my father's insatiable appetite for current affairs, I think politics and the doings of the world soaked into me by osmosis. It has to be remembered that this was an Ireland where the price heavy store bullocks made in Ballinasloe was prime time viewing on the telly (*Mart & Market*). Most aspects of Irish life deemed suitable for young ears and eyes were there in your face. If you wanted to watch the telly, listen to the radio or flick through the newspaper, you were cornered – only the odd copy of the *Beano*, and *Wanderly Wagon* provided some escape.

Like many families in rural Ireland in the 1960s/'70s we were net producers rather than consumers. Our house on a one-cottage acre supported a cow, poultry and a kitchen garden which, due to my parent's fear of idleness, provided more than the house could consume, so the rest was sold. The local co-op even had to give us a milk quota when they were first introduced.

It could be said that this background is not one conducive to fostering a political identity different from anything around you. I was always politically conscious and was acutely aware of the power our political system has in our democracy and how it affects everyone's lives.

From this vantage I remained a political spectator for many years. I did go to one or two Fianna Fáil fundraisers but I don't think that amounted to political activism. During my years at Bolton Street, I remained a spectator, never got involved in any of the myriad societies promoting or protesting. Staying up all night watching the returns from the general elections was the height of my involvement for years.

Around 1992 I took a conscious decision to join a political party and requested information from Fine Gael, Labour, Greens, Sinn Féin and Fianna Fáil. The only one that didn't reply was Sinn Féin. 1992 was a year I won't forget. My father died. I became a father. The Bishop Eamon Casey scandal broke. There was a general election. Trevor Sargent was elected to the Dáil and as usual, Dan Boyle in Cork wasn't. Our country was changing and I wanted to try to ensure that the change would be for the better. I clinically appraised the information I had received from the parties on managing and controlling the inevitable change Ireland would go through.

It was not a decision I took lightly. The greens I guessed would be as popular as smallpox in a rural constituency west of the Shannon, but I had listened to and read Trevor and Dan, and as an avid reader of realistic economic assessments the greens seemed to me to be the only hope of influencing the change to longer-term needs of this society. The others, though well-meaning, did not consider long-term consequences of their polices, so some time in 1994 this twenty-six year old father of a baby girl joined the Green Party and it didn't impress anyone.

My electoral record is on the website if anyone wants it, so I am not going to go through it here, but I will finish by saying that I love politics and I have a great admiration for all politicians. The greens think out loud and tell people what they don't want to hear but it is part of what we are and those who adopt lazy positions in assessing us or are directly challenged by what we represent will recognise the value of our policies well before this party is fifty years old.

Brian Meaney joined the Green Party/Comhaontas Glas in 1994. He was elected to Clare County Council in 2004.

2004

In the new year the Dáil Constituency Commission announced the redrawing of some Dáil constituency boundaries. The new boundaries that were proposed increased the number of three-seat constituencies, which did not favour the interests of the smaller parties. Fortunately, the proposed changes did not materially effect the constituencies of any of the sitting green TDs.

During the first six months of 2004 the Irish government assumed the presidency of the European Union. When the Taoiseach announced the Irish government's programme for the presidency at a meeting of the European Parliament, it caused some difficulty for the Irish Green MEPs. This was after all a re-election year to the European Parliament. The green group as a whole were only given eight minutes to respond to the Irish government's programme. Three of these were allocated to Daniel Cohn Bendit, the leader of the greens in the European Parliament. Of the remaining five minutes, Patricia McKenna secured two minutes speaking time. Nuala Ahern expected that she might receive at least one minute's speaking time, in recognition of the fact that she would not be seeking re-election. Patricia felt that seeking re-election should be the sole criterion for participating in the debate.

A more unified approach was apparent when the greens in the European Parliament sponsored a seminar on food that was held at Dublin Castle. This brought together many prominent greens to debate a subject that is an important part of the green agenda.

In 2004 the next set of elections for the city and county councils and for the new town councils took place. The greens, in preparing for these contests, drew on many of the lessons they had learned in previous elections. Candidate selection took place well in advance and the party fielded a record number of candidates.

After the general election performance of 2002 expectations were high that substantial progress might be achieved. The party hoped to get in the region of fifty councillors elected. In the end, thirty-two local authority seats were won. Eighteen seats at city and county level, and fourteen on town councils.

While this result fell short of expectations, it was a significant increase on the number of seats that the party had held previously at local government level.

There was some satisfaction with the increased geographical spread of the seats, particularly on the western seaboard where Brian Meaney was elected to Clare County Council and Niall Ó Brolcháin was elected to Galway City Council in one of the most difficult and competitive wards in the city.

Town council seats were won for the first time in Donegal and Louth with new seats being won in Cork, Kildare and Kilkenny. On Bray Town Council the party won seats in each of the three wards. In Dublin county four seats were won in Dún Laoghaire/Rathdown, three on Fingal County Council and two on South Dublin County Council.

One area of disappointment was the decline of the party in Dublin city. The party's representation on the city council had fallen from four councillors in 1991 to only one representative, Bronwen Maher, who won a seat in the Clontarf ward.

In these elections the first of a new wave of councillors succeeded in getting elected for the party. Mark Deary for example topped the poll and was elected
to Dundalk Town Council. Mark had been active in environmental politics for a number of years before he joined the Green Party. He had been a member of the STAD group established in Dundalk to take a court case against the THORP reprocessing plant in Sellafield.

Elsewhere, Malcolm Noonan succeeded in being elected to Kilkenny County Council. Tom Kelly, a former independent councillor, joined the greens and succeeded in winning a seat on Meath County Council.

All told the party was satisfied with these elections. More councillors had been elected over a wider geographical spread throughout the country.

The party knew in advance that the European elections were going to be difficult. Due to the accession of ten new member countries into the European Union, the number of seats available to Ireland was reduced to thirteen. Nuala Ahern had decided for health reasons not to seek re-election as an MEP. Leinster (or Ireland East) was now a three-seat constituency. This made it virtually impossible for Mary White to retain Nuala's seat on behalf of the Green Party.

Nuala's ten years in the European Parliament had been ones of significant achievements. She had involved herself fully in the work of the European Parliament and had achieved prestigious and effective positions on a number of committees. During her time in the European Parliament she influenced the European agenda on many issues, not only to do with the environment, but also concerned civil and human rights, as well as helping to define the idea of a social Europe.

In her first term, Nuala was Vice President of the parliament's Petitions Committee dealing with the rights of citizens from all over the European Union. During this time she also served as the green group's Co-ordinator for Energy and in her second term she was Vice President of the parliament's Committee on Industry, External Trade, Research and Energy. She brought the British Nuclear Inspectorate before the committee to explain their supervision and management at Sellafield, as well as the falsification of documents relating to MOX fuel pellet exports to Japan.

Nuala was instrumental in compiling the WISE Paris Report for the European Parliament. This report warned of a terror attack at particular installations such as Sellafield and of the possible consequences of an accident there. Although there were attempts to suppress this report, Nuala was successful in ensuring that the report was commissioned and was published.

Nuala also participated as a member on the Cultural Committee and the Legal Affairs Committee of the Parliament. She was president of the Parliamentary Group on Natural Medicine. This was in recognition of her campaigning work to try to prevent regulations being introduced in Ireland to make the herbal remedy St John's Wort a medicine requiring a doctor's prescription.

Within her Euro Constituency Nuala had been vocal on issues like the genetic modification of foods. She had taken part in peaceful protests in County Wexford on the subject, and was a witness to events at the proposed test sites for GM crops in the constituency.

In 2002 she took part in an Irish Sea flotilla against British Nuclear Fuels Nuclear transports to Sellafield. She also compiled a report on BNFL operations, a report which exposed the finances of the company and caused the British government to formally declare the company bankrupt.

As the green group's representative on the Industry, External Trade, Research and Energy Committee, Nuala produced a report that ensured that 'the polluter pays' principle was applied to the disposal of electrical waste.

On the issue of the future of the European Union, Nuala held a different position to that of Patricia McKenna. She often expressed her concern that the Green Party in Ireland was excessively Euro-sceptic and that the party should present its position in more positive terms. While she opposed many of the treaties on changing the structure and remit of the European Union, her criticisms tended to be more selective than those of Patricia McKenna.

During her ten years as an MEP Nuala Ahern accomplished herself as an elected representative for her constituency, and as a representative of the Green Party in Ireland.

Nuala's retirement meant that Patricia McKenna was the only green MEP seeking re-election in these European elections. At the selection convention she was challenged for the nomination by Deirdre de Burca but managed to prevail in spite of a significant level of support for Deirdre's candidacy.

The Green Party seat was the target for other political parties. Sinn Féin, for example which had been on the crest of an electoral wave since the signing of the Good Friday Agreement, made a conscious effort to win a European Parliament seat in Dublin. Its candidate, Mary Lou McDonald, was portrayed as a 'McKenna light' candidate.

When the votes were finally counted, Patricia finished fifth, fifteen thousand votes behind Mary Lou McDonald, who took the fourth seat.

The greens did not contest the Connaght/Ulster European constituency. In Munster, the green candidate was Cork City Councillor Chris O'Leary. He polled 10.000 votes, the same number of votes that the party had won in the two previous elections.

The government decided to hold a constitutional referendum on the issue of citizenship to coincide with the European and local elections in 2004. The amendment sought to restrict the right to Irish citizenship of children born in the country and to only grant citizenship to those children whose parents met certain citizenship or residency criteria. The Green Party opposed the referendum, believing it to be more about peoples' fear than about dealing with any significant constitutional difficulty. It was passed by a huge majority.

The party was becoming more professional in its approach to elections. Its conference in Galway, which preceded the elections, was the first for which a special set was built. This was done in order to project the best possible visual image of the party in the live television coverage that RTE gave the party for the first time ever. This facility provided Trevor Sargent with the opportunity of making his first live broadcast of the 'Leader's Speech' to the convention. The large attendance of party members in the hall ensured that positive visual images of the Green Party were portrayed to the public.

A special guest at the conference was Reinhard Bütikofer, co-leader of the German Green Party, Die Grünen. Reinhard spoke of the experience of the German greens in becoming part of the government. He put particular emphasis on the hard choices and compromises that had to be made.

President Mary McAleese's first term of office expired in November 2004. Speculation began as to whether or not there should be an election. There seemed to be little likelihood that McAleese would be defeated if she were to seek a second term. Some people felt that an automatic return to office, without the benefit of an election, had not benefited the office of the President in the past, and that an election should be held.

Fine Gael were unwilling to contest the Presidential election and seemed happy to see Mary McAleese continue in office without an election. Sinn Féin adopted a similar position. The leader of the Labour Party, Pat Rabbite, had earlier spoken of the need for a contest. Michael D. Higgins made known his willingness to be the Labour Party candidate. Dana (Rosemary Scanlon) sought but failed to secure the required support from sufficient city and county councils to allow her to be nominated.

The greens got to thinking of possible candidates who might represent their point of view. I suggested Denis Halliday, a former Assistant General Secretary at the United Nations. As a person of principle who had represented Ireland with distinction on the international stage, I felt that this was a person who could and should be considered for the position of President of Ireland. Several people involved with non-governmental organisations supported the possibility of the Halliday candidacy. However, my proposal failed to achieve critical mass and other names began to be mentioned.

In September Eamon Ryan suddenly announced that he would be willing to be the Green Party candidate. This caused a mixture of excitement in the media and panic among the Green Party TDs. Eamon's decision had been made without any consultation with anyone in the party.

The parliamentary party was divided on Eamon's initiative. Ciarán Cuffe and I supported his bid to be a candidate. Paul Gogarty was adamantly opposed, believing that this would deflect the party from more important issues. Trevor was concerned that it might not be the right political move to make. John Gormley had similar concerns but was closer to being neutral on the issue. Many party members became excited at the prospect of contesting the presidential election and with having Eamon as their candidate.

It so happened that a National Council Meeting had been arranged to be held in Darrara, near Clonakilty in West Cork. At this meeting, which was to deal with other items of party business, it was agreed that a decision on whether or not the party should contest the election should be on the agenda. The Parliamentary Party agreed to go to that meeting, and support Eamon's candidacy if the party's National Council agreed that sufficient resources existed within the party to allow such a campaign to be undertaken.

In the meantime Pat Rabbitte changed his mind on the desirability of the Labour Party contesting the presidential election. The administrative council of the Labour Party decided by one vote not to contest the election.

Pat Rabbitte made it known that if Eamon Ryan was to pursue his candidacy then he himself and other Labour Party TDs would be prepared to sign the nomination papers to allow Eamon enter the contest, as long as more than half the signatures were non-Labour Oireachtas members. Among the Green Parliamentary Party there was uncertainty as to whether this offer should be accepted. Twenty Oireachtas signatures are required for a nomination to become a presidential candidate. The Green Party, with only six TDs, could not make up this number on its own. A number of independent TDs, including Tony Gregory, Seamus Healy and Finian McGrath, indicated their willingness to co-sign Eamon's nomination papers.

At a meeting between Pat Rabbitte and Trevor Sargent with Eamon Ryan, it became clear that nine Labour Party members of the Oireachtas would be willing to co-sign the nomination papers. This, combined with the independents and the greens, would give eighteen of the twenty names needed. Within the green parliamentary party however there were some misgivings about relying on another political party to provide the majority of the signatures required.

As the date of the Green Party National Council meeting in Darrara approached, it was uncertain what Eamon would do. None of his Parliamentary Party colleagues knew, and given the pressure Eamon had come under in the preceding days, it was not known what he was likely to say in his contribution to the meeting.

Eamonn addressed the meeting and outlined the situation as he saw it. He announced that, given all the circumstances that an election would involve, he had changed his mind and had decided not to proceed with his candidature.

Despite this setback, the majority of the party members who attended this meeting were still in favour of the Green Party contesting the election. Some of the green TDs who spoke in favour of Eamon's decision to withdraw gave many present the impression that they had made an agreement among themselves and that the party's membership was being by-passed.

When the meeting concluded, Eamon, Trevor and Mary White explained to a large media gathering (many of whom had come quite a long distance to Darrara) that there would be no Green Party candidate, and that in all probability there would now be no presidential election.

The 'what ifs' about such a campaign still remain. It could have been an opportunity to achieve a significant vote for a Green Party candidate. It could have been an opportunity to get access to media time to highlight Green Party issues. On the other hand it could also have been a disaster.

Towards the end of 2004 Stiofán Nutty resigned as General Secretary of the party. He had served for little more than a year in that position, but had played a pivotal role in putting the party on a professional footing. He had overseen a successful party conference in Galway and had managed the move of the party's national headquarters from Fownes Street to a new location on Suffolk Street. However, the demands of the job were such that they were imposing to an inordinate degree on his family life. Stiofáin was replaced by Dermot Hamilton, who brought a great deal of business management experience to the position.

In the Dáil the party moved the 'Sustainable Communities Bill', which sought to put in place appropriate agencies that would encourage measures in the area of sustainability. The party also used its private members time to debate particular motions. One motion was a vote of No Confidence in Martin Cullen, the Minister for the Environment and Local Government. A second motion was on the government's failure to meet its commitment on overseas development aid. This motion was timed to coincide with the G8 Summit meeting being held at that time in Scotland.

At local government level Green Party representatives were making an impact. At a meeting of Wicklow County Council, Deirdre de Burca was found to be tape-recording the proceedings. The meeting was discussing the passage of the Wicklow County Development Plan. Deirdre was concerned that in the case of one rezoning proposal some members of the council had not declared their personal interest in what was being discussed. As with most Irish local authorities, Wicklow County Council did not maintain verbatim minutes. Instead of recognising Deirdre's case for greater accountability, many of her county council colleagues turned on her instead.

European greens gathered for a second time in Dublin that year when the Congress of the European Green Party was held in Gresham Hotel in Dublin. The European Green Party had been established earlier in the year in Rome and Trevor Sargent had signed the charter establishing the party on behalf of An Comhaontas Glas. The Dublin congress was the first working meeting of this European-wide party. Discussion centred around a green approach to the European Union Constitutional Treaty.

Deirdre de Burca, Wicklow

At a meeting of Wicklow County Council on October 2004, controversial zoning decisions on the draft Wicklow County Development Plan were being revisited. Shortly after the council meeting began, I was approached discreetly by a council official.

The atmosphere at the meeting was very tense because of the controversy. Negative publicity had arisen since a previous meeting of the council in July when the draft County Development Plan was first voted upon.

At that meeting, seventeen last-minute and controversial zoning decisions had been made by a majority of councillors. As the only Green Party councillor on Wicklow County Council, I had been very critical of those rezoning decisions and previously asked questions about them in the local and national media. This had provoked the ire of some of my fellow councillors. I was subjected to a torrent of verbal abuse by at least one high-profile fellow-councillor. The war of words that ensued played itself out in the media over the intervening weeks. This was the context in which the October meeting of the council occurred.

The official who approached me pointed out that other councillors had made a complaint. They said that I was using a recording device in the council chamber. Wires had been seen emerging from paperwork in front of me and councillors were concerned that I was recording the proceedings of the meeting. I was informed that any recording of meetings was not permitted under the standing orders of Wicklow County Council. The council official had been asked to take the device from me and to remove it from the council chamber.

I conceded that I had such a device on my person and asked the official to confirm that audio-recording of council meetings was prohibited under the council's standing orders. He conferred with the County Secretary. In the meantime other councillors demanded to know whether the proceedings of the meeting were being secretly taped. The council meeting was suspended. I was approached and asked to hand over the tape-recorder to the official. I complied and the meeting resumed.

Any objective third party who heard an account of that day's proceedings of Wicklow County Council could legitimately have asked what on earth an elected representative was doing privately recording the proceedings of the council of which she was a member. In fact, the behaviour of such a representative would have appeared to have been so unorthodox as to invite serious questions about her suitability for public office. I *was* that councillor, and the response of the political party to which I belong was to offer me immediate and unquestioning support. When I switched my mobile phone on later that evening, I heard unconditional messages of support from three of the six Green Party TDs in Dáil Eireann. Having heard an account of the Wicklow County Council meeting during the RTE news that evening, they rang to offer me moral support.

There must be moments in the lives of all public representatives when they question whether they are in the right political party or not. On the evening of that meeting of Wicklow County Council, when I received messages of support from my party colleagues, I knew for certain that I had made the right choice. My Green Party colleagues were aware of the controversy that had surrounded the process of adopting the draft County Development Plan for County Wicklow. They had followed the media coverage of the marathon meeting of Wicklow County Council on 12 July 2004 at which the series of questionable re-zonings, some of them in the early hours of the morning, were agreed by members of the council. They were aware that I had publicly questioned many of the proposed re-zonings, and, in doing so, had provoked the anger of many of my fellow councillors.

Trevor Sargent, while a member of Dublin City Council in the mid 1990s, drew attention to a cheque that he had received from a developer seeking to have his land rezoned. When Trevor publicly questioned whether other councillors in the council chambers had received similar payments, he was physically attacked by some of his fellow councillors. Over the years, details of the corruption endemic on Dublin City Council in the early 1990s have emerged through the various tribunals. Looking back, it is hard not to admire Trevor's willingness to put his head above the parapet and to draw attention to the corruption of the planning process that was so widespread at the time. Other Green Party public representatives over the years have had the courage of their convictions. They have not been afraid to question apparent irregularities that applied to the conduct of the business of their local authority.

Public trust in politics and politicians has been badly damaged over the past two decades. There is a real need to restore the confidence of the ordinary voting public in the concept of public service. They need to be sure those they elect to public office are motivated by a genuine commitment to work on their behalf, in order to create a better society for all. One of the fundamental impulses behind the emergence of the Green Party as a political force was a recognition of the need for a total renewal and even re-invention of politics and the political process.

I joined the Green Party initially not just because I agreed with its policies, but because there was a very definite sense of integrity that applied to its public representatives. As an elected representative for the past seven years, I have developed an appreciation of the pitfalls and pressures that make the pursuit of political power such a challenge, even for greens. I am reassured to note that, to date, at each point when the Green Party's integrity has been tested, it has passed with flying colours.

I know the public appreciates the party's integrity. I believe that this is one of the reasons why the number of those who vote for the Green Party continues to increase.

If the Green Party allows its sense of integrity to guide it in its decision- and policy-making, it will have the potential to fill the moral vacuum that currently exists at the heart of our political system.

Deirdre de Burca has been an active member of Wicklow County Council since she was first elected in 1999. She was re-elected in the local elections of 2004 and was also one of three Green Party councillors to be elected to Bray Town Council for the first time. She was Cathaoirleach of Bray Town Council for 2005-2006.

2005

Charlie McCreevy TD, who had served for many years as Minister for Finance in various Fianna Fáil-led governments, became Ireland's next member of the European Commission. This promotion necessitated the holding of a by-election. A second by-election was also required when John Bruton, a former leader of Fine Gael, accepted the nomination to become the first European Union Permanent Representative in Washington. The by-elections in Kildare North and Meath were held in early March of 2005. The Green Party contested both by-elections. The issues that predominated, such as planning, infrastructure, and the lack of childcare support, were issues that could rightly be seen as green issues. However, the protest vote against the government gravitated towards Fine Gael in the case of Meath and to the independent candidate Catherine Murphy in Kildare North. The Green Party support at these by-elections was unchanged from the percentage won by the greens in the 2002 general election.

In Northern Ireland local elections were held in May. Consideration had been given to the establishment of an all island Green Party and a motion to this effect had been endorsed by the Green Party/Comhaontas Glas. Debate continued within the Green Party of Northern Ireland about the wisdom of such a move. Several party members from Comhaontas Glas, mainly from the Fingal greens, travelled across the border to give assistance to the Northern Irish greens. This group was led by Cadogan Enright. Three members of the Northern Ireland Green Party, Brian Wilson, Bill Corry and Ciarán Mussen, were successful in winning the party's first ever council seats.

Towards the end of 2004 the EU heads of government reached an agreement on the draft text of the proposed Constitutional Treaty. This was submitted to member states for ratification, to be completed by the end of 2006. Following this summit meeting, some countries (particularly those of the new member states) whose ratification process was by way of a parliamentary vote, began to ratify the treaty.

The first country to hold an indicative referendum was Spain, where a large majority approved of their government's position on the Constitutional

Treaty. In Ireland the Green Party decided to consult its membership on the position the party would adopt on the Constitutional Treaty.

To this end a number of public seminars were organised by the party in Cork, Galway and Dublin. These seminars were addressed by prominent members of the pro-European lobby. These speakers included Pat Cox, a former president of the European Parliament, and Professor Bridget Laffan, Jean Monnet Professor of European Studies.

These seminars were held early in 2005. At that stage, the Irish Government had not yet decided when the Irish Referendum would be held. Anxious to avoid the mistake that had been made with the Treaty of Nice, the government waited for the results of the first referenda on the issue, which were held in France and the Netherlands. Both countries voted No. These results undermined the future of the European Constitutional Treaty.

In May the Green Party held its 2005 convention in Cork. Media interest in this convention was aroused when the list of motions revealed that there seemed to be a conflict between a motion tabled by the parliamentary party and another presented by the Cork South Central constituency group. Both motions sought to adopt a strategy in relation to the part the greens might play in the formation of any future government after the next election.

The parliamentary party motion asked delegates to defer making a decision for as long as possible. The Cork South Central motion on the other hand, asked the delegates to make a clear statement that it would fight the election as an independent party, standing on its own platform, and that it would not negotiate with any other political party (about the formation of a government) until after the election had taken place. The convention accepted the Cork South Central motion. Some political commentators reporting on the convention stated that the party had made a significant decision in relation to its election strategy for the next general election.

The guest speaker at the conference was the former Finnish Minister for the Environment, Pekka Haavisto. He recounted the Finnish greens' experience of going into (and of coming out of) government. The Finnish greens had withdrawn from their government on a point of principle – the building of a new nuclear power station. Pekka described what the greens had achieved in government in Finland. His talk to the delegates reinforced many of the messages that had been given by Reinhard Bütikofer at the previous year's convention.

During 2005 some of the benefits of the Green Party success in the 2004 local elections began to bear fruit. Bronwen Maher, the only Green Party Councillor on Dublin City Council was in a position to determine who would be elected Lord Mayor in the city. She secured an agreement whereby if she was to support the Fine Gael candidate for Lord Mayor that year, she would received their support for the office of Deputy Lord Mayor from June 2005 onwards. Up to the last moment it was uncertain as to whether Fine Gael would follow through on this commitment. Ultimately Bronwen became Deputy Lord Mayor of Dublin.

Other Green Party representatives were also succeeding in attaining office on their respective councils. Deirdre De Burca was made chairperson of Bray Town Council and Malcolm Noonan served as Deputy Mayor of Kilkenny Borough.

In September the party was shocked to learn that its General Secretary Dermot Hamilton had died suddenly as a result of a heart attack. Dermot had continued the work of Stiofáin Nutty in improving the party's organisation and increasing its professionalism. His death was a tremendous setback for the party as well as a personal tragedy for his family and friends.

The party decided to honour Dermot by naming a special internal committee in his honour. This committee, originally inspired by the talk of Reinhard Bütikofer, examines the priorities that the party will pursue in the aftermath of the next general election.

During 2005 the Houses of the Oireachtas Commission decided to allocate an additional parliamentary researcher to each TD. This brought the party's staff complement to twenty-six people. This was a far cry from the total reliance on volunteer effort that had sustained the party through most of its history.

In the Dáil the Green Party put forward another Private Members Bill, this time on the question of climate change targets. Green Party spokespersons availed of this opportunity to criticise the government on the failure of its National Climate Change Strategy. This bill sought to commit the government (and any future government) to set targets that the country would need to put in place over a long period of time in order to bring about effective change to ameliorate the effects of climate change.

Earlier in the year, the party had moved and debated the Fur Farming (Prohibition) Bill. There were some raised eyebrows that the Green Party would 'waste' its valuable private members time on this subject. It did, however, provide an opportunity of publicising green animal welfare concerns. As with previous Green Party private members bills, opposition parties and a number of independent deputies supported the greens.

Andrew Murphy, Galway

There was a time when I was not a fan of the Green Party. Being a member of another party I felt the greens had taken a fringe issue 'above its station'. From an early age I had taken an interest in environmental issues but only saw them as peripheral to more immediate matters such as health, housing and the economy.

My 'conversion' came about in a very green way. As an oarsman, while at secondary school I spent more time on the River Corrib than I did behind the books. While training on the river I became aware of how integral it was to the web of life in the city: from the fields that fed it, the bridges that crossed it, to the flora and fauna that thrived off it. Not to mention the water plant that served the city. I noticed that the river was slowly being poisoned by over-development and pollution. I began to realise that the greens were right to be concerned about our immediate environment and that the other parties were criminal in their neglect.

I announced the switch in my political allegiance to some bemused fellow oarsmen at an Irish bar in Belgium. I paid my €5 membership and set about looking for what I could do to help. As I was sitting my Leaving Cert in 2004, I was not able to help my local candidate, Niall O Brolcháin. I remember sitting by a small radio on counting day though, while he squeezed out a forty vote victory over the Fianna Fáil candidate. That five-hour saga the day before my history exam certainly did nothing to help my grades, but was a nice break from the study.

I was determined to help the greens and decided to set up a branch of the Young Greens at NUI Galway. I approached the college authorities to enquire as to the procedure about setting up a society at UCG. I needed fifteen signatures to be allowed have a stall at Societies Day and ran around campus looking for the required number of friends to sign the form.

The first meeting pulled together an eclectic mix of students who formed the nucleus of what was to become one of the most active societies on campus.

Members from all walks of life brought issues and concerns to our meetings that the mainstream parties had ignored. We worked together to bring these concerns to the attention of the public and try to bring about change. We also studied a whole range of issues, from human rights in Colombia to energy conservation on campus.

In my short time with the party I've held a number of positions, but each one has had, for me, the same theme – a community of activists.

I am currently serving as the Chair of the Young Greens and as a member of the National Executive Committee of the Green Party. I have the chance to get involved in so many issues and meet so many people. The day doesn't seem long enough to work on everything. It appears to me that there will always be a threat to our ecosystem, our quality of life and our planet. As long as there is, there will be a need for the greens to save it.

Andrew Murphy joined the Green Party/Comhaontas Glas in 2004. He is Secretary of Galway West greens, Chair of the Young Greens and is a member of the National Executive Committee of the Green Party.

2006

The Green Party entered its twenty-fifth year shaken by recent events but confident that a stronger future awaited it. A new General Secretary, Donal Geoghegan, was appointed. Donal did not have any previous involvement with the party but he had considerable experience in community and youth work, and his participation in the social partnership process on behalf of the community and voluntary sector brought valuable expertise to the party.

Steve Rawson, who had served the party as Press Officer for many years, left the party early in 2006 to pursue a career in public relations. Steve had been pivotal in the party's struggle to 'change the hearts and minds' of the Irish electorate. He was replaced as Communications Manager by Gerry Mullins, who had served as Parliamentary Assistant to Trevor Sargent. Soon afterwards, an entirely new Press Office team was put in place when Elaine Walsh, who had also given the party sterling service, left to pursue a personal project.

Despite these personnel changes, the restructured office staff rose to the challenge of organising a number of events that have helped to raise the profile of the party and solidify its support. A conference on climate change was held in the Mansion House, and an energy fair at Leopardstown racecourse was attended by several thousand people

In March another private members motion was tabled by the party's TDs. This time the motion had to do with the question of planning corruption, an issue with which the greens had taken issue with Fianna Fáil in particular. Around this time a portfolio of position papers were published. These included policies on childcare, taxation, pensions and energy.

The government's response to this renewed confidence in the party was to resort to their usual tactic of name-calling and the introduction of legislation that would curtail public accountability in regards to the planning of major infrastructural projects. An example of this was the Strategic Infrastructure Bill. The government's urgency to 'fast track' the construction of controversial road projects and waste incinerators was at the heart of this proposed bill.

Proposals to build incinerators had been made in many of the constituencies represented by Green Party TDs. In my own constituency of Cork

South Central an application to locate a national toxic waste incinerator at Ringaskiddy had been approved. There were further plans to build a similar domestic waste incinerator on the same site. The largest proposed incinerator was to be located in Poolbeg, in John Gormley's constituency. The incinerator that was most advanced in the planning and waste licence processes was in Duleek, County Meath. This is close to the Dublin North constituency of party leader Trevor Sargent. In June a Green Party private members motion sought to put pressure on the government regarding this issue.

The name-calling against the Green Party was mostly carried out by the Minister for Justice, Equality and Law Reform, Michael McDowell. His reaction to a riot that erupted on Dublin city centre streets, after an attempt to hold a pro-Unionist parade, was to claim in the Dáil that the riot had been caused by 'Deputy Gormley's (Green) type of people'. Party members reacted stridently to these snide remarks and this type of abuse. McDowell's appointment later in the year as Tánaiste and leader of the PDs has only served to 'raise the ante' between the parties.

One of the persistent criticisms of the greens made by the present government, and by other opposition parties, has to do with the credibility of the Green Party's economics policies. There has been a perception that the greens are a high-taxation party. A motion put to the Kilkenny convention this year committed the party to not increasing income tax rates or the levels of corporation tax, but instead to tackle the growing anomalies that exist within the taxation system. This motion was readily accepted by members and is seen by some political commentators as another step forward on the party's journey towards possible participation in a future government.

In July, Niall Ó Brolcháin, the sole Green Party member on Galway City Council, was elected Mayor. He had only been elected in 2004, but because of his pivotal position on the council he succeeded in being elected to the office. It was a magnificent achievement on his part and it places him in a good position to be a serious candidate in the next general election. His election as mayor is an important stage in the development of the Green Party west of the Shannon.

During 2006 Joe Corr, an able lieutenant of Trevor Sargent, was also elected the first ever Green Party Cathaoirleach of Fingal County.

From its inception in 1981 the Green Party has encountered sustained resistance to its ideas and policies. In the past, this took the form of mockery and public insult. Recently however the attacks on party activists have become more physical. During 2006 vicious attacks, in the form of exploding gas cylinders and an attempted arson attack, occurred at the homes of Mary White in Carlow and Councillor Chris O'Leary in Cork city. These attacks show that being forthright in representing ones constituents' interests may constitute a danger in itself.

In August the party was plunged into grief when news came from China of the death in a motor accident of the party's Lucan councillor, Fintan McCarthy. He died, along with his girlfriend Sonya Rabbitte, in a minibus that was taking them to visit the Great Wall of China. Fintan was a close friend and political partner of Paul Gogarty TD, and had replaced Paul as a councillor on South Dublin County Council. He had retained the seat in his own right in 2004. Fintan was replaced as councillor on South Dublin County Council by Billy Gogarty.

Within the past few months the Green Party has been happy to welcome to its ranks Betty Doran, of Mullingar Town Council.

In the final private members time available to the greens in the Dáil this year, the party introduced its 'Neighbourhood Noise Bill'. This was moved by Ciarán Cuffe TD, and has been a bread and butter issue for greens for many years. The motion emphasises the distinctiveness of the Green Party and its role in Irish politics.

A series of opinion polls during 2006 have shown support for the Green Party to be creeping steadily upward, and being maintained at those higher levels. Commentators are beginning to talk positively about the possibility of the greens being key in the formation of the next government.

At the end of September the revelation that Bertie Ahern had received payments from Irish and British businessmen while he was Minister for Finance in 1993 and 1994, rocked the political establishment. It severely soured relations within the government parties, but highlighted once again issues that the Green Party had sought to address since the foundation of the party, issues such as the corrosive nature of corporate fundraising in Irish politics and the skewed approach to public appointments.

The Green Party has lasted for twenty-five years, it has stood the test of time and has grown stronger over the years. It has been a real achievement to come from nowhere and start with nothing and now be part of an international movement that has developed deep roots in Irish politics. With thirty-four constituency-based groups, the party has almost achieved a full geographic representation throughout the country and is now in a position to offer the Irish electorate a real political choice in the future governance of this country.

The greens have never been in government in Ireland. This is the next challenge that faces the party. After the next general election, the other political parties will have to consider the greens as potential coalition partners. Whether or not this will result in the greens finally entering government only the next twenty-five years can tell.

Trevor Sargent
'Greening Communities in Preparation for a Post-Oil Era'

One sure way of annoying a green (and of demonstrating one's own ignorance) is to assert that green politics is about a single issue. It may be the fact that green policies are so wide-ranging that causes commentators to try to simplify a whole political philosophy as something to do with 'snails and swans', as An Taoiseach Bertie Ahern might say.

Early societies had fairly basic politics, where the tribe was led and dominated by the physically strongest individual in the group. Dictatorships have much in common with this model. As time went on and social structures developed, a number of strong individuals tended to form a dominant class and wield influence for their narrow mutual benefit, even competing against each other to increase their fraction of the tribe's total wealth. Feudalism, and later capitalism, have much in common with this model. The early industrial revolution saw capitalism become the dominant political model in Europe and America.

Capitalism has a slightly wider ethical circle than a dictatorship, in that it benefits a few individuals rather than just one. However, the atrocious working conditions of the poor during the industrial revolution, and the lack of help for those injured while working, created public pressure to widen the circle of ethics even further. Socialism came to be identified with the belief that no person should be excluded from the means to enjoy a basic standard of living.

However, the industrial revolution did not just exploit former farm workers who had come to the cities to work in the factories, mills and mines. It also took for granted the natural world on which all life, and indeed manufacture, ultimately depends. Landscapes were denuded of wildlife habitats, rivers were poisoned, species wiped out, and the chemical make-up of the atmosphere altered over time. In 1900, the concentration of carbon dioxide in the air was 260 parts per million (ppm). Since then the levels have risen to 380 ppm, due mainly to the burning of fossil fuels, making the climate warmer than it has been for over 10,000 years. Scientists working on the International Climate Change Taskforce say that 450 ppm would be the tipping point to trigger runaway climate chaos, after which the only political philosophy worth talking about would be Survivalism, the least ethical philosophy of all, in that it involves a 'Mad Max' type straight fight for the slim chances of survival.

Meanwhile, the concentration of carbon dioxide in the atmosphere worldwide continues to rise by 3 p.m. every year, thanks to the narrow economic systems supported by left- and right-wing parties. The need to widen that circle of ethics further still to the extent that green politics requires is literally a matter of life and death, if not for us, then increasingly for our children.

Roger Garland, in his inaugural Dáil speech as the first Green TD in 1989, said that green politics was about the 'security of socialism, combined with the freedom of capitalism'. At the moment, we have the bureaucracy of socialism combined with the inequality of capitalism. Thus, in their endeavours to find common ground in the centre, both right and left combine the worst elements of both ideologies, whereas we in the greens take the best. Much of the struggle between left and right in 'first world' countries is a struggle over the spoils of exploitation in the 'third world'. With this in mind, the motto of green parties worldwide is 'think globally, act locally'. Green local action seeks to assist people as well as other species, taking account of urban and rural concerns, and in a holistic way, the economic, social and environmental health of our respective countries.

My own interest in what became known as green politics began in the mid-1970s when I was a student at The High School in Dublin. The more I read

about species becoming extinct, the more I knew a way had to be found for
humans to live in harmony with the natural world. My own family and my
interest in scouting instilled in me an appreciation of nature. I have a vivid
memory of setting off on a ferry heading for a summer camp in Guernsey
with Rathfarnham Scout Troop. While others brought along novels by Wilbur
Smith and Terry Pratchett to pass the time, I struggled with *The Social Contract*
by Jean-Jacques Rousseau and *The Origin of Species* by Charles Darwin.

Darwin is quoted by some capitalists to support their contention that competition is a political version of 'natural selection'. Just as a lion picks off the
weakest zebra from the herd, so a big retail store sets up and forces the closure
of the long-standing corner shop.

However, Darwin saw evolution as being more than a process of natural
selection. Darwin refers to 'conditions of existence' as being also critical to
the evolution of 'all organic beings'.

Capitalism and socialism require conditions of existence which we can
now see are out of balance with the fundamental characteristics of a finite
planet. Both depend on plentiful cheap energy. (The peaking of oil production makes that a non-runner.) Both depend on a stable climate. (Energy
demand, which drives globalisation is, within ten years, expected to end this
'condition of existence' due to climate change.) Both left and right depend on
global inequality to maintain supplies of cash crops, such as coffee, tea, exotic
timber, animal feed and out-of-season food. (Poverty, where there is no social
protection and poor education, causes parents to have more children, driving
up the world population, thus causing an even greater global demand for
energy, food and water.)

It amazes me how politicians from left and right revert to 'rates of growth' as
a solution for whatever political problem is being discussed. I have yet to hear
an interviewer question properly what this means. Does this mean growth in
consumption of energy and a widening gap between rich and poor? (It generally does in Ireland.) Would such growth be causing more problems than it
solves? (The growing numbers of homeless people and those depending on
charities would say, 'Yes'.) Can we have growth in quality of life without con-
suming greater and greater quantities of energy, fresh water and other finite
resources? (Yes, if we implement sustainable green economic policies.)

I first read about green economics in the Church of Ireland College of
Education in 1979 although it was not on the course. The principal at the
time, Dr Kenneth Milne, a very well-read man, was a good listener. I told
him that I felt humanity was on a collision course and that there had to be
a political response. He suggested I take a look at *Small is Beautiful,* a book

by Fritz Schumacher, former Economic Advisor to the National Coal Board in Britain from 1950 to 1970 and a former farmer, businessman and journalist. The book is subtitled *Economics as if People Mattered* and it continues to inspire me to this day. Many books and articles on green and sustainable economics have since been published. Many greens were delighted when FEASTA, an organisation which carries out research into the economics of sustainability, was established.

Articles in newspapers about green parties in England and Germany caught my eye, giving a political voice to the economic analysis in Schumacher's book. As there was no Green Party in Ireland in 1980, I wrote to the Ecology Party (now called the Green Party) in London to get more information. The reply I received was obviously typed by a very busy person in the middle of an election campaign. It told me to effectively go away and if I was really interested, I should start an Ecology Party in Ireland. As I was busy preparing for exams, I determined to pass those first, before taking up the challenge of politics. Meanwhile, I was delighted to see a letter from Christopher Fettes in *The Irish Times* announcing that he and some friends had established The Ecology Party of Ireland and interested persons were invited to join. I signed up immediately.

Having qualified as a primary school teacher in 1981, it was now time to spread my wings. My first post was in The Model School, Dunmanway, in beautiful West Cork. Cultural diversity and biodiversity for me are two sides of the one coin. My interest in speaking Irish drew me in the direction of Joan and Seán Ó Duinnín, a family from Gaeltacht Mhúscraí who gave me accommodation. This was as close as I got to realising my dream of teaching in a Gaeltacht school.

Later, when I got to know the area, I moved west to Drimoleague and purchased a second-hand Honda 125. This gave me the means to attend meetings in Bantry of HOPE (Help Organise Peaceful Energy), which later became Earthwatch, before becoming Friends of the Earth Ireland. Meeting such dedicated campaigners was a real inspiration and further strengthened my resolve to become an active green. During this time, the successful campaign to stop the dumping of nuclear waste off the south-west coast was in full swing.

Notwithstanding the fact that meetings of the nearest Ecology Party group took place fifty miles away in Cork city, I reckoned my trusty Honda 125 was up to it. Lucky enough, meetings were on a Saturday during the day so the round trip was mostly done in daylight. A member from Douglas, Seán Ó Flynn, and his family were particularly kind in putting me up overnight when meetings ran late. Having come off the bike in bad weather going to one meeting, I was only too happy to accept the offer of a warm bed in Cork city.

The greens in Cork were a formidable group with such impressive members at the time as Seán Dunne, Adi Roche, Owen Casey, Pat Madden and many others including Seán Ó Flynn who, with Dan Boyle, is largely responsible for making this publication a reality. This group named itself 'The Cork Green Movement' while other green groups around the country meekly described themselves as 'branches' of The Ecology Party of Ireland. The national party newsletter *Eco-news* carried reports from each 'branch' but the report from Cork carried the title 'The Cork Green Movement'. However, the editor (from Dublin) provided a footnote to the report explaining that 'The Cork Green Movement' is the Cork Branch of The Ecology Party of Ireland. Blood boiled in the 'rebel county', the 'southern capital', the 'true republic'. How dare Dublin tell Cork how it must describe itself! After all, the principles of the party supported decentralisation. It was time to face down Dublin and so a National Convention was called to be held in Cork, where the structures of the party would be made to fit the founding principles of the party. The seven principles which still underline The Green Party/Comhaontas Glas are as follows.

1. The impact of society on the environment should not be ecologically disruptive.

2. Conservation of resources is vital to a sustainable society.

3. All political, social and economic decisions should be taken at the lowest effective level.

4. Society should be guided by self-reliance and co-operation at all levels.

5. As caretakers of the earth, we have the responsibility to pass it on in a fit and healthy state.

6. The need for world peace overrides national and commercial interests.

7. The poverty of two-thirds of the world's family demands a redistribution of the world's resources.

This convention was something of a cultural shock for me, as it was the first time I met greens who spoke with a strong Dublin accent. Everyone united behind the principles. Decisions were reached largely by consensus. The Cork Green Movement had been vindicated, and An Comhaontas Glas, a Green Alliance of largely autonomous green groups, was born. Each group developed structures, policies and indeed names appropriate to their own areas. We had for example, the Rathmines Radicals, the GANG (Green Action Now Group) and the group I was involved in founding when I moved to Dublin North in 1983, the Fingal Greens/Glasaigh Fhine Gall.

The years 1982 and 1983 saw the Ecology Party holding national conventions in the Glencree Centre for Reconciliation in County Wicklow. Attending these was a very enjoyable and thought-provoking experience. I recall meeting late great Seán Mc Bride, the former Minister for Foreign Affairs who expressed great interest in the fledgling green movement. I remember him telling me in conversation that 'the most patriotic thing anyone can do in Ireland is to plant trees, lots of trees'.

The move from West Cork to Fingal was an emotional one. I had made good friends in Cork but my younger sister Cheryl was diagnosed with lung cancer and I needed to be nearer to the Adelaide Hospital in Dublin. The offer of a job as principal teacher in St George's National School, Balbriggan, made this move possible. Cheryl died on 10 January 1984, leaving my brother, our parents and myself to try and make some sense of what had happened to our lovely sister who at eighteen years of age had just begun her first job.

The Balbriggan Breakaway festival in June 1984 coincided with the European Parliament Election campaign in that year. Christopher Fettes was the Green Alliance candidate for Dublin. I invited him to meet the people lining the streets for the Breakaway parade and so the seeds of electioneering for me, and green politics in Dublin North were sown.

My first political news coverage came soon afterwards in an equally memorable way. A journalist from the *Fingal Independent* rang me to get my reaction to a decision by Balbriggan Town Commission to reject a motion from Carrickmacross Urban District Council which had sought their support for a ban on hare coursing. I cannot abide cruelty to people or any creature and am a longstanding member of the Irish Council Against Blood Sports (ICABS). Naturally, I expressed my disgust at the callous disregard by local public representatives of activities which cause such distress and painful death to wild hares. I announced that if I found a corpse from a victim of coursing, I would bring it in to the next meeting of the commissioners and lay it on their table to let them see what they were endorsing. My comments made the front page under a headline, 'Local Teacher Lashes Commissioners over Coursing'. Balbriggan has a very active Coursing Club. Notwithstanding that, local people approached me to offer support and to join ICABS. Before long, we had a strong branch of ICABS in the town and a number of annual peaceful protest marches to the Coursing Field were organised, attended by such luminaries as Hugh Leonard, the playwright and Roger Garland as the sole Green Alliance TD at the time.

Nowadays, dogs used for coursing must be muzzled, by law. Unfortunately, coursing still takes place, involving blooding of dogs and fatal injuries to some of the captured hares. It is still a cruel activity, in my view, and has no place in a humane society.

With the local elections in June 1985 approaching, it was time to organise a green group in Dublin North. Colm Ó Caomhánaigh, from Malahide (now Parliamentary Secretary to the Green Party in the Oireachtas) and myself convened a public meeting in the Grove Hotel, Malahide. The dedicated attendees decided to establish the Fingal Greens and both Colm and I stood as candidates in the Malahide and Balbriggan wards respectively.

The closure of Sellafield was one of the campaign issues and, early on, the party was the only political party making this call. I recall that we organised a demonstration to highlight the need for government action against Sellafield when the Minister responsible, Ray Burke TD, visited Balbriggan. This was the first of many exchanges I had with Ray Burke.

The profile of the anti-nuclear campaign reached the eyes and ears of British Nuclear Fuels Ltd. An invitation was received for me to meet the management and workers at Sellafield. The first visit was low-key, travelling with fellow green and physicist Fran McKeagney by ferry, train and our bicycles. It was a low-budget trip too. We slept in a hay barn at Ravenglass, a bird sanctuary on the Cumbrian coast. When morning came, we were shocked to see men in white protective clothing walking the beach monitoring the local environment for radiation levels. Bird numbers had been falling year by year at Ravenglass. BNFL told us this was nothing to do with Sellafield. We were not so sure.

The 1986 Chernobyl disaster created even more concern about the risks associated with nuclear power. The direct effect of contamination on Ireland caused restrictions for sheep farming in particular, and highlighted the cross boundary nature of all pollution. The green motto, 'Think globally, act locally', made us think more and act more. Adi Roche moved on from green politics and CND to establish the Chernobyl Children's Project as soon as she saw a fax from survivors of the disaster pleading for help.

In Fingal, we had highlighted what we were against, but we needed to work harder at setting out the solutions. There were no bottle banks in Fingal at this time so action was needed. I organised to have a skip adapted and painted to do the job. It was a labour-intensive operation however. When full, the bottlebank had to be brought by me as navigator in the skip lorry to Irish Glass Bottles, twenty-two miles away, in Ringsend, Dublin. The load was weighed, emptied and the glass cullet sold. The proceeds from cullet covered the cost of door to door leaflets to re-establish a Tidy Towns Association in Balbriggan with the help of local celebrities Linda Martin and comedian

Frank Carson. This pioneering bottlebank, festooned with bunting, was then entered as a float in the local St Patrick's Day parade to highlight its existence. In the end, it won a prize as the best commercial entry.

The damage being done by CFC gas from fridges, spray cans and other products was the focus of another successful campaign. Colm Timmins, a particularly artistic member made a large anti-CFCs notice that ensured a good picture was published in local papers.

Before long, another election campaign was upon us. This was the first chance for the Green Alliance/Comhaontas Glas to go before all the people of Dublin North in a general election. Many people were still new to green politics. While canvassing in Swords one evening, a child answered the door. I introduced myself as being from the Green Alliance. She went off shouting to her mother, 'Mammy, the 'green lions' are at the door!' An elderly lady, having heard that the Green Party in Germany was doing well, wondered if we had any connection to 'Hitler Youth'!

Following this election, I felt strongly the need not just to talk about green solutions to improve people's quality of life, but to visit a place where I could see green technologies, live in a greener way and get tips about how Ireland could demonstrate the benefits of the changes the Green Alliance/ Comhaontas Glas was advocating in Ireland.

I found this 'green Mecca' in Wales. The Centre for Alternative Technology (CAT) was established by an intelligent bunch of green-minded idealists in the mid-1970s. They leased a disued slate quarry near Machynlleth in mid-Wales. They harness wind, hydro and solar power. They boast the best-insulated house in Britain. They have a water-powered train that climbs a gradient of forty-five degrees. They farm organically and have a prize-winning restaurant and accommodation. They run courses up to MSc level and are currently building WISE (The Welsh Institute of Sustainable Education). The MSc course is in Advanced Environmental and Energy Studies, and is linked to the University of East London. The demand for residential courses is growing all the time, and has doubled in the three years between 2003 and 2006. Fifty to sixty thousand visitors per annum pay admittance to experience the kind of quality of life we could all experience if everyone voted green.

I went to work in CAT as a short-term volunteer after the 1987 election to help, among other things, in the building of what is today called the 'Self-Build House'. This project was a way of marking the UN Year of Shelter. In the evening time, after dinner, I wrote postcards – ninety in all – to people I knew at home who I felt would be interested in an ecological centre of this sort being established in Ireland. I put out a general invitation to attend a public meeting in Balbriggan on my return where I presented a slide show from photographs I had taken at CAT. That slide show gave rise to a working group. I was then told of a dilapidated complex of buildings and a two-acre walled garden and orchard with rare apple varieties on the banks of the River Nanny near Laytown, County Meath. Myself and two friends, Anna Doran of the Fingal Greens and Tommy Simpson of Dublin North West went to meet Luc Van Doorslaer, the farmer who owned the buildings and land in question. Luc was very interested in the idea of an ecological centre, but the main challenge was to convince him, over many very relaxing meetings, that this was a long-term commitment. To ensure this commitment was not compromised, a number of greens, such as Anna Doran, left the party to concentrate their efforts on developing Ireland's answer to CAT.

CAT has great regard for the Welsh language, with all signs displayed in Welsh and English. I wanted a similar regard for the Irish language, so I came up with Sonairte as a name for the Laytown project. Sonairte means 'of positive strength' and forms a handy acronym for the objectives of the centre:

S – sustainable living

O – organic growing

N – nature conservation

A – appropriate technology

I – intercultural exchange

R – reconciliation & inner peace

T – trading fairly

E – educational resource

FÁS, the state training authority, helped Sonairte to restore many of the buildings, the garden and nature trail. But since the community employment schemes have been stopped, the centre is now totally dependent on volunteers. Even so, it welcomes visitors and school groups. Every Saturday in the Dublin Food Co-op, the organic produce from Sonairte is eagerly awaited and the money made is ploughed back into paying for the renewable energy displays and the general upkeep including the terribly expensive public liability insurance.

Whatever time I had to devote to Sonairte before the 1989 European Elections campaign certainly diminished afterwards. I was selected as the Green Party/Comhaontas Glas candidate for Dublin, while Seán English from Naas stood in Leinster. Printing a good, inexpensive leaflet on recycled paper was the first priority. A friend from the marketing business, Seán O'Halloran, and myself spent most of a Saturday in my house scribbling and testing ideas until we came up with an eye-grabbing design (we thought!) where unfolding the design revealed the words, 'The Earth is dying, save it, vote Green'.

Early on in the campaign, my second-hand car reached the end of its useful life, so as candidate I took the bus, the train, cycled, walked and sometimes got a lift. From Balbriggan to Ballybrack and from Clondalkin to Connolly Station, from January to June 1989 I was on the trail. Meanwhile, a multitude of lobby groups wrote to me personally looking for a response to particular concerns or inviting me to public meetings. These letters were often critically important as responses were published. One such letter was from Earthwatch to all candidates, in the form of a questionnaire to check how ecological the Green Party/Comhaontas Glas was.

One question from Earthwatch asked how we would respond if sea level rise due to climate change inundated coastal areas. Being under pressure, I responded brusquely that the whole point of implementing green policies is to prevent such a tragedy happening. For this off-hand response, I was penalised 2 per cent and accordingly the Green Party was deemed 98 per cent ecological! Thankfully, we were ahead by a good distance of all the other parties and the correlated results were widely published in the media. Imagine, however, if I had not opened that particular letter in time!

The 1989 General and European elections were a watershed for the Green Party/Comhaontas Glas. I was a candidate in both but was elected in neither! However, Dublin South returned Roger Garland as Ireland's first Green Party TD, and I felt very satisfied to have shocked the establishment with a sizeable vote in the European Election. From 227 votes in 1985 to outpolling a well-known politician like Mary Harney was certainly going in the right direction. The healthy green vote was due to a combination of factors. This included the successful campaigning of the Green Parties 'across the water', which spilled over wherever British television in Ireland was received. On the ground, active greens in Dublin like John Gormley were upping the ante to end the smog problem in Dublin. This clean air campaign had won huge public support. It is little wonder, given the support the Green Party was attracting, that Mary Harney saw the importance of taking the Minister of State job at the Department of the Environment. Smog in Dublin became history thankfully and the Green Party continued setting the agenda.

I had stood for three elections now and next time I was determined to take a seat. With the local elections expected soon, I made a habit of attending Dublin Council meetings in O'Connell Street, Dublin. From the public gallery, it was obvious that the ubiquitous Section 4 motions were dominating the agenda. Motions that would benefit the whole community were hardly ever reached, because councillors had stacks of Section 4 motions to force the City Manager to allow building in locations which were totally at variance with the Development Plan. There was a whiff of corruption emanating from a number of councillors going by their inexplicable actions, but I had no proof, at that point in time.

June 1991 was set as the date of the next Local Elections. I had a great team, with Dave Cronin my Election Agent. The late and very sadly missed Eithne O'Donnell from Daingean Uí Chúis, who lived in Balbriggan with her family, would not take no for an answer and set a high standard in canvassing all over the ward. Our banners were hand-painted in my back garden. They certainly stood out from the rest, given that each included ivy that was stapled to each roadside billboard. The ivy was not so much a decoration as shorthand for creating a tree image, the logo of the party at that time.

Success at last. I took the second seat in the Balbriggan Ward and we got a good vote in the Swords ward with Tony Nolan and in Malahide with Alan Nagle. David Healy was elected in Howth, which gave the Fingal area two new green councillors. One of our members in Rush, the late and very sadly missed Dermot Hamilton, was selected to stand in Whitehall, where he had grown up in Dublin, and narrowly missed taking a seat also.

When the dust settled, there was a Green group of six on Dublin County Council. The experienced councillors from Fine Gael and Labour tried to outmanoeuvre us newcomers in any way they could. With our numbers, we were entitled to various positions on the VEC, the Health Board and as Chairs of Committees. I was offered the Chair of the Fingal Area Committee. I accepted but expressed a preference for year three, four or five to allow me to learn the ropes. This was refused, and I was told that only year one was available. So, on my first day in the Fingal meeting, I was Cathaoirleach! If this was supposed to trip me up, however, it did not work. The following year, a row between Dessie O'Malley and Albert Reynolds brought about a general election in November 1992. My profile as Cathaoirleach was very helpful and I was elected as a TD, thanks to a very energetic team of canvassers and transfers from all other parties, but mainly from Labour.

Whatever about being new to the council, being new to the Dáil was even more daunting. Unfortunately, Roger Garland had lost his seat, but, even more unfortunately, he told his Parliamentary Assistant that I would employ her. With several people who had worked voluntarily for me expecting to be considered, I advertised the PA position. Roger's PA did not apply and

I appointed Mairéad Ní Oistín, who could work as effectively in Irish as in English.

Looking back, I now appreciate just how rare it is to find a mutilingual Parliamentary Assistant in Ireland. As a result, Mairéad was later in demand from TG4 and more recently Údarás na Gaeltachta. The Constituency Office in Swords, the capital of Fingal, has also become very busy. I am fortunate that Madeleine Farreally and Paula Evans are available there to share the work and to deal with constituency matters, as well as more general issues relating to my job as Green Party Leader. More recently, Conor Little has taken up a PA position in my Dáil office which will become even more hectic in the run-up to the general election.

Following my election as TD in 1992, a second invitation was issued by BNFL after I had highlighted the dangers of nuclear power again and again, especially after the Chernobyl nuclear disaster in 1986. Dave Cronin, (now a journalist living in Brussels and former PA to Patricia Mc Kenna MEP) had done an excellent job as my Director of Elections in 1991. Dave and I prepared for this visit by inviting school children to make cards in the shape of fish that we could hand-deliver to the BNFL people at Sellafield. BNFL were ready for us this time. Sellafield management greeted us with camera crews from BBC and ITN when we arrived. We presented the hundreds of protest cards, which made a very eye-catching display for the cameras. They then gave us white coats to wear and gave us a tour before our meeting. The TV news that evening claimed we were happy with Sellafield! We had to correct that blatant falsehood. Next morning we joined a Greenpeace protest blocking a ship-ment of plutonium nitrate which was preparing to unload at Wokington port near Sellafield. I was arrested, kept in custody, but not charged. Fortunately, the same cameras were there to record the arrest. It was clear to TV viewers that I did not just want an end to Sellafield but felt strongly enough about the issue to be arrested.

The Green Party was alone at that time in advocating the end of the dual mandate that allowed TDs to also serve as councillors. Had there been a trained replacement selected, I could have resigned earlier than the end of 1993. However, the Development Plan was being decided during that year and I felt duty-bound to see it through, especially with the questions being raised in the media about whether some of the decisions were corrupt.

The planners were at their wits' end trying to warn FF and FG council-lors in particular that ignoring planning advice was going to cost the council dearly and damage people's quality of life for years to come. In the middle of all this, one of the many letters sent to the Green Party seeking support to rezone a piece of land had attached to it a £100 cheque made out to the party. There was no reference in the letter to the cheque and the green councillors felt that this bizarre practice might be the tip of an iceberg.

So I went in to the council, having taken a few days to consider how best to deal with our mystery cheque. Making clear that the question was not related to the specific proposal before the council, I asked if any councillors had received an unsolicited cheque such as the one I displayed.

Instead of getting a yes or no answer, I was mobbed by an apoplectic ad hoc coalition of Fianna Fáil and Fine Gael councillors with shouts of 'Get the cheque, somebody get the cheque'. Senator Don Lydon (FF) lost it altogether and grabbed me in a headlock from behind, pulling me back so another councillor could prise open my fist which held on tightly to the offending cheque, which I have since passed on to the Flood (now Mahon) tribunal. That was 19 February 1993, a date I will never forget. Noel C. Smyth, the well-known solicitor, later accosted me in the corridor of the 'Councillors Only' restricted area of the council offices. He threatened he would 'get me', before Cllr David Healy and Larry Gordon from the Green Party, as well as Cllr Joe Higgins and Cllr Pat Rabbitte TD came to my rescue and reminded him that he was trespassing in the restricted area.

Very soon after that I received a solicitor's letter from Monarch Properties threatening to sue me unless I apologised for the cheque incident. To this day I am grateful to the late Senior Counsel Michael Gray for reminding me I had nothing to apologise for. Tragically, Michael lost his life in a small aeroplane accident not long after this time.

Elsewhere, in Dublin City Council, where four Greens had been elected in 1991, John Gormley was selected to become the first Green Lord Mayor of Dublin in 1994. The party was now preparing to contest the 1994 European Elections. Patricia McKenna had huge experience already representing the party at meetings in Brussels and elsewhere. Early on, my Dáil office was an administrative base for Patricia to deal with the copious amounts of correspondence that accompany European Election campaigns as I well knew from my own outing in 1989. This time, however, Patricia won in style, topping the poll thanks to the help of so many people like Grattan Healy and Steve Rawson who positioned a few hundred posters around Dublin and made it look like we had thousands of posters everywhere. Also impressive was the success of Nuala Ahern who took a seat in Leinster. Dan Boyle established a good base in Munster where we had not run before and likewise Richard Douthwaite from Westport, better known as an economist and founding member of FEASTA, did Trojan work as a candidate in the vast constituency of Connaught-Ulster.

The successes in the European Elections created the unique situation among Irish political parties where we had more parliamentarians in Brussels than we had in Dublin. Being in the Dáil on my own did cause huge frustration. As a former teacher, I wanted to cover education, given the overcrowding in classrooms. In Dublin North there were many issues needing attention at Aer Lingus, inadequate public transport, lack of ambulance and GP services after hours, poor harbour facilities for the fishing community, lack of local employment opportunities, low farm-gate prices driving farmers into the arms of land speculators, illegal dumping, lack of Gardaí, care for the elderly, childcare facilities, unaffordability of houses, and the general rise in the cost of living, among others. In the Dáil, these issues were raised through Parliamentary Questions and Adjournment Debates. Some received positive responses. The Minister for the Marine, David Andrews, for example, prevented the further infilling of the renowned bird habitat Rogerstown Estuary for a dump after he accepted my invitation to visit the area.

A question from me in 1994 to Minister for Finance Ruairí Quinn for a small levy to dissuade the over-use of plastic bags was rejected initially, but it pays to be persistent. It took nearly ten years for my proposal to be accepted, but better late than never.

I found that the most satisfying work took place trying to amend proposed legislation in committee. I was a member of the Finance Committee, which gave significant powers to the Minister in the Waste Management Act 1996 to reduce waste at every opportunity. To see the Minister for the Environment and Local Government ignore many of these powers while other countries are endeavouring to incrementally reduce their waste levels eventually to zero was very frustrating.

Mary O'Rourke, as Minister for Enterprise, was a pleasure to work with, as she listened. I proposed an amendment to favour the place of renewable energy in a deregulated energy market. The civil servants advising the Minister did not like my suggestion, but the Minister thought it was a good idea and accepted it. As a result, the wind power industry in Ireland took off as a better investment opportunity than previously had been the case.

The election of John Gormley as TD in 1997 and my re-election was a great day. I had a great canvassing team and the legendary organising skills of my Director of Elections, Dr Ray Ryan from Skerries, which ensured Dublin North held on to the Green seat. At last, I was a member of a Parliamentary Party rather than being regarded as an Independent by the rules in the Oireachtas. John and I divided the portfolios between us so that we could better mark the Taoiseach and the various ministers.

Having two TDs also entitled me to meet President Bill Clinton, his wife Hillary and their daughter Chelsea during their visit to Ireland. I raised various issues, but in particular the growing problem of climate change and the need for the USA to show international leadership to tackle it. He accepted my point, declared we had a huge problem facing us and then told me the Everglades in Florida would be gone in his lifetime due to rising sea-levels caused by the melting of the polar ice-caps. When I suggested he set a personal example to reduce carbon emissions by perhaps cycling or walking or using public transport whenever possible, he said he really wanted to do that, but his security staff would not allow it.

The Fingal Greens in Dublin North, meanwhile, were growing in membership. In 1993, I resigned from Dublin County Council. Earlier that year, a selection convention took place to choose a replacement councillor. Two men, Dave Cronin (Balbriggan) and Seán Mac Aonghusa (Rush) as well as one woman, Thea Allen (Balbriggan), went forward. Thea was selected and commenced an induction period helping me and sitting in the Council public gallery to observe meetings. Thea found being a councillor with two small children was tough going after a while. In due course, Therese Fingleton took over the seat, having been elected a Balbriggan Town Commissioner. Previously, Colm Timmins had been the first ever Green Cathaoirleach of the Town Commission and Therese became the second person to hold the office. Therese also put a huge amount of time and effort into the Special Olympics, making the Pakistani team feel very at home in Balbriggan, with help from such warm-hearted people as Kathleen and Martin Fanning.

Meanwhile, in 1998, I married Heidi Bedell. We first met at a crowded Fingal Green constituency office meeting at 35 Main Street, Swords. Heidi's green credentials, not to mention her charm, quickly won over not just me, but many other greens too. Heidi was elected a county councillor for her native Malahide Ward. She became very involved later with Sonairte, the ecology centre in Laytown, County Meath. This took up more and more time. Eventually, Heidi felt she should resign her council seat and Robbie Kelly, also from Malahide, was selected as her replacement and successfully won the seat in his own right at the subsequent local election in 2004.

Another fantastic person to join the Fingal Greens after 1997 was Eve Jenkins from Skerries. I had worked with Eve to push the case of aviation workers who had retired and were short-changed in their pension entitlements. Eve also was a great campaigner for the RNLI. A number of Fingal Greens were persuaded by Eve to build a raft and take part in the RNLI raft race in Skerries. As it was all for fun and for charity, it is immaterial how well we did in the races. However, if you guessed we came fifth one year and last the next, you would not be far off! Eve was by now Secretary of the Fingal Greens and she drove her team hard because she drove herself even harder. In canvassing for the 2002 General Election, she told me I had to top the poll, as no other result was acceptable to her.

Tragedy struck suddenly just ahead of our first televised Ard Fheis live broadcast. Eve was taken in to hospital for tests and died following medical complications. The Fingal Greens had a special memorial ceremony at her graveside at Ardla, Skerries, with her husband, David, and her grown sons, Andrew and Mark. We are thankful for her wonderful but short life, and we all know there will never be another Eve Jenkins.

The 2002 General Election exceeded all green expectations. My election in 2001 as Leader/Ceannaire created clear accountability in the party, which helped us to increase our seats. Also helpful in this regard was the election of Cllr Mary White (Carlow/Kilkenny) as Deputy Leader/Leas Cheannaire. As well as John and myself being returned, we were joined in Dáil Éireann by Dan Boyle (Cork South Central), Eamon Ryan (Dublin South), Paul Gogarty (Dublin Mid-West) and Ciarán Cuffe (Dún Laoghaire). This was a bittersweet election for me. With six TDs we had done well but narrowly missed out on the magic seven seats needed, to get full recognition as a party in Dáil Éireann. Also, for all our attention to gender balance on party committees and in candidate selection, only males had been elected. All female MEPs in Brussels, all male TDs in Dublin!

The 2004 local elections increased again the strength of the Fingal Greens. My dear wife, Heidi Bedell, won a seat on Balbriggan Town Council. Joe Corr from Rush became the first councillor from the town since 1991 and joined Cllr Robbie Kelly (Malahide ward) and Cllr David Healy (Howth ward) on Fingal County Council. In 2005 Robbie became the first ever Green Leas-Chathaoirleach and in 2006 Joe became the first ever Green Cathaoirleach. The three greens together have achieved very significant improvements for the people of Fingal. For example, new house insulation standards in areas of the county have been set 60 per cent higher than the acceptable government standard, reducing the cost of living and improving quality of life for householders as fossil fuel costs continue to rise.

With the election of six TDs in 2002 came extra resources for the party, including the Leader's Allowance, which I hand over 100 per cent to be administered by the party. State funding therefore allows the employment of staff for research, communications and administration. The Green Party does not accept corporate donations, so this state funding is vital for us to organise and get our message out to the wider public. In charge of staff matters is the Ard Rúnaí/General Secretary of the party. Stiofán Nutty, who had been my very effective Director of Elections in 2002 was the first person to be appointed to this position. He resigned after a year to stay involved but pursue his business consultancy and broadcasting work.

We were fortunate then that Dermot Hamilton, again from Dublin North, became available. Dermot had great experience of being in charge of large teams in the world of business. He brought great ideas and strategy to the party. Tragically, the morning after Dermot had been handing out leaflets during European Car-Free Day 2005, he suffered a sudden heart attack. Our thoughts and prayers go out to Patricia, Dermot's wife, and their daughter, Kelly. Dermot left a legacy of great memories and excellent ideas. A key committee in the party, which is making preparations for government, has been named the Hamilton Committee in his honour. His inspiration as Ard Rúnaí is still very much with us day by day.

The current Ard-Rúnaí is Dónall Geoghegan, who has considerable experience working with the National Youth Council and in negotiating Social Partnership. Dónall heads up a very talented and enthusiastic team and is based at the National Office of the Green Party/Comhaontas Glas at 16/17 Suffolk Street, Dublin 2.

The challenge for the Green Party/Comhaontas Glas is to be a party that people can rely on to represent and realise their hopes, not their fears. We need to communicate a message of hope. In the face of the failure by government to adjust to changed economic realities, it is fear, rather than hope, that grips people when they are faced with escalating fuel costs, doubts about job prospects, the relocation of jobs by trans-national corporations to low wage economies, and the unaffordability of housing that is forcing people to live further and further away from amenities and employment.

TK Whitaker, as Secretary General at the Department of Finance in the 1950s and 1960s, introduced new economic ideas that offered people hope at a time when for many, emigration was seen as the only way to survive. TK Whitaker saw how Ireland had to change from being inward-looking and protectionist to becoming an open economy, competing with other countries to win direct foreign investment. The plan suited the time perfectly, as energy was relatively cheap and Ireland had many links with the USA and other countries from which investment was attracted.

Almost fifty years on, it is time for the old plan to make way for the new again. Global trading is a legacy of cheap energy. The peaking of global oil production will change all that very fast, as demand increasingly outstrips supply. Already the Swedish Government, in which the Swedish Green Party plays a significant role, is preparing to be free from oil dependency by 2020. This is being planned with Swedish parties, key industrialists and social partners working together over the period in question. Success in Sweden will give that country a competitive advantage in business and self-reliance, as well as self-confidence, for the Swedish people. Along with having a sustainable quality of life, the Swedish people will have played an effective role in counteracting the catastrophic effects of climate chaos caused largely by the burning of the remaining fossil fuels.

Responsible government is needed to develop the 'conditions of existence' as Darwin might say, to allow communities to meet their needs for the most part through local economic activity with international trade where necessary. Instead of seeing globalisation as desirable, the triple challenges of peak oil, climate change and global inequity will require that localisation be promoted as the road to prosperity for the next fifty years.

The seven principles of the Green Party/Comhaontas Glas have stood the test of time. Cúig bhliain is fiche ag fás. Of all the countries worldwide where greens are organised, Ireland is particularly well-suited to the transition we can make to a clean, green and lean economy.

We can produce wind-generated electricity at half the price that Germany can. We have more coastline per capita than most countries, for harnessing wave and tidal power. We have the best growing conditions of any European country for biomass, such as timber for construction and elephant grass for fuel.

We have the remains of a once-extensive railway network, which could be re-opened, modernised and electrified for freight as well as passengers. We have housing stock, which needs retrofitting to high insulation standards, giving worthwhile employment in the process. We have sufficient solar power levels to heat water by retrofitting solar panels on the south-facing roof space of houses all over the country.

Traditional rights to hold farmers' markets exist in most towns and villages around the country. Where such markets operate, local traders also benefit and the local community has healthy food, security and sociable interaction.

Childcare

Green politics is not just 'clean politics' it is 'life politics' – politics that address the everyday issues of life here in Ireland. In government, we will make sure that parents have the necessary free time and resources to get the crucial first years of parenting right. To give them a choice, a parent should be able to afford to spend three years with their children as well as having the option of decent childcare available close to where they live. We want neighbourhoods designed – from the earliest stage in the planning process – to be safe for children and their parents. That means designing streets for children rather than just cars. That means more playgrounds and parks. At the moment, Ireland has just over 200 playgrounds – roughly the number you would find in one London borough.

Let us give our children an alternative to locking themselves away in front of computer games. National and local government must take some responsibility for driving children off the streets, as a result of the drab and dangerous environments created in many communities. We also need a proper education system starting with smaller primary classes; classes of twenty rather than classes of thirty.

Health

To ensure children and adults alike have healthy lives, we also need a proper health system. The Green Party in government will concentrate on getting our primary health system right and taking the pressure off the expensive high-tech medical services. Green public representatives around the country are campaigning in support of local health clinics and community hospitals and are campaigning against the downgrading of local hospitals proposed in the Hanly Report.

The Fianna Fáil election promise to end waiting lists by 2004 stands as another classic example of a disgraceful broken promise. All governments over the last three decades share responsibility for the chronic shortage of bed capacity. During the 1980s, the number of beds fell from about 18,000 to 12,000. Even the FF/PD Health Strategy with its promise of 3000 beds over ten years will not come close to restoring those beds, not to mention keeping up with population growth. However, even that promise is on course to be broken. *Quelle surprise!*

We have seen huge advances in society but there has been a downside of increases in asthma, allergies, obesity and stress, alcohol and drug abuse and the resulting violent crime. Suicides are also on the increase. In spite of all this, the current government spend on health promotion and disease prevention is less than 0.1 per cent of the Department of Health budget.

We need to embrace a new vision – a new emphasis on prevention could deliver massive financial savings in our health budget and offer the prospect of longer and healthier lives. We believe that government should have responsibility for the nation's health, not just the health budget. The Green Party is different from other parties in that we believe that in the long run, prevention is better than cure.

Transport

We have also become the most car-dependent country in the world. Irish cars now drive 15,000 miles each year – more than in the USA and twice the German average. More schoolgirls are now driving themselves to school than are cycling to school. The biggest plan Minister Cullen has is the further building and widening of motorways. The fact that petrol is not going to be so widely available in twenty years time is being ignored by this irresponsible government.

Long before the Al Gore film *An Inconvenient Truth* was made, the scientific community was saying that carbon emissions from our transport and other sectors must be cut 60-80 per cent urgently, as our planet warms and our seas rise due to the amount of pollution we are putting into the atmosphere. There is a clear moral imperative, therefore, to massively invest in efficient and clean trains, trams and buses to solve our traffic problems. The Green Party will bring in light rail in Cork, an extended metro in Dublin, the Western Rail Line and we will deliver new rural and urban bus services throughout the country.

Housing

The difficulty in getting affordable housing is also something that young people in both rural and urban Ireland share. Has anything really changed from the days when it took wads of cash as thick as bricks to deliver corrupt rezoning? Young people are becoming slaves to a thirty- or forty-year mortgage, praying that interest rates will not continue rising. Meanwhile the large landowning friends of the FF/PD administration still hoard their land banks without fear of any action from government. The Green Party is campaigning for a right to housing in the Irish Constitution. We will ensure that local authorities can purchase land and build quality housing.

A telling question is, why are the rules that allow obscene profiteering from land rezoning still in place? The Green Party in government will implement the recommendations of the 1973 Kenny Report, which proposes a windfall tax on development land, a proposal based on the principle that communities rather than developers should benefit from the rezoning.

It is a disgrace that under the FF/PD administration the numbers of people on the housing lists have doubled. The Green Party in Government will build 10,000 social housing units per year until the waiting lists are cleared.

Energy

Adult illiteracy is an indictment of an under-resourced education system, but a more widespread form of illiteracy is to be found especially in this current government. I refer to energy illiteracy. For example to call an incinerator, a 'waste-to-energy' plant is a fraudulent description. To manufacture anew the material burned in the incinerator takes on average twice the energy that is derived from the burning process.

Instead, the Green Party knows that we could create thousands of jobs through enterprises that re-use and recycle waste materials rather than burning them. Meanwhile, it is a fact that even more jobs could be developed from the renewable energy economy. For example, in Germany, where the Green Party was elected and re-elected to government, 35,000 people are employed in wind energy, 18,000 are employed in solar power and 50,000 are employed in the renewable biomass industry.

It is alarming that over 80 per cent of the energy consumed in Ireland has to be imported. The track record of this government reminds one of a pilot flying a plane without a fuel gauge. More worrying still is the assumption implicit in a reply given to me in the Dáil by An Taoiseach, that 'the supplies of gas coming from Russia are infinite'.

We have no choice but to wean our society off its growing oil dependency, given that the global peak in oil production is expected in 2010 and gas soon afterwards around 2015. If we are to secure our children's future, we need to grow the Green Party, implement energy conservation measures and harness renewable sources of wind, wave, solar and tidal power. Every community, and especially the farming community, has a huge role to play in meeting these needs by growing crops and harnessing windpower.

The vision and work to bring about a sustainable future is about building competent communities, which do not just survive the challenges ahead, but thrive. Having worked in the Centre for Alternative Technology (CAT) in Wales all those years ago, I have seen this vision become a reality on a small scale. The challenges of peak oil, climate change and global inequity mean we need to replicate our own 'Centre for Alternative Technology' on a national scale.

Everyone has heard of the Celtic Tiger. However, the conditions that gave us the Celtic Tiger are changing fast. It is time we developed our collective vision and plan to bring about the Celtic CAT. Ireland could lead the world again as the Celtic Centre for Alternative Technology. For anyone who thinks that a Celtic CAT is smaller than a Celtic Tiger, remember *small* is beautiful, (and then read the book).

The Green Party/Comhaontas Glas represents a set of ideas whose time has come. From globalisation and the inequities of international trade to the creation of safer, child-friendly and sustainable communities, the Green Party is a party of tried and tested solutions.

We want to ensure that the planet is passed on in a fit and healthy state to our children. Ours is a good news story. Green politics is the politics of hope. Together we can create a caring, compassionate and sustainable Ireland for the twenty-first century.

Trevor Sargent TD, Leader of the Green Party/Comhaontas Glas.

Bibliography

Bomberg, E. *Green Parties and Politics in the European Union*, London, Routledge, (1998).

Carson, R. *Silent Spring*, London, Hamilton, (1963).

Carter N. 'Mixed Fortunes: The Greens in the 2004 European Parliament election', *Environmental Politics*, Vol. 14 No.1 103-111. London, Frank Cass & Company (2005).

Donnelly, S. *Poll Position (An Analysis of the 1991 Local Elections)*, Ireland, Published by Author, (1991).

Donnelly, S., *Elections '99 (All Kinds of Everything)*, Ireland, Published by Author, (1999).

Farrell, D.,'Ireland: The Green Alliance', in Ferdinand Muller-Rommell (Ed), *New Politics in Western Europe: the rise and success of Green Parties and alternative governments*, Ireland, Weltrier Press 123-130, (1989).

Gallagher, M. and Laver, M. (eds.) *How Ireland Voted 1992*, Ireland, Folens/PSAI Press, (1993).

Gallagher, M. and Marsh M. *Days of Blue Loyalty (The politics of membership of the Fine Gael party)*, Ireland, PSAI Press, (2002).

Gallagher, M., Marsh M. and Mitchell P. (eds.) *How Ireland Voted 2002* Ireland, Palgrave, (2003).

Handy, C. *The Future of Work*, UK, WH Smith, (1993).

Kavanagh, R. *Spring, Summer and Fall (The Rise and Fall of The Labour Party)* Ireland, Blackwater Press, (2001).

Leonard, L.'Green Nation: the Irish Environmental Movement from Carnsore Point to the Rossport Five', *Ecopolitics* vol. II, Ireland, Greenhouse Press:London, (2006).

Marsh, M. and Mitchell, P. (eds.) *How Ireland Voted 1997*, Ireland, Westview Press/PSAI Press, (1999).

Mullally, G., ' "Treading softly" on the political system? The Irish Greens in the 1997 general election', *Environmental Politics*, vol. VI, No 4 winter, pp165-171, (1997).

Murphy, S. Murphy E., *Brennan's Key To Local Authorities* Ireland, Landscape Press, (1986).

O'Neill, M., *Green Parties and Political Change in Contemporary Europe* England, Ashgate, (1997).

Robertson, J. *The Sane Alternative*, River Basin Publishing Company, UK, (1983).

Schumacher, EF., *Small Is Beautiful: Economics As If People Mattered*, New York, Harper and Row, (1973).

Sinnott, R., *Irish Voters Decide (Voting Behaviour In Elections And Referendums Since 1918)*, Manchester University Press, (1995).

Whiteman, D.,'The Progress and Potential of the Green Party in Ireland', in *Irish Political Studies*, 5, 45-58, Galway, PSAI Press, (1990).

'The Limits to Growth', Club of Rome Report, London, Earth Island Ltd, (1972).

Debates of the European Parliament No 4-451/40, 27 September 1994.

Debates of the European Parliament No 4-451/18, 27 September 1994.

Historical Dáil Debates Volume 391, 6 July 1989.

Historical Dáil Debates, Volume 425, 14 December 1992.

'Alternative Votes', Michael Viney, *The Irish Times* 13 February 1982.

'Ecology Party seeks "citizen's dividend"', Willy Clingan, *The Irish Times,* November 1982.

'Ecology Party formed' *The Irish Times,* 22 March 1982.

'Much more than just cleaning up our image', Frank McDonald, *The Irish Times*, 30 June 1989.

'The other parties ought to have seen it coming' Frank McDonald, *The Irish Times*, 29 June 1989.

'Join the Greens instead, new party is urged' Alison O'Connor, *The Irish Times,* 11 July 2000.

'Plastic bag query ends in uproar' *The Irish Times,* October 2000.

'First leader ready to take hold of the Green rudder', *The Irish Times*, 8 October 2001.

'Lord Mayor targets air and water' Stephen McGrath, *Irish Independent,* 5 July 1994.

'Green Mayor plans to 'get on his bike' in new post', *Irish Independent,* 18 April 1994.

'Uproar over cheque from a builder' Lara MacMillan, *Irish Independent,* 20 February 1993.

'Shatter risks his position over coursing' Gene McKenna, *Irish Independent,* 30 June 1993.

'Greens dance to an offbeat tune', *Irish Independent,* 13 June 1991.

'Green surge vote against cynicism' Willie Dillon, *Irish Independent,* 13 June 1994.

'Greens wasn't to get and hold power' Denis Coughlan, *The Irish Times,* April 1997.

'Greens accuse Government over waste Bill' Alison Healy, *The Irish Times,* 7 July 2001.

'McKenna Judgement targeted in orchestrated campaign' Patricia McKenna, *The Irish Times,* 6   December 2001.

'Party sets out terms for its support in a coalition after election' Mark Hennessy, *The Irish Times,* 10 October 2001.

'Greens embrace change in bid too widen appeal' Mark Hennessy, *The Irish Times,* 26 May 2001.

'Green Party focus on jobs as key issue in local elections' Gerard Ryle, *Irish Press,* 13 May 1991.

'Green Party urges devolution of power to local communities' Maol Muire Tynan, *The Irish Times*, 13 May 1991.

'Little progress outside Dublin for Greens' Paul O'Neill, *The Irish Times*, 1 July 1991.

'Ireland's Green Movement,' Kevin Mills, *Cork Examiner,* 22 November 1982.

Irish Times 27 November 1981 (letters page).

Appendix I

Chronology of principal Green Party conventions held to date

March 1982 Glencree Reconciliation Centre, County Wicklow
October 1982 Glencree Reconciliation Centre, County Wicklow
April 1983 Glencree Reconciliation Centre, County Wicklow
May 1983 Ennismore Retreat Centre, Mayfield, Cork
October 1983 Foulksrath Castle Youth Hostel, Jenkinstown, County Kilkenny
April 1984 Ray's Restaurant, Dublin
April 1985 Limerick
October 1985 Glencree Reconciliation Centre, County Wicklow
April 1986 Seville Lodge, Kilkenny
October 1986 Mary Bower's Restaurant, Dublin
April 1987 Smarmore Castle, Dundalk
October 1987 Seville Lodge, Kilkenny
October 1988 Cranagh Castle, County Tipperary
1989 Metropole Hotel, Cork
April 1990 Wexford
December 1990 St Andrew's Hall, Dublin
1991 Skerries, County Dublin
March 1992 Kingston Hotel, Dún Laoghaire
October 1992 Mother RedCap's
1993 St Andrew's Centre, Pearse Street, Dublin
1994 Firkin Crane, Cork City
1995 Howth, County Dublin
1996 Westport Woods
1996 Series of Constitutional Conventions, Dublin
1997 Grand Hotel, Malahide, County Dublin
1997 Wynns Hotel, Dublin
1998 Central Hotel, Dublin & University College Cork
1999 Central Hotel, Dublin
2000 Dolmen Hotel, Carlow
2001 Central Hotel, Dublin
May 2001 Wynn's Hotel, Dublin
2001 Kilkenny – special convention to elect leader
2002 Silver Springs Hotel, Cork
2003 Woodstock, Ennis
2004 Galway Bay, Galway
2005 Silver Springs Hotel, Cork
2005 Special Convention, Hilton Hotel, Dublin
2006 Newpark Hotel, Kilkenny

Appendix II

Green Party Candidates and Elected Representatives

Key
Elected in Bold and Italics

Acronyms
EE – European Elections
GE – General Election
BE – By-election
SE – Seanad Election
LE – Local Election
TU – Togachain an Udaras

Barry Ahern
LE 1991, Bray Electoral Area, Wicklow CC

Nuala Ahern
LE 1991, Greystones Electoral Area, Wicklow CC
GE 1992, Wicklow Constituency
EE 1994, Leinster Constituency
EE 1999, Leinster Constituency

Catherine Ansbro
GE 2002, Longford/Roscommon
LE 2004, Boyle EA, Roscommon CC

Eamon Ansbro
LE 2004, Ballaghadereen EA, Roscommon CC

Cecilia Armelin
LE 1991, Ballyfermot Ward, Dublin Corporation

Leo Armstrong
LE 1999, Leixlip TC
LE 1999, Leixlip EA, Kildare County Council
LE 2004, Clane EA, Kildare CC

Judith Ashton
LE 2004, Thomastown EA, Kilkenny CC

Alison Badrion
LE 1985, Glencullen Electoral Area, Dublin CC
LE 2004, Tullamore TC
LE 2004, Tullamore EA, Offaly CC

Jo Baker
LE 1991, Cabra Ward, Dublin Corporation

Bridget Banham
LE 2004, Roscommon EA, Roscommon CC

Jim Bartley
LE 1991, Mallow Electoral Area, Cork CC

Heidi Bedell
LE 1999, Malahide EA, Fingal CC
LE 2004, Balbriggan TC

Vincent Beirne
LE 1999, Boyle TC
LE 1999, Boyle EA, Roscommon CC

Sean Bell
LE 1985, Midleton Electoral Area, Cork CC
LE 1991, Midleton Electoral Area, Cork CC

Maggie Blake
LE 1991, Ballybrack Elect Area, Dún Laoghaire

Gerry Boland
GE 1997, Dublin South

Robert Bonnie
LE 1999, Mulhuddart EA, Fingal CC
GE 2002, Dublin West
LE 2004, Mulhuddart EA, Fingal CC

Selina Bonnie
LE 1999, Ballyfermot Electoral Area, Dublin Corporation

Mary Bowers
GE 1989, Dublin South Central
LE 1991, Crumlin Ward, Dublin Corporation
GE 1992, Dublin South Central
LE 1999, Tallaght Central EA, South Dublin CC

Dan Boyle
LE 1991, South East Ward, Cork Corporation
GE 1992, Cork South Central
SE 1993, Cultural and Educational Panel
EE 1994, Munster Constituency
BE 1994, Cork South Central
GE 1997, Cork South Central
SE 1997, Industrial and Commercial Panel
BE 1998, Cork South Central
LE 1999, South Central Ward, Cork Corporation
GE 2002, Cork South Central

Olive Brady
LE 1991, Kildare Electoral Area, Kildare CC

Ted Bradley
LE 1999, Kanturk Electoral Area, Cork CC
LE 1999, Newcastle EA, Limerick CC
LE 2004, Kanturk EA, Cork CC

Vincent Bradley
LE 1994, Naas UDC

Michelle Brett
LE 2004, Blarney EA, Cork CC

Marcus Briody
GE 2002, Limerick West

Anne Brogan Young
LE 1999, Blackrock EA, Dún Laoghaire-Rathdown CC

Rorie Brophy
LE 1991, Letterkenny Elect Area, Donegal CC

Louise Burchill
LE 1991 Naas UDC
LE 1991 Naas EA, Kildare CC

Brendan Burke
LE 1991, North Central Ward, Cork Corporation

Liam Burke
LE 1994, Youghal UDC
LE 1999, Youghal UDC
LE 2004, Youghal Town Council

Caroline Burrell
LE 2004, Bray No.3, Bray TC

Parvez Butt
LE 2004, Longford TC
LE 2004, Longford EA, Longford CC

Teresa Butterfield
LE 1985, Dún Laoghaire Elect Area, Dublin CC

Geraldine Callinan O'Dea
LE 2004, Carlow No.2, Carlow CC

Rosie Cargin
LE 2004, Bandon EA, Cork CC

Patricia Carolan
LE 2004, Tullow EA, Carlow CC

Owen Casey
GE 1982 (Nov), Cork South Central

Nessa Childers
LE 2004, Blackrock EA, Dún Laoghaire Rathdown CC

Neil Clarke
LE 2004, Letterkenny UDC
LE 2004, Letterkenny EA, Donegal CC

Phyllida Clarke
LE 1999, Kilkenny Corporation
LE 1999, Callan EA, Kilkenny CC

Eamon Collins
LE 2004, Newcastle EA, Limerick CC

Bernie Connolly
LE 2004, Skibbereen EA, Cork CC

Enda Connolly
GE 1989, Dublin Central

Fintan Convery
LE 1999, Galway No.3, Galway Corporation

William Cooke
LE 1985, Clontarf Ward, Dublin Corporation

Donna Cooney
GE 1997, Dublin North East
LE 1999, Donaghamede Ward, Dublin Corporation
LE 2004, Donaghamede Ward, Dublin City Council

Terence Corish
LE 2004, Glencullen EA, Dún Laoghaire Rathdown CC

Joe Corr
LE 2004, Balbriggan EA, Fingal CC

Dorothy Corrigan
LE 2004, Clondalkin EA, South Dublin CC

Sean Corrigan
LE 2004, Mullingar TC
LE 2004, Mullingar East EA, Westmeath CC

Dave Cotter
GE 1992, Dublin South Central

Pat Cotter
LE 1985, South Central Ward, Cork Corporation

Marcus Counihan
LE 1985, Killarney UDC
GE 1987, Kerry South

Afra Cronin
LE 1999, Piltown EA, Kilkenny CC

Therese Cronin
LE 1985, South Inner City Ward, Dublin Corporation

Ann Crowley
GE 1997, Mayo
LE 1999, Westport EA, Mayo CC
GE 2002, Mayo

Ciarán Cuffe
LE 1991, South Inner City Ward, Dublin Corporation
GE 1997, Dublin Central
LE 1999, South East Inner City Ward, Dublin Corporation
GE 2002, Dún Laoghaire

Pat Culhane
LE 2004, Rathkeale EA, Limerick CC

Elizabeth Cullen
GE 1997, Donegal South West

Maggie Cullen
LE 1999, Carlow TC

Romie Cullen
LE 1991, Athy Electoral Area, Kildare CC

Patrick Cummins
LE 1991, Trim Electoral Area, Meath CC

Kieran Cunnane
LE 2004, Galway No.1, Galway City Council

Michael Cuthbert
LE 2004, Enniscorthy TC
LE 2004, Enniscorthy EA, Wexford CC

Simon Curtis
LE 2004, Stillorgan EA, Dún Laoghaire Rathdown CC

Daragh Davenport
LE 1991, Clane Electoral Area, Kildare CC

Elizabeth Davidson
LE 2004, Tallaght South EA, South Dublin CC

Carol Davis
LE 2004, Slane EA, Meath CC

Deirdre De Burca
LE 1999, Bray No.2, Bray UDC
LE 1999, Bray EA, Wicklow CC
GE 2002, Wicklow
LE 2004, Bray No.1, Bray UDC
LE 2004, Bray EA, Wicklow CC

Mark Dearey
LE 2004, Dundalk No.1, Dundalk TC

Denis Deasy
LE 1985, Terenure Electoral Area, Dublin CC

Conor Delaney
GE 1989, Dublin South West
LE 1991, Clondalkin Elect Area, Dublin South

Jillian Delaney
LE 1991, South West Ward, Cork Corporation

Liam De Siun
GE 1982 (Nov), Wicklow Constituency
GE 1987, Wicklow Constituency

Carole Doherty
LE 2004, Trim TC
LE 2004, Trim EA, Meath CC

Florence Doherty
LE 2004, Bundoran TC
LE 2004, Donegal EA, Donegal CC

Ger Doherty
LE 1999, Clondalkin EA, South Dublin CC

Tony Dolan
LE 1991, Edenderry Electoral Area, Offaly CC

Dominick Donnelly
LE 2004, Passage West TC
LE 2004, Carrigaline EA, Cork CC

Peter Doran
LE 2004, Buncrana TC
LE 2004, Inishowen EA, Donegal CC

Richard Douthwaite
EE 1994, Connaught/Ulster Constituency

Matt Diskin
LE 2004, Carlow No.1, Carlow CC
LE 2004, Luggacurren EA, Laois CC

Ken Duffy
LE 2004, Swords EA, Fingal CC

Sean Dunne
LE 1985, South West Ward, Cork Corporation

Michael Dunphy
LE 1991, Blackrock Elect Area, Dún Laoghaire

David Edler
LE 1999, Bruff EA, Limerick CC

Paul Edson
LE 1994, Kilrush UDC
LE 1999, Kilrush UDC
LE 1999, Kilrush Electoral Area, Clare CC

Sean English
GE 1989,
EE 1989, Leinster Constituency
LE 1991, Naas Electoral Area, Kildare CC

GE 1992, Kildare
LE 1994, Naas UDC
GE 1997, Kildare North

Tess Enright
LE 2004, Arklow TC
LE 2004, Arklow EA, Wicklow CC

Ciarán Fallon
LE 2004, Dundrum EA, Dún Laoghaire Rathdown CC

Monique Federsal
GE 1997, Dublin South West

Patricia Feldwick
LE 1994, Greystones TC
LE 1999, Greystones TC

Christopher Fettes
EE 1984, Dublin Constituency
GE 2002, Laois Offaly

Therese Fingleton
LE 1999, Balbriggan TC
LE 1999, Balbriggan EA, Fingal CC

Conor Fitzgerald
LE 1991, Tralee Electoral Area, Kerry CC
LE 1994, Tralee UDC
LE 1999, Tralee UDC

John Fitzgerald
LE 2004, Piltown EA, Kilkenny CC

Mary Fitzgerald
LE 2004, Kells TC

Shane Fitzgerald
LE 2004, Leixlip TC
LE 2004, Leixlip EA, Kildare CC

Ger Fitzgibbon
LE 2004, Newbridge TC
LE 2004, Kildare EA, Kildare CC

Pat Fitzpatrick
GE 1997, Galway West
LE 1999, Galway No.2, Galway Corporation

Ann Marie Flanagan
LE 2004, Ennistymon EA, Clare CC

Brian Flanagan
LE 2004, Navan TC
TU 2005, Rathcairn

Sheila Fogarty
LE 1999, North Inner City Ward, Dublin Corporation

Maureen Foister
LE 1999, Gorey TC
LE 1999, Gorey EA, Wexford CC

Danny Forde
LE 1999, Wexford Corporation
LE 1999, Wexford EA, Wexford CC
LE 2004, Wexford Corporation
LE 2004, Wexford EA, Wexford CC

Trish Forde Brennan
LE 2004, Castleconnell EA, Limerick CC

Patricia Gardiner
LE 2004, South West Inner City, Dublin City Council

Fiona Garland
LE 1985, Rathfarnham Electoral Area, Dublin CC

Roger Garland
GE 1982 (Nov), Dublin South
GE 1987, Dublin South
GE 1989, Dublin South
GE 1992, Dublin South

John Garvey
LE 1985, Castleknock Electoral Area, Dublin CC

Noel Giles
LE 1999, Bandon Electoral Area, Cork CC

Paula Giles
LE 1991, Bandon Electoral Area, Cork CC
GE 1997, Cork South West

Cathal Gogan
LE 1999, Navan EA, Meath CC

Johnny Gogan
LE 2004, Dromahaire EA, Leitrim CC

Paul Gogarty
LE 1991, Castleknock Electoral Area, Fingal CC
GE 1992, Dublin West
BE 1996, Dublin West
GE 1997, Dublin West
LE 1999, Lucan Electoral Area, South Dublin CC
GE 2002, Dublin Mid-West

John Goodwillie
BE 1994, Dublin South Central
GE 1997, Dublin South Central
LE 1999, Crumlin-Kimmage Ward, Dublin Corporation
BE 1999, Dublin South Central

Larry Gordon
LE 1991, Stillorgan Elect Area, Dún Laoghaire
LE 1999, Stillorgan Elect Area, Dún Laoghaire

John Gormley
GE 1989, Dublin South East
SE 1989, National University Panel
LE 1991, Rathmines Ward, Dublin Corporation
GE 1992, Dublin South East
GE 1997, Dublin South East
GE 2002, Dublin South East

Claire Gould Fielding
LE 1999, North East Ward, Cork Corporation

Patricia Greene
LE 1985, Greenhills Electoral Area, Dublin CC

Richard Greene
LE 1991, Clonskeagh Elect Area, Dún Laoghaire

Stephen Gregory
LE 1985, Bray North Ward, Bray UDC

David Grey
LE 2004, Tralee TC
LE 2005, Tralee EA, Kerry CC

Ger Griffin
LE 1994, Athy UDC

Patricia Griffin
GE 1989, Dún Laoghaire Constituency

Sieneke Hakvoort
LE 1999, Artane Electoral Area, Dublin Corporation

Dermot Hamilton
LE 1991, Drumcondra Ward, Dublin Corporation
LE 2004, Ballymun-Whitehall Ward, Dublin City Council

Joe Hardin
LE 1985, Lucan Electoral Area, Dublin CC

Natasha Harty
LE 1994, Midleton UDC

Carol Hayes
LE 1985, Bray West Ward, Bray UDC

David Healy
LE 1991, Howth Electoral Area, Dublin CC
GE 1992, Dublin North East
LE 1999, Howth EA, Fingal CC
GE 2002, Dublin North East
LE 2004, Howth EA, Fingal CC

Imelda Healy
LE 1994, Bantry TC

Simon Herbert
LE 2004, Artane Ward, Dublin City Council

Denis Higgins
LE 1999, Monaghan UDC
LE 1999, Monaghan EA, Monaghan CC

Jacqueline Hodgson
LE 2004, Bantry EA, Cork CC

Elma Holahan
LE 1985, Crumlin Ward, Dublin Corporation

Stephen Hollinshead
LE 2004, Ferbane EA, Offaly CC

Robert Hopkins
LE 1994, Kilkee TC
LE 1999, Kilkee TC

Timothy Hourigan
GE 2002, Limerick East

Patricia Howard
LE 1994, Wicklow UDC

Shauna Hutchinson Edgar
LE 2004, Tallaght Central EA, South Dublin CC

Tom Hyland
LE 1991, Cork Rural North Elect Area, Cork CC

Kealin Ireland
LE 2004, Dún Laoghaire EA, Dún Laoghaire Rathdown CC

Sarah Iremonger
LE 2004, Cobh TC
LE 2004, Midleton EA, Cork CC

Philip Jones
LE 2004, North East Ward, Cork City Council

Geffery Kane
LE 2004, North West Ward, Cork City Council

Nora Keane
LE 1985, Artane Ward, Dublin Corporation

Vincent Keaney
LE 1999, Cobh TC
LE 1999, Midleton Electoral Area

Phil Kearney
LE 1985, Ballybrack Electoral Area, Dublin CC
LE 2004, North Inner City Ward, Dublin City Council

Kevin Kelly
LE 2004, Carlow TC

Mary Kelly
LE 1999, Glenties Electoral Area, Donegal CC

Robert Kelly
LE 2004, Malahide EA, Fingal CC

Tom Kelly
LE 2004, Slane EA, Meath CC

Liam Kieran
LE 1999, Dundalk South EA, Louth CC

LE 2004, Dundalk No.2, Dundalk TC
LE 2004, Dundalk South EA, Louth CC

Evelyn Kingston
LE 1994, Clonakilty UDC
LE 1999, Clonakilty TC

Catherine Kinsella
LE 1999, Waterford No.3, Waterford Corporation
LE 2994, Waterford No.3, Waterford City Council

Tom Kivlehan
LE 2004, Ballybrack EA, Dún Laoghaire Rathdown CC

Kevin Knox
LE 1999, Thomastown EA, Kilkenny CC

Murrogh Lacy
LE 1985, Dundrum Electoral Area, Dublin CC

Alison Larkin
GE 1987, Dublin North West
GE 1989, Dublin North West
LE 1991, Greenhills Elect Area, Dublin South
LE 1999, Finglas Electoral Area, Dublin Corporation

Eddie Lawler
LE 2004, Athy EA, Kildare CC

Declan Lehane
LE 1985, Bruff Electoral Area, Limerick CC
GE 1987, Limerick East

Bernard Lennon
LE 2004, Clonmel Borough Council
LE 2004, Clonmel EA, Tipperary South CC

Dominick Leonard
LE 1999, Dundrum EA, Dún Laoghaire-Rathdown CC

Chris Lordan
LE 1985, Midleton UDC

Jan Loughney
LE 1985, Ballyfermot Elect Area, Dublin Corporation

Ted Lucey
LE 2004, Mallow TC
LE 2004, Mallow EA, Cork CC

Mary McAdam
LE 1999, Cavan Electoral Area, Cavan CC
LE 1999, Cavan TC

Mecky McBrearty
LE 1999, Bantry Electoral Area, Cork CC

Marcus McCabe
GE 2002, Cavan/Monaghan

Aoibheann McCann
LE 2004, Galway No.2, Galway City Council

Brendan McCann
GE 1997, Waterford
LE 1999, Waterford No.2, Waterford Corporation
GE 2002, Waterford
LE 2002, Waterford No.2, Waterford City Council

Neil McCann
GE 1997, Louth
LE 1999, Ardee EA, Louth CC
LE 2004, Dundalk No.3, Dundalk TC
LE 2004, Dundalk Carlingford EA, Louth CC

Áine McCarthy
LE 1999, Limerick No.2, Limerick Corporation
LE 1999, Castleconnell EA, Limerick CC

Eddie McCarthy
LE 1999, Tralee EA, Kerry CC

Fintan McCarthy
LE 2004, Lucan EA, South Dublin CC

Donogh MacCarthy Morrogh
LE 1991, North East Ward
GE 1992, Cork North Central

Anne McCormack
GE 1992, Meath
GE 1997, Meath
GE 2002, Kildare North

Tony McDermott
LE 2004, Terenure-Rathfarnham EA, South Dublin CC

Vincent MacDowell
LE 1991, Dún Laoghaire Elect Area, Dublin CC

GE 1992, Dún Laoghaire
GE 1997, Dún Laoghaire

LE 1999, Dún Laoghaire EA, Dún Laoghaire-Rathdown CC

Kristina McElroy
LE 1999, South West Inner City Ward, Dublin Corporation
GE 2002, Dublin South Central
LE 2004, Crumlin-Kimmage Ward, Dublin City Council

Martin McEnroe
LE 2004, Athlone TC
LE 2004, Athlone EA, Westmeath CC

Adrian Mac Fhearraigh
LE 2004, Glenties EA, Donegal CC

Anne McGoldrick
GE 1987, Dún Laoghaire

Brigid McGonagle
LE 1991, Donegal North East

Anthony McGuinness
LE 1991, Mulhuddart Elect Area, Dublin CC

Madeline McKeever
LE 2004, Skibbereen TC

Patricia McKenna
LE 1991, North Inner City Ward, Dublin Corporation
GE 1992, Dublin Central
EE 1994, Dublin Constituency
EE 1999, Dublin Constituency
EE 2004, Dublin Constituency

Michael McKeon
LE 1999, Drogheda No.3, Drogheda Corporation
LE 1999, Drogheda West EA, Louth CC
LE 2004, Drogheda No.3, Drogheda Corporation
LE 2004, Drogheda West EA, Louth CC

Alistair McKinstry
LE 1991, Glencullen Elect Area, Dublin CC

Hilary McLoughlin
LE 1985, Donaghmede Ward, Dublin Corporation

Nicholas McMurray
GE 2002, Cork North Central

Bronwen Maher
LE 1991, Artane Ward, Dublin Corporation
LE 1999, Clontarf Ward, Dublin Corporation
GE 2002, Dublin North Central
LE 2004, Clontarf Ward, Dublin City Council

Bernadette Martin
LE 1999, Drogheda East EA, Louth CC
GE 2002, Louth
LE 2004, Drogheda No.1, Drogheda Borough Council
LE 2004, Drogheda East EA, Louth CC

Duncan Martin
LE 2004, Limerick No.2, Limerick City Council

Paul Martin
BE 1998, Dublin North
LE 1999, Swords EA, Fingal CC

Andrew Mason
LE 1999, Bray No.3, Bray UDC

Ingrid Masterson
LE 1903, Clonskeagh Elect Area, Dublin CC

Ryan Meade
LE 2004, Rathmines Ward, Dublin City Council

Aidan Meagher
GE 1982 (Nov), Dublin North West
LE 1985, Finglas Ward, Dublin Corporation
LE 1991, Finglas Ward, Dublin Corporation
LE 2004, Finglas Ward, Dublin City Council

Brian Meaney
GE 1997, Clare
LE 1999, Ennis Electoral Area, Clare CC
GE 2002, Clare
LE 2004, Ennis Electoral Area, Clare CC

Gene Meegan
LE 1985, Castleblaney Elect Area, Monaghan CC

Ian Mitchell
LE 2004, North Central Ward, Cork City Council

Diarmuid Mulcahy
LE 2004, Conamara EA, Galway CC
TU 2005, Gaillimh

Máire Mullarney
GE 1982 (Nov), Dublin South East
LE 1985, Rathmines Ward, Dublin Corporation
GE 1987, Dublin South East
GE 1989, Dublin North East
LE 1991, Rathfarnham Elect Area, Dublin South

Cillian Murphy
LE 2004, Kilkee TC
LE 2004, Kilrush EA, Clare CC

Fiona Murphy
LE 1985, Dundalk South Ward, Dundalk UDC
LE 1985, Dundalk Electoral Area, Louth CC

Jim Murphy
LE 1991, Terenure Electoral Area, Dublin South
GE 1992, Dublin North West

Malachy Murphy
LE 1991, Tallaght/Oldbawn EA, Dublin CC

Vincent Murphy
LE 1985, North Inner City Ward, Dublin Corporation

Colm Murray
LE 1999, Castleknock EA, Fingal CC

Pat Murray
LE 2004, South West Ward, Cork City Council

Liam Murtagh
LE 1999, Castleblaney UDC
LE 1999, Castleblaney EA, Monaghan CC

Mick Murtagh
LE 2004, Killaloe EA, Clare CC

Alan Nagle
LE 1991, Malahide Electoral Area, Dublin CC

Stan Nangle
LE 2004, Tramore TC

Francis Neary
LE 2004, Greystones TC
LE 2004, Greystones EA, Wicklow CC

Siobhan Nevin
LE 2004, Tuam TC
LE 2004, Tuam EA, Galway CC

Sinéad Ni Bhroin
LE 2004, Ballyfermot Ward, Dublin City Council

Una Ni Bhroin
GE 2002, Galway East

Tony Nolan
LE 1991, Swords Electoral Area, Dublin CC

Malcolm Noonan
LE 2004, Kilkenny Borough Council
LE 2004, Kilkenny EA, Kilkenny CC

Ben Nutty
LE 1999, Waterford No.1, Waterford Corporation
EE 1999, Munster Constituency

Donal O'Bearra
LE 1999, Ennis TC
LE 2004, Ennis TC

Ciarán O'Brien
LE 2004, Bray No2, Bray TC

Colm O'Brien
LE 2004, Scarriff EA, Clare CC

Eugene O'Brien
LE 1999, Ballymun-Whitehall EA, Dublin Corporation
GE 2002, Dublin North West

Kate O'Brien
LE 1985, Tallaght/Rathcoole EA, Dublin CC

Paul O'Brien
SE 1989, Dublin University Panel

Niall O Brolcháin
GE 2002, Galway West
LE 2004, Galway No.3, Galway City Council

Fergal O'Byrne
LE 1999, Slane EA, Meath CC
GE 2002, Meath
LE 2004, Navan EA, Meath CC

BE 2005, Meath

Colm Ó Caomhánaigh
LE 1985, Malahide Electoral Area, Dublin CC

Hannah O'Cinneide
LE 1994, Skibbereen UDC

Bridin O'Connor
GE 1987, Dublin West
GE 1989, Dublin West
LE 1991, Lucan Electoral Area, Dublin CC

Patrick O'Doherty
LE 1991, Ward No.2, Limerick Corporation
LE 1991, Rathkeale Electoral Area, Limerick CC

Mary O'Donnell (Jordan)
LE 1991, Skibbereen Electoral Area, Cork CC
GE 1992, Cork South West

Enid O'Dowd
LE 1985, Pembroke Ward, Dublin Corporation

Roderick O'Gorman
LE 2004, Castleknock EA, Fingal CC

Martin O'Keeffe
GE 2002, Cork East
LE 2004, Fermoy TC
LE 2004, Fermoy EA, Cork CC

Chris O'Leary
LE 1999, South East Ward, Cork Corporation
LE 2004, South East Ward, Cork City Council
EE 2004, Ireland South Constituency

Donie O'Leary
LE 1999, North Central Ward, Cork Corporation

Kieran O'Leary
LE 1999, Skibbereen Electoral Area, Cork CC

Antoin O'Lochraigh
LE 2004, Dunshaughlin EA, Meath CC

Bea O'Neill
LE 2004, Killarney TC
LE 2004, Killarney EA, Kerry CC

Frida O'Neill
LE 1985, Tallaght/Oldbawn EA, Dublin CC

Sadhbh O'Neill
LE 1991, Donaghmede Ward, Dublin Corporation
GE 1992, Dublin North East

Donal O'Riordan
LE 1994, Bandon TC
LE 1999, Bandon TC

Eugene O'Shea
LE 1991, Killarney Electoral Area, Kerry CC
LE 1994, Killarney UDC

Lucille O'Shea
LE 1999, Castlebar EA, Mayo CC
LE 2004, Westport EA, Mayo CC

Pauline O'Shea
LE 2004, South East Inner City Ward, Dublin City Council

Deirdre O'Sullivan
LE 1991, Clane Electoral Area, Kildare CC

John O'Sullivan
LE 1991, North West Ward, Cork Corporation

Tom O'Sullivan
LE 1999, South West Ward, Cork Corporation

Marie Percival
GE 1997, Wexford
LE 1999, Celbridge EA, Kildare CC
LE 2004, Celbridge EA, Kildare CC

Alex Perkins
GE1997, Wicklow
LE 1999, Greystones EA, Wicklow CC

Pat Pidgeon
LE 2004, Baltinglass EA, Wicklow CC

Shirley Piggins
LE 2004, Westport TC

Catherine Power
LE 1991, Celbridge Electoral Area, Kildare CC

Jane Power
BE 1994, Cork North Central
GE 1997, Cork North Central
JJ Power
LE 1999, Naas UDC
LE 1999, Naas EA, Kildare CC
GE 2002, Kildare South
LE 2004, Naas TC
LE 2004, Naas EA, Kildare CC
BE 2005, Kildare North

Michael Power
LE 1999, Tramore EA, Waterford CC
LE 2004, Tramore EA, Waterford CC

Richard Power
GE 1982 (Nov), Limerick East

Patrick Quinn
LE 1999, Tallaght South EA, South Dublin CC
GE 2002, Dublin South West

Steve Rawson
LE 1991, Clontarf Ward, Dublin Corporation
GE 1997, Dublin North Central

Betty Reeves
LE 1985, Blackrock Electoral Area, Dublin CC
LE 1991, Blackrock Elect Area, Dublin CC

Deidre Reynolds
LE 2004, Kells EA, Meath CC

Caroline Robinson
LE 2004, Macroom TC
LE 2004, Macroom EA, Cork CC

Ben Ryan
LE 1994, Westport UDC
LE 1999, Westport UDC
LE 1999, Ballinrobe EA, Mayo CC

Eamon Ryan
SE 1997, National University
LE 1999, Rathmines Ward, Dublin Corporation
GE 2002, Dublin South

Jim Ryan
LE 1991, Dundrum Electoral Area, Dún Laoghaire

Tony Ryan
BE 1983, Dublin Central

Mary Ryder
LE 2004, South Central Ward, Cork City Council

Elizabeth Ryder
GE 1982 (Nov), Cork South West

Trevor Sargent
LE 1985, Balbriggan Electoral Area, Dublin CC
GE 1987, Dublin North
GE 1989, Dublin North
EE 1989, Dublin Constituency
LE 1991, Balbriggan Electoral Area, Dublin CC
GE 1992, Dublin North
GE 1997, Dublin North
GE 2002, Dublin North

Jane Sexton
LE 1991, Dún Laoghaire EA, Dublin CC

Eric Sheppard
GE 1997, Limerick East
BE 1998, Limerick East

Martin Shiels
LE 1999, Wicklow UDC
LE 1999, Wicklow EA, Wicklow CC

Andrew Shorten
LE 1999, Terenure-Rathfarnham EA, South Dublin CC

Tara Skakie
LE 1999, Glencullen EA, Dún Laoghaire-Rathdown CC

Jennifer Sleeman
LE 2004, Clonakilty TC

Mary Sleeman-Power
LE 1999, Mallow Electoral Area, Cork CC

Tommy Simpson
GE 1997, Dublin North West
LE 1999, Cabra-Glasnevin Ward, Dublin Corporation
GE 2002, Dublin Central
LE 2004, Cabra-Glasnevin Ward, Dublin City Council

Emer Singleton
BE 1995, Wicklow

Caroline Smith
LE 1994, Kinsale UDC

Joe Snow
LE 1994, Passage West TC
LE 1999, Passage West TC

Isabelle Sutton
LE 2004, Kinsale TC

Catherine Sweeney
LE 1999, Ballybrack EA, Dún Laoghaire-Rathdown CC

Peter Sweetman
LE 1991, Naas Electoral Area, Kildare CC
GE 1992, Longford/Roscommon

Joe Thorton
LE 1985, Stillorgan Electoral Area, Dublin CC

Colm Timmins
LE 1994, Balbriggan TC

Brian Torode
LE 1985, Cabra Ward, Dublin Corporation

Vincent Treanor
LE 1991, Ballybrack Elect Area, Dublin CC

John Tully
LE 2004, Muinebheag TC
LE 2004, Muinebheag EA, Carlow CC

Irene Tyrell
LE 1994, Naas UDC

Michael Wall
LE 1994, Tipperary UDC

Bernadette Walsh
LE 1999, North East Ward, Cork Corporation

Helen Walsh
LE 1994, Clonmel Corporation

Claire Wheeler
LE 1991, Pembroke Ward, Dublin Corporation
SE 1993, Dublin University Panel
LE 1999, Pembroke Ward, Dublin Corporation
LE 2004, Pembroke Ward, Dublin City Council

Mary White
GE 1997, Carlow/Kilkenny
LE 1999, Borris Electoral Area, Carlow CC
GE 2002, Carlow/Kilkenny
SE 2002, Industrial and Commercial Panel
LE 2004, Borris Electoral Area, Carlow CC
EE 2004, Ireland East Constituency

Carolyn Wilson
LE 1985, Drumcondra Ward, Dublin Corporation

Appendix III

Former Green Party Co-ordinators and members of the Co-ordinating Committee included:

Janice Spalding
Tim Spalding
Rosemarie Rowley
Joe Dunne
Roger Garland
Kevin Stanley
Paul O'Brien
Roger Garland
Margie Bach
Dermot Hamilton
Patricia McKenna
Vincent MacDowell
Patricia Howard
Steve Rawson
Mary Bowers
Angela Boyce
Bronwen Maher
Phil Kearney
Marie Percival
Heidi Bedell
Shane Fitzgerald
Terry McDonough
Dominick Donnelly

Appendix IV

Green Party Private Members' Bills Introduced in Dáil Éireann

Neighbourhood Noise Bill 2006
This Bill provides for effective control of noise emitted from various sources.

National Pensions Reserve Fund (Ethical Investment) Amendment Bill 2006
This bill provides for an ethical investment policy for the national pensions reserve fund.

Fluoride (Repeal of Enactments) Bill 2006
This bill stops flouride from being added to Irish drinking water supplies.

Twenty-eighth Amendment to the Constitution (No. 3) Bill 2006
This bill shortens the term of the Presidential office, changes the rules for nomination and provides for changed procedural matters.

Twenty-eighth Amendment of the Constitution (No. 2) Bill 2006
This bill provides for every citizen over 18 to have the right to run for Dáil, Seanad and Presidency elections.

Climate Change Targets Bill 2005
This bill provides for a longterm partnership approach to Ireland's climate change obligations.

Sustainable Communities Bill 2004
This bill provides for the empowerment of local government and citizens opening the way to sustainable local communities that are actively involved in the decision-making processes for their future and able to exercise ownership and choice over their economic, social and political environment.

Fur Farming (Prohibition) Bill 2004
This bill prohibits the keeping of animals solely or primarily for slaughter for the value of their fur or for breeding progeny for such slaughter.

Planning and Development (Amendment) (No.2) Bill 2004
This bill provides for a mandatory requirement to preserve and list public rights of way, in particular rights of way which give access to the seashore, mountain, lakeshore, riverbank or other places of natural beauty or recreational utility.

Planning and Development (Amendment) Bill 2003
This bill provides for measures to discourage land speculation

Broadcasting (Amendment) Bill 2003
This bill strengthens the role of the broadcasting commission regarding its health-related responsibilities in regulating advertising output and its impact on the public, especially children.

National Transport Authority Bill 2003
This bill provides for the amalgamation of the National Roads Authority and the national Rail Procurement Agency.

Waste Management (Amendment) Bill 2002
This bill provides for enhanced duties regarding waste management plans at local authority level.

Planning and Development (Wetland Habitats) (Amendment) Bill 2002
This bill prohibits development involving land reclamation and public areas.

Organic Food and Farming Targets Bill 2000
This billl makes provision for the setting and achievement of targets for organic farming and food consumption.

Twenty-first Amendment of the Constitution Bill 1999
This bill seeks to ensure that the public will be consulted by way of referendum should the government decide to join a military body or alliance.

Road Traffic Reduction Bill 1998
This bill seeks to maintain sustainable levels of traffic on roads.

Public Office Bill 1997
This bill prohibits the holding of dual local, national and European mandates.